Discovering
Lewis and Harris

Other titles in this series

Discovering Lewis and Harris

JAMES SHAW GRANT

JOHN DONALD PUBLISHERS LTD
EDINBURGH

For Cathie
The Good Companion

© James Shaw Grant 1987

ISBN 0 85976 185 1

Exclusive distribution in the United States of America
and Canada by Humanities Press Inc.,
Atlantic Highlands, NJ 07716, USA.

Phototypesetting by Newtext Composition Ltd., Glasgow.
Printed in Great Britain by Bell & Bain Ltd., Glasgow.

Contents

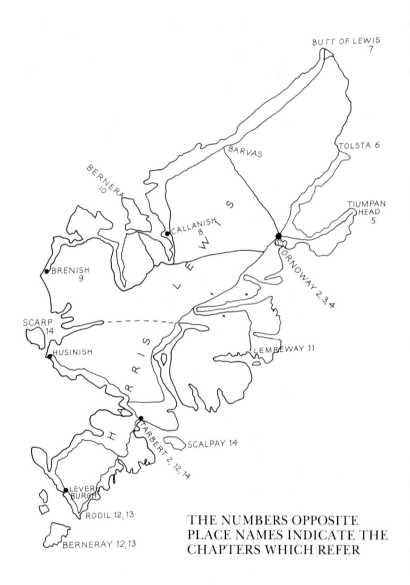

BUTT OF LEWIS
7

TOLSTA 6

BARVAS

BERNERA
10

TIUMPAN
HEAD
5

CALLANISH
8

L
E
W
I
S

STORNOWAY 2, 3, 4

BRENISH
9

SCARP
14

H
A
R
R
I
S

HUSINISH

LEMREWAY 11

TARBERT 2, 12, 14

SCALPAY 14

LEVER-
BURGH

RODIL 12, 13

BERNERAY 12, 13

THE NUMBERS OPPOSITE
PLACE NAMES INDICATE THE
CHAPTERS WHICH REFER

Introduction

I have tried in this book to give a general picture of the history of Lewis and Harris, especially those events and influences which have formed current attitudes and may shape the future. Instead of following a chronological sequence, however, I have related what I have to say to the island's road system, because this is the way in which the visitor will move around. From Chapter 5 onwards each chapter follows one of the island's main roads so that the reader can associate closely the events described and their physical setting.

I have also mentioned as many as possible of the books to which an interested reader can turn for more detailed and authoritative information. If I have whetted appetites, I will have achieved my aim.

The decision of Comhairle nan Eilean – the Islands Council – to use only Gaelic names on many of the road signs presented a problem. Should I use the English names which appear on the Ordnance Survey map, or the Gaelic which the visitor will find on the road signs as he travels around?

I finally decided to use the Ordnance Survey spellings because these are the spellings used in most of the books to which I refer, but, in an Appendix, I give a list in both languages of the main village names where the Gaelic spelling is different from the English. In this way, I hope, the visitor will be able to move freely around the maps and the literature as well as the roads. His interest in Gaelic may perhaps be sharpened by the parallel listing.

There are other spelling problems at the Gaelic-English interface. Just as Russian names like Chekov are variously spelt in English so Breitheamh is sometimes rendered Breve in English and sometimes Brieve. W.C. Mackenzie favours Rodil for Roghadal while Dr I. F. Grant favours Rodel. Mackenzie introduces a further complication by using hybrid names, e.g. the English Torquil – Gaelic Torcul – with Gaelic adjectives like dubh (black). My aim has been to make it easy for the reader to pursue my theme through the authorities I refer to rather than maintain strict consistency within the framework of this book.

It would not have been possible to write the book without a

great deal of assistance. I would like in particular to acknowledge information, advice, the loan of books and documents, and/or the use of photographs from Acair; Sandy Matheson, Convener of Comhairle nan Eilean; the family of the late Angus M. Macdonald; Paul Cowan, editor of the *Stornoway Gazette,* and his award-winning photographer, Sam Maynard; the family of the late T. B. Macaulay; George Smith; Donald Macdonald, Bunavoneadar; Peter Cunningham; Colin MacIver of Lewis Off-shore; Professor Derick Thomson; William Matheson, Edinburgh University; Iain MacIver, National Library of Scotland; Angus Smith Photographic; Dr Alexander Fenton; the Scottish Ethnological Archive, National Museums of Scotland; John M. Macleod, Ness & Stornoway; John M. Macmillan; Mr and Mrs C. Scott Mackenzie; Baroness Macleod of Borve; Dr Alastair Fraser; D. J. Mackay of the Harris Tweed Association Ltd; John Macleod, formerly Principal of Lewis Castle College; Murdoch Macleod, General Manager of the Stornoway Pier and Harbour Commission; Professor D. W. Harding, Edinburgh University; Professor E. J. Clegg, Aberdeen University; James Cumming RSA; the late Alex. Macleod (Princey); Edward Young, Rector of the Nicolson Institute; Donald Stewart, P.C., M.P; Iain G. Macdonald of the Ness Football Club; Mrs Mary Macdonald, Valtos, Uig; Dr J. L. Campbell of Canna; D. M. Smith, Factor to the Stornoway Trust; Donald Macdonald FEIS, FSA (Scot); Gerald and Margaret Ponting; John Macleod of Macleod; Mrs Nan Maclean; Elizabeth Blight of the Provincial Archives of Manitoba; and above all my wife, Catherine M. Grant, who participated at all stages of the work, and finally undertook to decipher my hieroglyphics and produce a clean typescript for the printer.

CHAPTER 1

What Are We Looking For?

I used to boast that Lewis and Harris was more than three times larger than the Isle of Man. Nearly six times larger than the Isle of Wight. I was wrong! Not in my calculation but in the yardstick I used.

An island is not an area of land. An acreage. An island is people. A community. Completely unlike any mainland community, but also unlike any other island community, however closely related to it.

The difference between Lewis and Orkney, or Lewis and Shetland, is well recognised and generally overstated. The categorisation of Orkney and Shetland as the Viking Isles, and the Hebrides as the Celtic Isles, conceals many similarities. It has led to much loose thinking, even in St. Andrew's House. Perhaps, especially in St. Andrew's House. Those who miss the similarities between the Northern and the Western Isles also miss the differences within the Western Isles.

Lewis is unlike Skye, not only in the configuration of the land but in the flavour of the community. In attitudes and responses. In its legacy from the past and aspirations for the future.

The difference between Lewis and Barra is more obvious because one is wholly Catholic and the other rigidly, almost rabidly, Presbyterian. Yet in some ways the difference between Lewis and Skye is greater than the difference between Lewis and Barra. Or let us say, the differences are different.

There are differences even between the Siamese twins, Lewis and Harris, solidly joined at the spine to form the Long Island, but looking in opposite directions.

Three hundred years ago the Dutch cartographer Blaeu put it on record in Latin: 'Leogus et Haraia insulae ex Aebudarum numero quae quamquam isthmo cohaerant pro diveris habetur'. In his own translation, 'Lewis and Harray of the number of the Westerne Yles which two, although they ioyne by a necke of land, ar accounted dyvers Ylands'.

A paradox so long and so widely recognised must have a substantial basis. But what?

The difference between Lewis and Harris is not as great as the difference between whisky and wine, or even the difference between whisky and other ardent spirits. It is rather like the difference between two neighbourly malts. Marginal, and almost indefinable, but very real to the connoisseur.

If we wish to discover Lewis and Harris we must catch the subtle flavour, the idiosyncracy, the essence, of each: the basis for Blaeu's Latin paradox. That will involve us in a hunt more exciting than for buried treasure; more tantalising than a whodunit. There is no crock of gold at the rainbow's end. There may be something less tangible but more enduring.

At Knockan, on the border between Ross and Sutherland, scientists were puzzled by the unusual stratification of the rocks, and so, in an almost unpopulated corner of the Highlands, looking at mountains which are insignificant by any international standard, geologists discovered how the Himalayas, the Andes, and the Rockies were formed.

In the same way, searching for the quiddity of the Siamese Islands, on the periphery of Europe, we may learn more about the influences which shape communities than we could in a crowded metropolis, blinded by the scurrying multitude; deafened by the chatter of a million tongues.

At the very least, we will learn how the rest of Britain looks from the north-west corner of Scotland, which is just as valid a viewpoint as the south-east corner of England, although there are fewer people to enjoy it and they don't have the same power to impose their parochialism on others.

CHAPTER 2
Ports of Entry

There are three ports of entry to the Long Island, as Lewis and Harris are sometimes called. Confusedly, the name Long Island is also used of the whole of the Outer Hebrides which, from the sea, appear as one unbroken line. More confusedly still, the whole of the Outer Hebrides was called Lewis – or its Norse equivalent – in Viking times. Even into the Gaelic era, Harris was referred to occasionally as 'Ardmeanach' of Lewis, that is: the high ground in the middle of Lewis; which increases the mystery why they came to be regarded as separate islands.

For our purpose the Long Island means always the Siamese twins: Lewis to the north and Harris to the south. And 'Lewis', in spite of the Vikings, means only the northern part.

That is not quite the end of the confusion. Lewis is sometimes referred to as Lews or even the Lews. In fact the three spellings are used almost interchangeably, while the local authority, in pursuit of its bilingual policy, prefers a fourth variant, the Gaelic Leodhas. The Lews was used as early as the sixteenth century and was favoured by W. C. Mackenzie, the local historian. The Gaelic Leodhas, however, has the better claim to authenticity: according to Mackenzie himself the name is Celtic, signifying a marshy place, and pre-dates the Norse occupation.

For Harris the local authority prefers the Gaelic Na Hearadh: the definite article before the name being a reminder that it originally indicated a district or part of a larger entity.

The Long Island is within easy reach of anyone who wants a taste of 'foreign' travel in his own country: a journey into a different life style, without problems of language, currency or passport.

Lewis is linked with Ullapool, on the mainland of Ross-shire, by car ferry to Stornoway. Harris is linked with Uig in Skye by car ferry to Tarbert. Stornoway airport, a few miles from the town, is linked with Benbecula, Inverness, Glasgow and beyond, by air.

The sound of Gaelic on the ferry, or in the airport, alerts us

5

A view c.1890 by George Washington Wilson showing Stornoway before the old castle was demolished to make way for the main wharf. Courtesy of Aberdeen University Library.

to the difference but, when we speak to the islanders, we quickly find their English is better than our own. They have two windows on the world, giving them a binocular view of life which most of the rest of Britain lacks. They have free access to the English-speakers' world. English-speakers have to discover theirs.

The air route to the Long Island is quicker but the ferries are more interesting. On a summer evening, when there is almost no night in northern latitudes, the sail across the Minch is an adventure into fairyland. It is also a voyage into history, telling us how one island became two.

Seven hundred years ago, when Norway finally relaxed its hold on north-west Scotland, there was a scramble for the loot. The Macleods succeeded in grabbing Lewis, Harris, Raasay, a large swatch of Skye and parts of the mainland coast. But who were the Macleods, and why did the family separate into two main branches? That's where the mystery and the argument begin.

The usual version of the story is that Leod (progenitor of the Macleods) was a descendant of the Royal House of Man, who married a descendant of Rollo, the first Duke of Normandy, ancestor of the present Royal line in Britain. On his death, his possessions were divided between his two sons, Tormod and Torquil. Tormod got the clan lands in Skye and Harris. Torquil got Lewis, Raasay and parts of the northwest mainland.

William Matheson, lecturer in Celtic at Edinburgh University and a leading authority on island genealogies, disagrees. In a well-argued paper presented to the Gaelic Society of Inverness, and which reads like an Agatha Christie, he suggests that the Macleods are descended from Olvir the Unruly, a Viking mentioned in the Sagas, who flourished in Caithness around 1135, and that Tormod and Torquil were not brothers, but great-granduncle and great-grandnephew. Leod and his son Tormod successively held part of Skye and Harris, but Lewis was held by the Nicolsons.

According to Matheson, one of Tormod's sons, Murdoch, married a daughter of the chief of the Nicolsons. In a sea mist, near the Shiant Islands, the galley of the Nicolson chief and the galley of his Macleod son-in-law were in collision. The father-in-law was drowned, leaving Murdoch Macleod in control of the Nicolson lands.

In some versions of the story the drowning was accidental. In others, according to Matheson, the bride whispered to her husband, when he tried to avoid her father's galley, 'Sink him and our son will succeed!' The son was Torquil.

The one point which is beyond dispute is that one branch of the Macleods, known in Gaelic as 'the seed of Tormod' ('Norman' in English) held Skye and Harris while another, known as 'the seed of Torquil', held Lewis and Raasay.

It may seem an odd division of territory but, if we make the round trip, coming in by one ferry and leaving by the other, we will learn why history prevailed over geography.

During the whole period of Macleod supremacy in the Long Island, which lasted many centuries, the sea was the highway because there were no roads. By sea Harris is closer to Dunvégan, Tormod's stronghold, than to Stornoway, where Torquil held sway; and Raasay, although it lies close to Skye, is just as accessible by sea from Stornoway as from Dunvégan.

Logistically, the association of Skye with Harris, and Lewis with Raasay made sense, whether it came about because old Leod divided his territory between two sons, Tormod and Torquil, or because, at a later date, as Matheson suggests, a descendant of Tormod obtained the land of the Nicolsons by marriage and patricide.

That, of course, is long in the past.

The descendants of Tormod still hold sway in Dunvegan.

Stornoway's new and powerful lifeboat shows its paces in the placid waters of the inner harbour. The call normally comes in the worst weather and from the most exposed localities. Courtesy of *Stornoway Gazette*.

Their castle is one of the oldest buildings in Britain continuously inhabited by the same family, with relics going back to the Crusades. Two hundred years ago, however, they sold off Harris to reduce the family's debts.

As for the descendants of Torquil: the last of them to hold sway in Lewis died 'verie Christianly' in 1613, on the scaffold in Edinburgh, after his conviction in the High Court of Justiciary, on charges of fire-raising, theft, piracy and murder. We will meet him again, and perhaps see him in a more favourable light.

Although it is nearly two hundred years since the (Tormod) Macleods sold Harris and nearly four hundred years since the (Torquil) Macleods lost Lewis, they are still a formidable presence in both islands. Macleod is far and away the commonest surname. Perhaps one in ten of the whole population is a Macleod, much to the confusion of those who do not know the Gaelic patronymics or the abundant and

Caledonian MacBrayne's new and well-appointed car ferry draws into the pier at Tarbert after its voyage of one hour forty minutes from Uig in Skye. The new Road to the Isles is quick and comfortable.

sometimes startling island nicknames.

In a bilingual community nicknames can pass from one language into the other, sometimes getting mistranslated in the process. As a nickname may persist in a family for three or four generations, and undergo a few transmutations in its progress, tracing back to the original significance can involve a major feat of linguistic detective work.

Behind the common surname, the divergent history of the two branches of the Clan Macleod has left subtle differences in attitudes to chiefs and landlords, and perhaps to all authority, as between the two sections of the Long Island. These we will try to identify as we go around.

Much more obvious are the physical and historical differences between Stornoway and Tarbert, our two ports of entry to a fabled land.

Stornoway is the largest town in the Hebrides and the administrative capital of the Western Isles. Tarbert is a modest village, perched picturesquely on the steeply raked sides of a narrow valley between two long fiords: east Loch Tarbert, opening on the Minch, and west Loch Tarbert, opening on the Atlantic.

The name Tarbert tells us that it was a place of portage where the Vikings manhandled their long ships from sea to sea.

Here we discover that Blaeu was wrong and misled some very reputable modern writers, who have picked up his phrase about a narrow neck of land, without examining the map to see precisely where it is.

The narrow neck links North Harris with South Harris. The link between Lewis and Harris consists of eight solid miles of the highest hills in the Western Isles.

Today the Harris hills rise to a modest 2622 feet, calling for no great climber's skill to reach a summit. They offer, when we get there, long vistas of Skye and the Scottish mainland on one side, and the lonely islands of the St Kilda group on the other: thrusting up from the wide horizon of open sea, like two or three blue-black teeth in an aged empty jaw.

In their prime, the Harris hills were as high as the Himalayas, John Barber tells us in his book *The Western Isles*. Consisting as they do of the oldest rock exposed in Britain, they have been worn down to stumps by the rain and ice of a thousand million years.

If the boundary between Harris and Lewis had been the narrow neck of land between east and west Loch Tarbert it would have been clear and self-defining. The real boundary among the worn-down hills is not so sharp and has been the subject of some notable litigation.

Apart from size, there is another significant difference between Stornoway and Tarbert. Tarbert is a relatively modern village, established in 1779 as a fishing settlement. The historic capital of Harris and the old port of entry was Rodil, at the southern tip, where there is much of interest to pursue.

Stornoway, however, has been the capital and main port of Lewis as far back as the written record takes us, although not always as dominant as it is today. One of the safest harbours on the west of Scotland north of the Clyde, it has a long and eventful maritime history.

Despite the fact that Stornoway harbour is deep, sheltered

A moment of aviation history. The Provost of Stornoway, accompanied by Air Marshall Sir Brian Baker, welcomes the pilot of the first American jet to fly the Atlantic. In the same week the first British jets to make the crossing set off from Stornoway.

from every wind and accessible at all states of the tide, each rock and creek around it has its own story, of disaster. Even in sheltered water, the winter gales of the north Atlantic take their toll.

On New Year's morning 1919, the 'Beasts' of Holm, a well-named reef near the harbour entrance on the north-east side, was the scene of one of the most poignant calamities in the history of the sea. I will take the story up again when we visit Holm.

In January 1905, the Danish steamer *Alabama* dragged her anchors in a hurricane and drove on the rocks near the mouth of the River Creed. A few days later she slipped from the rocks and disappeared in deep water.

In June 1883 the Admiralty yacht *Lively*, with a Royal Commission on board, headed by Lord Napier, struck a rock off Chicken Head and sank. The Commissioners made an undignified arrival in Stornoway on the tramp which rescued them: the *Mary Ann* of Glasgow, carrying a cargo of herring!

Despite the mishap, the Napier Commission was one of the most important events in the history of the Highlands. For the first time, its report set on public record the plight of the people. It is one of the main sources in any attempt to 'discover' the islands. I will come back to it again and again.

The locally-owned sailing barque *Arrow* lay rotting on the beach at Goat Island for more than half a century, near where the slipway is today. She was not the victim of a storm or faulty navigation. She 'sank' in a legal wrangle involving Lewis, Lossiemouth and Elsinore, with an arrestment notice nailed to the mast.

Another sailing vessel, the *Gilsland*, was driven on Newton beach in 1887 during a week of gales of exceptional ferocity. Her cargo of wheat was scattered along the foreshore. The townsfolk gathered the unexpected harvest and kept the miller busy making flour.

The Sgeir Mhor – the Big Reef – off Battery Point has been the graveyard of innumerable vessels. The steamer *City of Waterford* perished there in the 1920s. Thirty years later the reef was the scene of a memorable rescue.

A little fishing boat from Park, the *Mamie*, was fast on the fang of rock: in imminent danger of being swamped or broken up. Stornoway lifeboat inched across to her despite the shallow water, while hundreds of people lined the shore and held their breath. The R.N.L.I. is sparing with awards. Courage and seamanship are taken for granted. But the *Mamie* rescue ranked for three. A silver medal and two bronze.

There has been a lifeboat in Stornoway since 1887. For half the period it was an open boat, propelled by oars and scarcely able to operate beyond the harbour limit.

Stornoway now has one of the most powerful lifeboats in the R.N.L.I. fleet, capable of 18½ knots, and with a range of 240 miles at full speed.

Its beat is the largest in the UK: south to Skye; north to Rona and Sulisgeir; and westward into the Atlantic as far as St Kilda. Some 8000 square miles of open sea in one of the stormiest regions in the world.

Successive lifeboat crews at Stornoway have saved more than

250 lives and earned five awards for bravery. The lifeboat – *Sir Max Aitken II* – mirrored in the still water on a summer evening, as it lies at its moorings near Sober Island, may seem 'as idle as a painted ship upon a painted ocean' but its presence reminds us of the great formative influence on the people of Lewis and Harris – the ever-present sea, warmed by the North Atlantic drift, giving milder winters than Kent, but whipped by winds that often exceed a hundred miles an hour and reach gale force for an average of twelve hours a day, in exposed places, in December and January.

There is no comprehensive record of those who came and went by the historic seagate which the lifeboat guards but we do know that at least three reigning monarchs used it.

James V of Scotland came in 1540, but not on pleasure bent. He had a fleet of twelve ships 'well equipped with artillery', according to W. C. Mackenzie in his *History of the Outer Hebrides*, who quotes a contemporary comment that the voyage 'bred great fear in those islanders and savages'.

When the King left Stornoway he had Ruaraidh Macleod, the Lewis chief, on board – a prisoner.

Ruaraidh, despite his imprisonment, cannot be dismissed as a savage. Next year he was free again, marrying the Lord Chancellor's daughter with the blessing of the King, and brandishing a new charter for his lands, erected for the first time into a free barony.

Edward VII came to Stornoway in 1902 – as many humbler citizens have done – on a convalescent cruise. After the operation for appendicitis which robbed his coronation of much of its ceremonial, the King, as the *Encyclopaedia Britannica* put it, 'spent several weeks recruiting his health . . . partly in a yachting trip round the coast and up to Stornoway'.

No hostages were taken on that occasion. The crowds cheered, schoolchildren sang the National Anthem – despite its anti-Jacobite overtones! – and at night the town was ablaze with lighted candles in every window.

Stornowegians still relish the story that, as the barge approached the quay from the Royal yacht – the spot is still marked by a plaque – a local docker thrust a boat hook into the hand of an astonished King with the sharp command, in good Stornoway slang: 'Hing on, cove!'

I have heard two elderly maiden ladies boast, in their declining years, that they had gone out in their rowing boat and got so close to the Royal yacht that they were able to peep through a porthole and see the monarch naked in his bath.

The present Queen has used the island seagate twice. On the second occasion she came to perform a quite historic duty in island terms – the official opening of the headquarters of the newly established Western Isles Islands Council.

On the Queen's first visit a Fleet Street editor, looking for a little local colour, phoned the *Stornoway Gazette* to ask: 'If all the people in the rural areas come to Stornoway to see the Queen, who will guard the villages?'

The old absurd equation of islanders with savages dies hard but it is in the media, and sometimes in the corridors of power, not in the Islands, that Hebridean myths abound.

William IV, the 'sailor king', visited Stornoway as a young midshipman and got into some sailorly scrapes ashore. Another royal seaman, Prince George, later the Duke of Kent, danced at the Castle with a local butcher's daughter, to the great delight of the egalitarian many and the deep chagrin of the aspiring few.

Famous politicians, too numerous to mention, have used the island seagate, among them John Bright and Joseph Chamberlain who came during the agrarian troubles which preceded, and followed, the Napier Commission and the Crofters Holdings Act of 1886.

Gladstone, whose Government passed the Crofters Act, didn't quite make it, but the yacht on which he was sailing with Lord Tennyson and other well-known figures paused at the harbour mouth, to let the famous statesman glimpse the town where his mother was born. She was one of the great formative influences on his career and he revered her.

Henry Brougham, who became Lord Chancellor and gave his name to a once fashionable vehicle, the brougham, spent some time in Stornoway as a young man. Long enough to be initiated into freemasonry in the local Lodge. Long enough also to get drunk in the Lewis Hotel and shoot the landlord's cat, thinking it was the devil.

In my own time, I have seen, among many others, a famous French explorer, M. Charcot; Estonian refugees, fleeing from the Russians at the end of the second world war; a Chinese murderer; a Bishop of Rangoon, bombed off the Butt of Lewis on a wartime journey to his diocese; seamen of every colour and almost every nation; and a party of a hundred Canadians and Americans, including well-known business men, travelling direct from Montreal by the C.P.R. liner *Minnedosa* to visit their ancestral island home.

The traffic in the other direction has been even greater and has spanned the centuries.

Donald Macdonald in *Lewis*, his excellent compendium of historical information about the island, says that in 1773, 840 people emigrated from Lewis, and the proprietor, Lord Fortrose, hurried north from London to stem the tide, without avail. The following year two vessels sailed from Stornoway with over a hundred more. One of them, a lad of twelve, left his mark writ large on the map of Canada. We will meet him in the next chapter.

The *Frances Ann*, outward bound from Ullapool in July 1817, cleared the Customs in Stornoway at the start of a remarkable pilgrimage which, like the children of Israel's sojourn in the desert, lasted forty years, linking the Highlands and Islands, Nova Scotia, Australia and New Zealand, and spawning a series of books in three continents, none of them, unfortunately, that I have seen, remotely worthy of the subject.

The ebbtide of emigrants continued unabated until after the First World War. In fact it reached a climax then, with the departure from Stornoway within a year of three Atlantic liners laden with young men and women, whose going left behind an apparently dying island, whose rise from the ashes, like the Phoenix of ancient mythology, is one of the themes of this book.

Of all the gatherings on Stornoway pier one of the most memorable took place on a Thursday evening towards the end of August, 1939.

In the Presbyterian churches communion is normally celebrated only twice a year and the different parishes celebrate on different dates. It is a specially solemn occasion and large crowds travel long distances to the centre where the services are currently being held.

The Thursday before the Communion Sunday is a day of

preparation, often referred to as 'Little Sunday'. In the 1930s it was still the custom for all the shops in Stornoway to close that day, and also most places of business. Even golf was taboo.

In August 1939 war was imminent. The Royal Naval Reserve had been mobilised. Seventeen hundred and fifty seamen in Lewis and Harris had received their calling-up notices – a quite disproportionate number out of a total population of less than 25,000. The first draft was due to sail after the Thursday evening service.

From all the churches hundreds of black-clothed worshippers made their way to the quay as soon as the service ended. They stood in utter silence watching the reservists file on board. The mail steamer *Lochness* began to list with the weight of men lining the quayside rail for a last glimpse of friends. The captain had to order them back, to trim the ship before he could cast off safely.

Suddenly, a lone voice was heard precenting, in the island fashion, the opening words of a Gaelic psalm. The crowd took up the line. The servicemen on board extinguished their cigarettes and joined in. The ship's telegraph bell rang and she slipped slowly into the darkness with the seamen on the crowded deck still singing in Gaelic:

> God is our refuge and our strength,
> In straits a present aid.

A few nights later another contingent sailed to the music of a pipe band and the lively banter of friends ashore.

To understand Lewis and Harris we must grasp the fact that solemnity and psalms, bagpipes and irrepressible gaiety belong equally to the tradition, and have their roots deep in the past.

Religion and roistering were certainly both represented 'on board' the most famous of all the 'wrecks' at the bottom of Stornoway harbour – the old castle of the Macleods, which stood on a rocky spit of land just beside the point where the ferry berths today.

According to tradition the site was fortified by the Nicolsons before the Macleods took over. How many successive defensive structures there may have been in the course of the centuries it is not possible to say but, according to W. C. Mackenzie's *Book of the Lews*, the last and most important was probably built in the fourteenth century and was not unlike Kismul Castle in the harbour of Castlebay.

It was besieged on many occasions, generally by forces sent by the Scottish kings to subdue the recalcitrant (or freedom-loving) Lewismen. It was the scene of a notorious banquet at which the guests were murdered at table by the host. It was once seized and held by a party of English fishermen against Scottish fishermen, in a row over a shipload of herring which was finally resolved by the local minister after some gunfire. It was more or less demolished by Cromwell's troops, under Col. Cobbet, during the Civil Wars and was finally 'sunk' in 1882 by the good folks of Stornoway who built a wharf across the ruins. All that remains to mark the spot is a plaque on the wall of the Maritime Buildings.

I sometimes wonder whether Stornoway would have had a harbour today if current legislation had existed a century ago and the heap of rubble left behind by Cromwell's guns had been protected as an ancient monument.

The airport, as a parvenu, lacks the glamour of the seaport. People slip in and out almost unnoticed. The crowds and the occasion are lacking.

When war broke out in 1939 Stornoway had an embryonic air service operated by tiny planes from grass runways on what was then the golf course.

The strategic location of the island, controlling the North Atlantic and the routes from Loch Ewe, where British convoys assembled, soon changed that.

The common grazings of three crofting villages – Steinish, Melbost and Branahuie – were taken over by the state. The fairways of sea pinks, daisies and machair grasses, which the golfers and aeroplanes had shared with the crofters' cows, were buried beneath tarmac runways. The bunkers were filled and the hummocks bulldozed flat.

Instead of a five-seater two or three times a week, the air was filled with the roar of heavy planes of Coastal Command on forays far into the Atlantic, or north-east to Norway.

Then suddenly, one day, a new and more insistent noise was heard as scores of American Lightning fighters, crossing the Atlantic by short hops by way of Newfoundland and Iceland, arrived to reinforce the hard-pressed British Fighter Command.

In a strange reversal of roles, an escort of Flying Fortresses gave 'fighter' cover to the Lightnings which, stretched to the limit of their endurance by the long sea crossing, could do nothing to defend themselves.

Stornoway airport is now an important and controversial N.A.T.O. base. It is also one of the best civil airports in Britain, with runways long enough to take anything that flies and almost completely free from fog.

On one of the few occasions when Stornoway airport has been closed by fog it made meteorological history: the fog was self-induced.

It was a cold bright day with a powdering of dry snow on the runways. When a civil plane started to taxi, the draught produced by the propellers created a dense white freezing fog. The thermometer plummeted well below zero, the pilot could see nothing and the plane had to stop. The control tower was above the fog in clear sunlight but the plane had vanished in the cloud below.

That was a freak; flying from Stornoway is normally easy and safe. The coming of the plane has dramatically altered the location of the town, which is now closer in time to London than many cities in between, still dependent on surface travel.

CHAPTER 3

Hebridean Capital

A good deal of the history of Lewis can be read from the street names of Stornoway, but it is a partial and distorted history, reflecting the whims of successive local authorities and showing that, even at the parochial level, the successful side in any struggle for power obliterates the history of the losers.

Many of the street names in the older part of the town commemorate the Mackenzies who, by force and guile, ousted the Macleods and, in 1610, added the island of Lewis to their extensive mainland estates. It was only comparatively recently that a street, on the fringe of the town, was called Macleod Road – a belated and rather cursory acknowledgement of the premier island clan, whose chiefs, despite their faults, had ruled the island for several centuries from within, as a territory in its own right, not as an appendage, or colony, of more extensive and wealthier mainland domains.

The extent to which the Mackenzies took over Lewis is revealed by John Wood's town plan of Stornoway, published in 1821. Wood lists sixty-five feu-holders. Fifty of them have local, or distinctively Gaelic, surnames. Of the fifty, eighteen are Mackenzies and, if we add in the Macivers, who were 'planted' in Lewis by the Mackenzies to control the 'natives', and the Morisons, who were the Mackenzies' allies within the island, the tally rises to thirty; while the Macleods, by far the largest clan numerically, are represented among the urban property owners by only five.

Kenneth Street and Francis Street have characteristic Mackenzie Christian names. Proby Street, an earlier name for Kenneth Street, is also, in a sense, a Seaforth name. The last Lady Seaforth was a daughter of Dr Baptist Proby, Dean of Lichfield. Mackenzie Street speaks for itself. Stag Road celebrates the Mackenzie crest and recalls the story of the chief who saved his king from an angry stag.

Keith Street commemorates the two remarkable Scotsmen – George and James Keith – who were associated with William Mackenzie, 5th Earl of Seaforth, in the abortive Jacobite rising

19

of 1719, launched from Stornoway. It fizzled out in a brawl, rather than a battle, in Glenshiel, near Eilean Donan Castle. The Castle was occupied by some of the conspirators' Spanish supporters, who defended it stoutly, but without avail, against the British navy.

After the failure of the 1719 rebellion, the Keiths fled to the Continent. James served as a soldier, with distinction, in the armies of Spain and Russia before being made a Field Marshal by Frederick the Great of Prussia. A statue to him was erected in Berlin and, more than a century after his death, the German Emperor named a regiment after him, as one of the heroes of the German state. His brother George – the hereditary Earl Marischal of Scotland – became Frederick the Great's ambassador in Paris and was a patron of Rousseau.

The main street is named after Cromwell, which seems odd in a town which Moray McLaren, in the *Shell Guide to Scotland*, has characterised, with a considerable element of truth, as 'the only example of a town purely Gaelic in its making and not one imposed by incomers'.

The original name was Dempster Street which still appears on Wood's 1821 plan. Why Dempster Street? I do not know: perhaps because the Town House and gaol were located there (dempster being a variant spelling of doomster, a judge); perhaps because George Dempster of the British Society was involved in establishing a fishing station at Stornoway. Whatever the explanation, Dempster Street is clearly the choice of one of the incomers who, over the years, did much to enrich the life of the town even if, as McLaren says, they did not create it or impose it on the indigenous population.

Stornoway's ability to accept and assimilate incomers from across the Minch, as well as the steady flow of incomers from its Gaelic-speaking hinterland, has always been its strength and its charm. It is, and has been for centuries, the most Gaelic town in Scotland and the most English part of the Hebrides. A town to which the mix and clash of cultures gives a unique and piquant flavour.

From Dempster Street the name was changed to Oliver Street, but quickly changed again to Cromwell Street, to avoid identification with the wrong Oliver. One of the most important figures in the life of the town in the first half of the

The modest building which constituted the Nicolson Institute in 1873. All has now disappeared except the clock tower which is embodied in the building which houses the school's swimming pool. The tower was preserved as an intellectual rather than a physical landmark: one of the most important in the island's history.

nineteenth century, when the street was named, was Captain Benjamin Oliver, commander of the revenue cutter *Prince of Wales*, despatched to the Hebrides around 1807 to suppress smuggling. In fourteen years he captured ten vessels with crews ranging from five to twenty-nine. An eleventh crew escaped, but Captain Oliver seized 147 tubs of gin, part of her cargo, which had been secreted ashore.

From the names of the vessels captured, it is clear that smuggling was not a local but an international trade.

Captain Oliver was the centre of a small English enclave in Stornoway. Two of his daughters married English members of his crew, while a third married another incomer, Alexander Rose Macleay, Collector of Customs, whom we will meet a little later, fighting a duel near the sands at Tong.

The Olivers were well integrated into the local community. The Captain was one of the guests when the foundation stone of Lews Castle was laid in 1841, and the incline outside his old home, on the outskirts of the town, is still known to older Stornowegians as 'Oliver's Brae'. The Captain of the revenue cutter was much better known in the island of Lewis than the long-dead Lord Protector.

At the time of the Civil War the natural sympathy of the people of Lewis would have been with the king rather than the Commonwealth, although their Jacobitism was always muted, because of the vacillation of the Earls of Seaforth and the fact that they were still regarded by many Lewismen as usurpers.

By the time Cromwell Street received its name, a revolutionary change had taken place in the islanders' attitude to religion and life. They had found a faith, a profound and egalitarian Presbyterianism, which would have made the Lord Protector a man to be revered; and which dominates the island down to the present day.

The 'conversion' of Lewis in the 1820s had social as well as theological overtones. It was, in part, a revolt against chiefs and landlords, although it was also part of a much wider national movement spilling over into Lewis, and, paradoxically, was given an impetus by the landlords themselves, who did not realise the power of the forces they had invoked or the direction they would take.

We will have a closer look at this when we get to Uig where it all began.

If it is surprising that the main street of Stornoway is called after a Huntingdon farmer, it is even more surprising to find one of the residential streets called after a Lancashire soapmaker.

Leverhulme Drive commemorates, in a modest way, the torrid love affair between the first Viscount Leverhulme and the people of Lewis and Harris.

It is difficult to think of the relationship in any other way. It had all the passion, the sudden changes of mood, of a love affair; the elements of pride and pique and self-regard; the misunderstandings; the clashes of interest and temperament. Generosity, too, on a lavish lover's scale, and ironies that belong to Greek tragedy.

When it was over, Lewis was left with the parting gifts of a great benefactor and the nostalgia expressed in the naming of a street. On the other side, Lord Leverhulme's descendants have been left with the hereditary title 'of the Western Isles' – although none of them has ever cared a button for the place. They carry the title like genes inherited from an ancestor one wishes to forget.

The simple message painted on a rock with red vermilion and grease which marked the end of Alexander Mackenzie's historic journey is now permanently maintained as one of Canada's national memorials. Courtesy Public Archives Canada/C3131.

We can learn more about Lewis and Harris from the Leverhulme 'affaire' than from any other single incident in the island's history. It illustrates the islanders' strengths and their weaknesses; the differences between Lewis and Harris relations with central government and the outside world in general; and the manner in which the attitude of the same people to the same events can change completely overnight – for very sensible reasons.

We will pick the story up here and there as we go along.

Leverhulme Drive came into existence when Stornoway was expanding and the Town Councillors were groping for names out of the island's past for their new streets.

Assaye Place belongs to the same vintage. It commemorates belatedly the battle in 1803 in which, according to the *Encyclopaedia Britannica* (14th edition), 'a Maharatta force of 50,000 men, supported by 100 guns served by French artillerymen, and entrenched in a strong position', was overcome by Wellington with only 4,500 men in 'the most complete victory that ever crowned British valour in India'. One man out of sixteen in Wellington's army – and one out of seven of his European troops – was a native of Lewis.

The Council drew back from the suggestion that they should commemorate the Battle of Maida in the same way. At Maida, just a year after Assaye, Sir John Stuart, with a small British force, inflicted on Napoleon's veterans their first defeat on the continent of Europe. One man out of twenty in Stuart's force was a raw recruit from Lewis, but the Council were afraid visitors might be reminded by the name of Maida Vale in London, rather than a historic, but almost forgotten, exploit of British arms, in Southern Italy, in which Lewismen played a notable part.

The island's contribution to the navy is just as disproportionate to the population as its contribution to the army. The naval connection is commemorated in the names Battery Road and Battery Park. They were names in popular use adopted by the Council rather than names thought up by the city fathers. They commemorate the fact that, for nearly half a century, the biggest training depot in Britain, for the Royal Naval Reserve, was at Stornoway.

Prior to 1874 large numbers of Lewismen went to Greenock as naval reservists, but, in that year, it was decided to establish a training camp and battery at Stornoway, which was then regularly visited by the Channel Fleet.

The abandonment of the Stornoway Battery, and the concentration of naval reserve training in the South of England, was a serious blow to the economy of Lewis. The abandoned Battery became Stornoway's first Labour Exchange, although the symbolism was not intentional.

Ripley Place belongs to the same period as Assaye Place. The name commemorates the founding of the town of Ripley in Ontario by a party of emigrants from Lewis. The association had been almost lost sight of in Lewis when Ripley's centenary celebrations brought the civic heads of the two towns into touch with each other.

In the same somewhat nostalgic mood, the Council decided to exhibit the street names in Gaelic as well as in English. A quarter of a century later Gaelic names were being used for new streets, in preference to English, not as a gesture towards the past but as a proclamation of faith in the future.

In 1974, when local government in Scotland was reshaped, Lewis was disjoined from Ross-shire, Harris and the other

Stornoway House, Ottawa, official residence of the Leader of the Opposition in the Canadian Parliament, is so called because a family which spent only 23 years in Lewis still regarded the island as home two generations after they had left. Courtesy Public Archives Canada/PA 113739.

islands were disjoined from Inverness-shire, and the whole of the Western Isles became a local authority area, independent of the mainland, for the first time in history.

The Western Isles Islands Council immediately decided that it would be known, for preference, as Comhairle nan Eilean, and a bilingual policy was adopted in an attempt to reverse the long decline in the Gaelic language. A decline due in part to the social and economic pressures of the majority culture in Britain, but also, more significantly, to the settled policy of central government to discourage the language: a policy actively sustained for three hundred years down almost to the present day.

In the Nicolson Institute – a public school in the Scottish but not the English usage – Gaelic is now positively promoted. Twenty years ago it was very different. Non-Gaelic speakers were given no encouragement, and indeed no opportunity, to learn the language, although it was the native tongue of the great majority of the inhabitants. Gaelic speakers, who wished to study the literature of their native language, could only do so by giving up some other major subject.

Despite the fact that, over the greater part of the school's history since its foundation in 1873, the majority of the pupils in the secondary department were taught in an acquired, rather than in their native, language, the school has a notable academic record.

It has won both the BBC's quiz programmes for schools – 'Top of the Form' on radio and 'First Class' on television – on the only occasions it has competed.

More importantly, it has produced a steady stream of distinguished scholars, including some of the highest rank – like the late Prof. Robert Maciver of Columbia University who must be regarded as one of the leading sociologists of his day.

The school in many ways encapsulates the history and the problems of Lewis. It began with an explosion in the engine-room of a ship in Shanghai. The engineer – Alexander Nicolson – was killed. Although still in his thirties, he had made a will leaving his very modest fortune for the foundation of a school in his native town.

His brothers subsequently supported the new school. One was a cotton planter in Mississippi. Another was a woollen manufacturer in Yorkshire. The third was a farmer in Australia and the fourth a chaplain in the Brigade of Guards. Not one was resident in Lewis, although they belonged to a clan which had been established in the island for at least seven hundred years, and had been dominant until the Macleods took over.

So with the pupils the school has produced. The great majority of them have been unable to find work in Lewis commensurate with their education and their talents. The school has helped hundreds of Lewis men and women to improve their positions in life but only by making it easier, and more necessary, for them to join in the great diaspora from the Gaelic-speaking islands. In social terms the school's great achievement has been to enhance the quality of the contribution Lewis has made to other places.

Although the Nicolson Institute owes its origin to the generosity of a widely scattered local family, it did not achieve real eminence as a school until it was absorbed into the state system. All the schools in Lewis, in the early years of compulsory education, required special aid because of the island's low rateable value. This aid is generally seen as charity extended by the wealthy south to the impoverished north. The truth is rather different.

View from the tower of Lews Castle. Castle grounds in foreground, Stornoway harbour in middle distance with Arnish in background. Courtesy *Stornoway Gazette*.

Until comparatively recently – and perhaps even yet – the state's investment in the education of Lewis children has enriched the mainland of Britain to a much greater extent than it has enriched Lewis.

Much the same applies to Lewis Hospital. It was built on local initiative and largely with local funds. Lewis people abroad, and even people of Lewis descent who had never seen the island, helped to support it. The state later recognised its special problems and assisted in its development through the Highlands and Islands Medical Service, which was established in 1916, and in many ways anticipated the National Health Service we now have.

The fact that the state's expenditure was an investment, as well as a grant, emerges from the fact that, of the first hundred patients treated at the hospital, more than 25% were ill or injured men landed from ships at sea. The hospital, at that time, was still a local hospital sustained by local funds but it was providing a national, indeed an international, service of succour.

One of the heaviest calls on the services of the hospital was made in 1904 when the Danish steamer *Norge* struck a reef near Rockall and sank with the loss of more than 600 lives: men, women and children – Danes, Swedes, Norwegians, Finns and Russians, emigrating to America.

Most of the 163 who survived were cared for at Stornoway, although small groups were landed at Faroe, Aberdeen and Grimsby. In Sandwick cemetery, on the outskirts of the town, there is a tombstone with the very unScottish names of Hinderson, Posansky, Jorgensen, Hansen, Reisman and Simmco, erected to those, mainly children, who died in Lewis Hospital, despite all the care that was lavished on them. They came from Norway, Sweden, Finland, Russia and USA, emphasising the importance of Stornoway's location, close to the shipping route from the Baltic to the New World.

Stornoway's location has also dictated – but not entirely – the nature of the burgh's industries.

James VI of Scotland, who became James I of Great Britain, had his eye on the 'store of fischeingis' in the Minch. He also had the strange idea that the soil of Lewis was more fertile than 'any part of the inland' (or mainland) of Scotland.

He tried to plant a colony in Lewis, as he later did in Ulster, under the pretext that he was civilising the natives.

His colonists were impecunious lairds, mainly from Fife, who became known to history as the Fife Adventurers. They didn't find the El Dorado that they sought!

The story is complicated. The details can be found in W.C. Mackenzie's *History of the Outer Hebrides* or I.F. Grant's *The Macleods*. In brief: the Lewismen would have none of it. The Macleods resisted the invaders of their island until they drove them out. In one affray they killed fifty or sixty of the armed men who had been sent to civilise them. Indirectly the Macleods were aided by the Mackenzies of Kintail, for devious purposes of their own, which only became clear when they ousted the Macleods and got possession of the island for themselves.

Charles I and Charles II both attempted to develop the fishings along the same lines as James I, but they planted

English 'colonists' rather than Fifers. For a period Stornoway was a Royal Burgh, and the representatives of the English fishing companies had the privilege of engaging in foreign trade, a privilege native Lewismen had been denied for centuries.

Charles I went so far as to authorise his London protégés to run a lottery in the capital to raise the money they required to exploit the Hebridean seas.

All these attempts failed. This time not so much because of the local hostility as bad management and international rivalry. Fishermen from the Low Countries, referred to in the records as 'Dunkirkers', seized the English fishing busses and carried off the crews as captives.

The situation changed, when the people of Lewis were given access to Colonial markets, by the Union of 1707, and were able to develop the fishing themselves.

When White, of the General Excise Office in Edinburgh, visited the island in 1790, he found that the Stornowegians had equipped themselves both with fishing boats and cargo vessels, and developed a profitable trade, carrying their own cured herring to the Indies.

White describes the town as a 'model of neatness and cleanliness', with many 'convenient mansions', in which the visitor was feasted on the finest local mutton, washed down with imported port and claret.

It is true the government gave a bounty to encourage the development of the fishing but that may have done more harm than good. As W.C. Mackenzie points out, the Bounty was based on the tonnage of the boats, which led the fishermen to design them for efficiency in catching the Bounty rather than efficiency in catching fish.

More than a century after White, R.M. Stephen, in his *Glimpses of Portrona*, describes Stornoway as a town dependent on inshore fishing and deep sea sailing. 'To be anything of consequence, one must own at least a schooner, which by dint of attentive pumping, could be kept afloat between Portrona' (his name for Stornoway) 'and Cronstadt.'

Rather regretfully Stephen adds, 'We used to build ships as well as sail them'.

The growth in size and scale of ships destroyed Stornoway's

shipbuilding industry and later its carrying trade.

The decline in the market for cured herring, and improvements in transport by road and rail, later transferred the fishing industry, very largely, from Stornoway to the mainland side of the Minch, leaving the town, in the late twenties, apparently on its beam ends. Stornoway, in the view of a well-known Scottish geographer, was at that time a dying town.

It was then that the islanders, deprived of their natural industries, created a new industrial base: manufacturing textiles, for which the island has no natural advantage whatever, except the native skill of the people. Even the raw material is imported.

The island fabric – Harris tweed – is unique. It is probably the only industrial product in the world whose methods of production are dictated by social considerations rather than industrial efficiency, as a chartered accountant would define it.

The tweed, at one time, was completely home-produced: hand-spun, hand-woven, dyed with vegetable dyes, and waulked (or shrunk to tighten the fabric) in communal songfests at which the women worked in unison to traditional Gaelic airs. The leading singer often improvised new verses as she sang, teasing the younger girls about their love affairs, or commenting on other events in the life of the village.

When the demand of the market for patterns that could be repeated precisely made the old system impracticable, design and spinning were concentrated in the hands of a few large firms – large, that is, by the standard of a cottage industry! – but hand-weaving, by independent craftsmen, was maintained.

In defiance of all accepted business practice, as soon as the wool has been dyed, spun and warped, it is taken off the production line, so to speak, loaded on a lorry and carried to a self-employed weaver, perhaps many miles away, in a crofting village, who works on a loom, which he himself has provided, in a shed, which he himself has built, to produce a high-fashion cloth commanding a premium in the world's market.

This compromise was protected in 1934 by the amendment of a trade mark originally registered in 1909. Every yard of cloth is now certified and stamped by the Harris Tweed Association, an independent body, none of the directors of

Carnival day in Stornoway, a lively island capital. Courtesy *Stornoway Gazette*.

which is permitted to have a financial interest of any kind in the industry. The Association directors are trustees, not entrepreneurs, but they work in close consultation with all sections of the industry.

The Association has frequently to take action to prevent the misuse of the name 'Harris Tweed'. In recent years 'poachers' in Canada, the USA, Italy and nearer home have been stopped in their tracks. In this way a viable industry has been sustained, so far, with the maximum spread of employment through the crofting townships. For the past fifty years it has been the island's most important industry.

In recent years Stornoway's geographical position, and the safety of its harbour, have reasserted their pull, drawing to the port an international fabrication yard serving the offshore oil industry.

I will pick that up in the next chapter in a quite improbable juxtaposition with one of the most romantic and over-exposed figures in Scottish history – Bonnie Prince Charlie!

Stornoway is also the headquarters of the Western Isles Tourist Association, set up to develop the great potential of one of the last unspoiled areas of Europe.

The experts are agreed the name Stornoway is Norse, but argue about the precise meaning. There is a mystery too about its use.

As in all similar communities, there is a rivalry between town and country, exacerbated perhaps by the fact that Stornoway is predominantly English-speaking while the rural areas are overwhelmingly Gaelic. Despite this, Lewis people living outwith the island almost invariably describe themselves as natives of Stornoway, even if their home village is forty miles away, in another parish, or even in another island. Why?

Is it that people from rural Lewis aspire subconsciously to a Stornoway superiority they deny, and a Stornoway snobbery they despise? I think not!

The answer may lie in the fact that all the island fishing boats are registered in Stornoway. Everyone connected with the fishing industry – and at one time that meant everyone in the island – was an 'S.Y.', a Stornowegian.

Again, the answer may lie in the fact that Stornoway, for its size, is one of the best-known towns in the kingdom, and the name has a resonance Lewis lacks. 'Stornoway – the name is like a banner,' wrote Dame Ethel Smythe. A banner which Lewismen have unfurled in every corner of the globe.

It is not by chance that the official residence of the leader of the Opposition, in the Canadian Parliament, is called Stornoway House. It arises from the fact that a family, whose residence in the town lasted a comparatively short time and ended disagreeably in a lawsuit, still cherished the name, and gave it to a house built 3500 miles from Stornoway, a generation after they had left it for good.

No one who has lived in Stornoway ever forgets it. There are houses called 'Stornoway' in almost every corner of the globe.

The town has an even more important link with Canada. A plaque, on the corner of Martin's Memorial Church, on Francis Street, marks the site of the house in which Sir Alexander Mackenzie, the great Canadian explorer, was born.

The Americans boast about the pioneering journey, across

the continent, completed by Meriwether Lewis in 1805, with the support of the army and 'almost without bloodshed'.

Alexander Mackenzie, from Stornoway, completed an even more difficult journey, in a more northerly latitude, more than ten years before Meriwether Lewis, without help from the army or government, and with no bloodshed whatever.

Another Stornoway man, Colin Mackenzie, a near contemporary of Sir Alexander, became the first Surveyor General of India, and a pioneer in recording the archaeology, history and traditions of the sub-continent. He was a close friend of Wellington and saved the Duke from an imputation of incompetence as a young man which might well have blighted his career.

There is a local tradition that James Morrison, one of the mutineers of the *Bounty*, was also a Lewisman, of the same vintage as the two great Mackenzies. I examine the evidence for this tradition more closely in my book *The Gaelic Vikings*.

Morrison has left an important record of the mutiny, and a fascinating account of life in Tahiti in the eighteenth century, now preserved in the Mitchell Library in Sydney, NSW.

At a time when Lowland Scots boasted of the Enlightenment, and regarded the Hebrides as a Gaelic backwater untouched by learning, Lewismen were adding significantly to the western world's knowledge of life in Canada, India and Polynesia.

CHAPTER 4

A Prince, an Outlaw and a Crock of Silver

Lews Castle, which looks across the Inner Harbour at the town in mock-baronial splendour, was built on opium and tea, dedicated to a genuine but sometimes flawed philanthropy, and finally inherited by the people of Lewis who put it to a proper use.

James Matheson, a young Highlander, was employed in his uncle's business in India until they quarrelled. One story is that he forgot to mail an important letter and was ordered home in disgrace. When he went to the docks to arrange a passage, the first captain he spoke to advised him to try his luck in China. That was in 1820.

He took the advice with dramatic consequences. At the age of 24 he arrived in Canton, for all practical purposes penniless. At the age of 36, along with a fellow Scot, he founded the firm of Jardine Matheson & Co. – one of the best-known firms in the history of British commerce. At the age of 46 he retired to Britain, with a fortune of over a million dollars, married an English aristocrat, entered Parliament, was elected a Fellow of the Royal Society, bought the Island of Lewis and received a baronetcy.

His fortune was even greater than appears. The million dollars was the stake he left in the firm. His dividends were paid in cargoes of tea, giving him a double profit. On his way home from China, eighty of the leading Parsee merchants in Bombay presented him with an illuminated address and a magnificent service of plate, for risks he took, on their behalf, during the Opium War.

Matheson made no secret of the source of his wealth. In an essay on the prospects for British trade in China, published in 1837, he spoke of the 'command of money' which British merchants in China derived from the opium trade and could hardly have 'derived from any other source'.

We cannot judge him by the standards of the present day. He made his fortune at a time when slavery still flourished in the United States and serfdom in Russia, and when the sale of

Lord Leverhulme (centre) with Sir Harry Lauder and Provost Roderick Smith at the opening of Stornoway Bowling Green. Sir Harry offered to play Lord Leverhulme for Lews Castle, but the canny comedian didn't say what his own stake would be. Photo by T.B. Macaulay, Stornoway.

opium to China was actively promoted by the British government in India for revenue purposes. Matheson's nephew left the firm in 1848 because he had conscientious scruples about the opium trade. The firm itself withdrew from the trade in the 1870s. It was nearly half a century later still – 1917 – before official British policy caught up with the moral scruples of the Mathesons and withdrew support from the opium traders.

The people of Lewis knew Matheson as a philanthropist and a developer. When he bought the island in 1848, there were only forty-five miles of very indifferent road and one wheeled vehicle. Forty years later there were two hundred miles of road, and the town of Stornoway had both water and gas. He even established a chemical works to produce paraffin from peat but the discovery of America's vast oil resources knocked the bottom out of the market and the experiment failed.

In addition Sir James reclaimed land and let it to the crofters at a reasonable rent; developed Stornoway harbour; established a brickworks and a slipway for building and repairing ships; improved the steamer service and the carriage of mails; built schools and supported schools established by others; imported bulls to improve the crofters' stock; and built curing stations to promote the fishing industry. He received his baronetcy for his munificence in providing food in the famine which struck Lewis, as it struck Ireland, in the middle years of the century. The presence of Sir James Matheson, with his opium millions, in Lews Castle may well have saved the people of Lewis from the fate of the Irish in those grim years.

Yet Sir James Matheson's regime in Lewis was marked by an unusual explosion of hostility which has become known in Highland history as the Bernera Riot. Practically all the able-bodied men in the island of Bernera, on the west coast of Lewis, came across to the main island in their boats and marched twenty miles to Stornoway with bagpipes playing, to lay their grievances before Sir James. It was one of the most remarkable incidents the Castle has known. The immediate problem was amicably resolved, but the Bernera Riot was the beginning of a tumultuous period of agitation which raises important questions about the relationship between crofters and their landlords and factors, and even more about the relationship between Lewis and central government.

We will pick up the pieces of the story as we go along: on the road to Tiumpan Head, on the road to Tolsta, on the road through the parish of Lochs and, of course, in Bernera itself. By the end of the book I hope the pieces in the jigsaw will begin to make a picture.

In the meantime, we must look at a later occupant of Lews Castle with whom the Lewis crofters played a variant of the same sad, discordant and confusing duet.

Towards the end of the First World War, Col. Duncan Matheson, Sir James' grand-nephew, who had inherited the Lewis estate, was compelled to sell it. He could no longer afford to keep it on. The island was bought by Lord Leverhulme.

Leverhulme had visited Lewis once before in 1884, the year of the Napier Commission. He was on a holiday cruise with his wife. An important cruise for him. It was in the course of it he decided to break out from the confines of his father's grocery business and become a soap manufacturer in his own right: the first step on the road to a Viscountcy and the creation of one of the great international business empires of the period – Unilever.

That recollection may have influenced Leverhulme's decision when Lewis came on the market but it is impossible to say with certainty whether it was the romantic association of the voyage with his wife, now dead, or the milestone in his own business career, now secure on a high plateau of success, which weighed with him – or indeed some other motive quite unrelated to the earlier visit.

Cautiously he made a reconnaisance of the island before taking the plunge. His first public – or pseudo-public – appearance in Lewis took place in the shop of Provost Roderick Smith on Cromwell Street.

The Provost found himself chaffering for his whole remaining stock of slightly shop-soiled postcards of Lews Castle with a blocky little man, rather hard of hearing, speaking with a strong Lancashire accent: and clearly out to strike a hard bargain.

As the stranger left with his purchase, the Provost followed him, curious, to the door. There he met Charles Orrock, the Mathesons' chamberlain. 'Do you know who that is?' he asked, pointing to the retreating stranger.

'Yes,' said Orrock. 'That's Lord Leverhulme. He's just bought the island.'

Later visits were different. Rockets were fired as the mail steamer approached with the new proprietor on board. There was a floral arch with the message – 'Welcome to your Island Home'. A flag flew from Lews Castle when Leverhulme was in residence and there was a constant flurry of activity, social and commercial.

Despite the difficulties of travelling to Lewis in the twenties, with a steamer only three nights a week, and no dining cars on the trains, Leverhulme was constantly back and fore, and the Castle was crammed with distinguished guests. The locals, too, were entertained, sometimes to dinner, sometimes to fetes in the grounds.

Leverhulme had no interest in fishing or shooting, although

Thanks to Lord Leverhulme's gift the grounds of Lews Castle are now a public park extending to nearly 1000 acres of woodland walks. Thanks to the use the people of Lewis have made of the gift the Castle itself is now an educational centre, geared specifically to the needs of an island coummunity. Courtesy *Stornoway Gazette*.

he now owned two of the best salmon rivers in Europe and two of the best deer forests. He had no wish to be a conventional Highland sporting laird. His purpose in buying Lewis, and later Harris, was to redeem the islands from poverty and make them rich. Not in the role of Santa Claus, handing out gifts to needy crofters, but as a businessman, in a strictly commercial relationship with the islanders, harnessing the almost boundless wealth in the seas around them.

Surprisingly, he had a passion for ballroom dancing, developed late in life. He was on the floor, keeping pace with the youngest guests, until ten or eleven o'clock. Then he went up the Castle stairs, two steps at a time, to show that he was not fatigued. He was at his desk by 5 am, having done his morning exercises with Indian clubs.

His bedroom had an unglazed window, open to the screaming Lewis gales. The floor was asphalt, with gutters to carry off the rain (or snow) the wind drove in.

Throughout his association with Lewis and Harris he wrote, on average, more than twenty letters a day about island affairs, while still controlling, in minute detail, one of the largest business enterprises then existing.

He refurbished the Castle. He planned to rebuild the town. Property after property was bought up to clear the way for the broad avenues he visualised, sweeping from the harbour front to a great Art Gallery on the summit of the hill.

He bought boats for his island fishing fleet; he created Macfisheries, a great chain of retail fish shops to sell the catch; he built a cannery and an ice-factory; roads and bridges; a light railway. He planned to use spotter planes to locate the herring shoals. He was decades ahead of his contemporaries in his vision of an integrated fishing industry, and his energy in pursuing his plans was boundless.

Yet it all blew up in his face. He abandoned his Lewis schemes. Put the island on the market and found it difficult to get buyers, even at a few pence an acre. He continued to operate in Harris, on a smaller scale but with much the same panache, although by now he was a disappointed man. Defeated, perhaps for the first time in his career. But by whom or by what? That is a mystery we must try to unravel. That is where the myths have proliferated. And the ghosts! We will meet them later on the Tolsta road.

Even Leverhulme's renunciation of his Lewis dream was high drama. In June, 1923, he invited Stornoway Town Council, Lewis District Council and Stornoway Parish Council to meet him. In a memorable speech he told them, 'I am like Othello with my occupation gone'.

He offered to hand over the island: crofts, farms, salmon rivers, deer forests, shooting lodges, the Castle and the Castle grounds, the gasworks, fish offal works and laundry, as a free gift, to the people.

He made only one stipulation. That the Castle policies should be named the Lady Lever Park, in memory of his wife, who had been with him when he first saw Lewis, forty-three years before.

Cracking jokes to hide the fact that he was close to tears, he told them, 'I am leaving Lewis with deep regrets', and asserted his desire, in parting, to do all within his power to secure the future welfare, prosperity and happiness of its people.

Thirty years after Leverhulme's dramatic valedictory, Lews Castle became a Technical College, giving instuction in navigation, textiles, catering, engineering, building construction and business studies, with a remarkable track record of success.

It is not the use Lord Leverhulme visualised for the building but he would have approved. Later we must look more closely at the manner in which the College came into existence and its achievements since. They are both important to any understanding of the historic predicament of the Long Island, the character of the islanders, and the role of government, both central and local.

One day, shortly after the new Technical College was opened by Lord Home, some of the students were scrambling down the steep gorge through which flows Allt nam Brog – the Shoeburn. One of them tried to steady himself on the slope by grasping what he took to be a stone. It was an old earthenware pot or craggan, worn by time, camouflaged by moss, and stuffed with silver coins. Over a hundred of them. British, Swedish and Spanish. Some from the reign of Elizabeth, others from the reign of Charles II.

No one has ever discovered where they came from.

It may have been the private cache of some rural merchant visiting the town on business. The Shoeburn got its name because Lewis people, before they had roads or public transport, used to walk across the moor barefooted, with their shoes or brogues slung round the neck. When they reached the Shoeburn, they washed their feet, put on their shoes, and crossed the inner harbour to the town, by huge stepping stones, which were still in use when I was a boy. Did some weary traveller lay down his craggan and forget it, as today we might mislay an umbrella? Or did he hide it deliberately, and so effectively, that he never found it again?

There is another possibility. The coins may be associated with the old Lodge of the Seaforths, which stood almost where Lews Castle stands today. It was there that the 5th Earl plotted with the two Keith brothers the 1719 rebellion, which was actively backed by Spain, and rather less actively by Sweden:

The Arnish yard of Lewis Offshore Ltd is the most flexible facility in the UK for the rolling of tubulars over a wide range of wall thicknesses. Most of the workforce in this highly sophisticated engineering establishment are recruited locally and have passed through the island's own training school. Courtesy Angus Smith/ Photographic.

two countries whose coins were represented in the hoard. The schoolboy's find may have been petty cash, purloined from the war chest, and hidden away for later use.

Or, although it is less likely, it may be associated with a mysterious figure from a later date, whose shadow haunts the Castle grounds, and whose memory bulks large in the folklore of Lewis.

Mac an t-Sronaich is an enigmatic figure. We know who he was. We know that innumerable crimes are imputed to him. But we have no idea what he really did. If anything!

Every village in Lewis has its own story of someone Mac an t-Sronaich murdered. Frequently a child. The detail is often precise as to location and sometimes as to the identity of the victim.

Surprisingly, we are often told what Mac an t-Sronaich said to the victim and the victim to Mac an t-Sronaich, although no witnesses were present and the victim was dead before anyone knew of the crime.

Mac an t-Sronaich, however, was more than a figment of the imagination. He was the son of an innkeeper at Garve. He had relatives in Lewis. The wife of a sea captain in Stornoway, for instance, and the wife of the minister at Keose.

The families of these people, and the families of their servants, can still identify the houses, sometimes even the windows, where food was left for Mac an t-Sronaich when he was on the run.

The Sheriff Court records show that a warrant was issued for someone unidentified, lurking in the moor and terrorising the inhabitants. It was never enforced.

The warrant described the suspect in English as a 'Fantom' and in Gaelic as 'Bodach no Mondach', which is badly misspelt but is intended to mean 'old man of the moor'. The warrant stated that the 'Fantom' was suspected of having committed some serious crime and to be a fugitive from justice. But the crime was unspecified and there was no hint of any offence committed in Lewis.

Near the mouth of the River Creed, on one of the many pleasant walks through the Castle grounds, there is a cave identified in local tradition as Mac an t-Sronaich's hiding place. One of his hiding places. Today it seems an unlikely spot for a fugitive from justice to choose. It would have been different a century and a half ago, before Sir James Matheson planted 'one of the finest woods in the west of Scotland' which, thanks to Lord Leverhulme's generosity, is now Stornoway's public park. The mouth of the Creed was then secluded, but reasonably near the town. The stepping stones of the Shoeburn would have brought Mac an t-Sronaich within a few yards of one of the windows he was reputed to be fed at, without passing through the town.

I examine the Mac an t-Sronaich story at some length in my book *The Gaelic Vikings*. The evidence suggests that the fugitive – Alexander Stronach – committed an offence, perhaps smuggling or even sheep stealing, which the authorities punished severely but the public condoned. He sought refuge in Lewis, and was protected by his relatives, many of them influential members of the community, until they were able to end their embarrassment, by secreting him on a vessel in Stornoway harbour, and shipping him safely abroad.

The story tells us quite a lot about the attitude of Lewis people to imposed authority. They are law-abiding in the main, remarkably law-abiding at times, despite considerable provocation, but their imperative loyalties are to people rather than institutions or ideologies. I have defined them elsewhere, with, I think, some truth, as law-abiding anarchists.

The Mac an t-Sronaich story also illustrates the process by which a folk tale grows from a germ of fact. When the outlaw flourished, Mac an t-Sronaich was a real name – the son of Stronach. Later generations treated it as a nickname, went back to the original meaning of Stronach – big nosed – and invented a physiognomy for a man whose appearance no one could really remember. In some versions of the tale the murderer (who never, as far as we know, murdered) had a terrifying nose 'like a shinty stick'.

For those who prefer real trees and living birds to phantoms from the past, the Stornoway Trustees, who own the whole parish of Stornoway and the Castle grounds, under Leverhulme's gift, have published a splendid little guide to the Stornoway woods and nature trails by W.A. Cunningham, a local naturalist.

The tug-of-war between loyalty to an individual and loyalty to an institution, which may have influenced attitudes to the outlaw Mac an t-Sronaich, arose more sharply for the people of Stornoway in May 1746, when a man and a boy, almost forgotten by history, arrived in town, to negotiate the charter of a vessel to take meal from Orkney to Skye.

The man was Donald Macleod of Gualtergill in Skye: Prince Charlie's pilot when he was on the run, after the battle of Culloden. The boy was Donald's son Murdoch, who ran away from school in Inverness at the age of fifteen, got himself a claymore, pistol and dirk, and fought for the Prince at Culloden.

After the battle, Murdoch followed the Prince across the Highlands, trailing him from hiding place to hiding place until he overtook him. When his father was summoned to provide a boat for the fugitive, he was astonished to discover that his own schoolboy son was one of the Prince's retinue.

Between them, father and son, they did more than anyone else – Flora Macdonald not excepted – to save the life of the Prince. He was the 'meal' they wished to convey, and the destination of the vessel they wished to charter was not Orkney but France.

To begin with, Donald's negotiations for a vessel went well. He struck a bargain with one of the Stornoway shipowners, Captain Macaulay, and sent word to the Prince to hurry north from Scalpay, where he had been hiding.

The Prince sailed from Scalpay to Loch Seaforth. Then crossed the moor on foot to Arnish, the peninsula which closes Stornoway harbour from the south. The night was dark, wet and stormy. There was neither road nor path. Wallowing through the bogs, the party lost their way. It was morning before they got to Arnish, soaked to the skin, famished and utterly exhausted. They slumped down to rest in the shelter of a rock.

When Donald Macleod heard of the Prince's arrival, he hurried back to Arnish to break the news that the deal was off.

Whether Donald had drunk too much and said too much, or whether information about the Prince's movements had been conveyed to Stornoway, by the Presbyterian ministers, who were hot on his trail, we cannot be sure, but Captain Macaulay's suspicions were aroused and he refused to sail.

While Donald made a fresh attempt to find a vessel, the Prince was given shelter in the home of a Catholic family who occupied a farm nearby – the Mackenzies of Kildun.

Colin Mackenzie of Kildun had been out in the rebellion of 1715. He was taken prisoner at the battle of Sheriffmuir, and incarcerated in Carlisle Castle, from which he escaped, disguised as his niece, Phoebe. Despite what his family suffered for the Jacobite cause on that occasion, his widow welcomed the Prince and did everything she could to help him.

By this time Stornoway was in an uproar. The rumour had spread that the Prince was marching north with five hundred men to burn the town, seize the cattle for provisions, and take a ship by force.

A drummer was sent out to assemble the townsfolk. Two

hundred armed men gathered, as a sort of impromptu militia, to defend the town. Their self-appointed officers held a Council of War. Into the middle of this assembly strode the redoubtable Donald, and a furious row broke out.

Donald, who knew the Islesmen, did a quite extraordinary thing. He told them the truth! With two hundred armed men assembled to repel an illusory Jacobite army, and a price of £30,000 on the Prince's head – well over a million in modern money – he told them the Prince was less than a mile away, with only two companions to defend him.

He knew that none of them would harm the Prince, but he placed them in a terrible dilemma.

The people of Lewis had suffered grievously for their part in earlier Jacobite risings. They had strict instructions from their chief to support the Hanoverian government. There was a naval vessel just off the harbour mouth, scouring the Minch for the Prince and his supporters. News was already circulating of the bloody aftermath of Culloden and the treatment that those who helped the Prince could expect.

The people of Stornoway would not harm the Prince but, equally, they would not help him. They asked him to go away.

It was not a courageous decision although it was an understandable one. Public meetings – as the Council of War appeared to be – cannot take courageous decisions. Individuals can.

When Donald returned to Arnish, Mrs Mackenzie killed a cow for provisions, gave the Prince's party meal, sugar and brandy, and saw them safely off again, in Donald's little fishing boat, under the very nose of the British Navy.

Her descendants still cherish the sheets in which Prince Charlie slept when he was her unexpected guest, the quaich he drank from, and the ring he gave her as a keepsake.

Donald Macleod was eventually captured, after the Prince had escaped. He spent eight months on prison ships, confined in total darkness without a candle, sleeping on the ballast, and exercised for only an hour a day in a pen with a flock of sheep – the ship's mutton, live on the hoof.

It is difficult to believe, but it is true, that many of the prisoners of the '45 were taken down from the gallows while still alive, revived with cold water, and then cut open so that the intestines of the living prisoner could be ripped out and burned, before the body was hacked in four and exhibited in a public place. This was the civilised society which regarded the Highlanders as savages.

Donald Macleod fortunately escaped this fate. After the blood-letting, reaction set in. Public opinion compelled the government to release the remaining prisoners.

As Ewan Barron writes in his book, *Prince Charlie's Pilot:* 'Flora Macdonald was the heroine of fashionable London; Donald Macleod found himself on a pinnacle of fame which must have well-nigh dazzled him'.

Ironically, the only memorial to this courageous Skyeman is a cairn in Lewis, looking across the bay to Stornoway, where he was refused a ship.

Arnish now is put to other purposes, more important to the people of Lewis than any change of dynasty could possibly have been.

In 1975 a Norwegian company, Fred Olsen Ltd., looking for a site from which to pursue their interest in the offshore fabrication industry, were encouraged, by the Highlands and Islands Development Board, to look at Lewis.

They chose Glumaig Bay, the deepwater harbour at Arnish which Lord Leverhulme had also planned to develop. Lewis Offshore Ltd., the firm Fred Olsen established, is now owned by the Dutch Heerema Group.

The labour force of around four hundred, including the management, is almost wholly local, which it probably would not have been if the firm had been in English, or even Scottish, ownership.

Nearly a tenth of the labour force are apprentices who get additional training at Lews Castle Technical College. Training is important in a high technology operation in which 60% of the work force are skilled, 30% semi-skilled, and only 10% unskilled.

Lewis Offshore Ltd. is equipped with an impressive range of heavy fabrication facilities, in a sheltered bay, with unrestricted access to open water. It has carried out work for many of the North Sea oilfields and in addition has built landing-craft and barges for Burma, Oman and Norway.

Symbolically, Lewis Offshore Ltd. has also designed and

constructed an inter-island passenger ferry for the Western Isles Islands Council.

For almost the first time in history, technological advance has brought work to the island instead of draining away local resources and local talent.

That is the sort of revolution the islands need. The sort of romance they understand.

The Eye of the Butt. According to local folklore a Viking reiver tried to tow the islands home. He tied his rope through this massive 'hawse hole' in the rocks. The rope broke, leaving the Western Isles strung out, fragmented, in the wake of his galley.

CHAPTER 5
The Westminster Abbey of Lewis

The Ui (or Eye) Peninsula – generally referred to as Point or the Rudha (perhaps more correctly Rubha), which is the Gaelic for headland – is almost completely detached from the rest of Lewis. The narrow isthmus of sand at Branahuie, which carries the road, would have been breached long ago if an extensive sea wall had not been built, and rebuilt; latterly with assistance from the EEC.

Thrust into the Minch as they appear to be, the villages of Point provide a series of viewpoints which command a magnificent sweep of mountains and open sea.

To the north there is modest little Muirneag, whose 800 feet seem magnified by its splendid isolation in the middle of the Tolsta moor. A far more prominent landmark than its height warrants, it is the Fuji-yama of Lewis: the semi-sacred mountain celebrated in the songs of scores of nostalgic emigrants.

Turning towards the west and south – in defiance of the old Celtic superstition that one should always turn 'deiseil' (or sunwise) – you pick up the Barvas hills and then, in succession, the mountains of Uig, Harris and Pairc.

Across the Minch from Pairc are the Cuillins of Skye, and then a magnificent procession of mainland peaks from Applecross and Torridon, almost to Cape Wrath.

On a clear day you can go into village after village, catching from each a different view of the great blue bowl of north-west Scotland. Away from the shore, and the sound of the sea, there are moments of intense peace. A silence you can hear – until the world intrudes in the noise of a passing car or, somehow more acceptably, a barking dog.

The peninsular situation of the Point villages has influenced the attitude of the rest of the island to the residents. The Rudhachs are looked on as a people apart – *sui generis* – although, in truth, the differences lie in imagination and mythology rather than historical fact.

The great majority of families in Point, as in the whole of

Lewis and Harris, outside Stornoway, live on crofts. Agricultural subjects too small to be called farms, too large to be called allotments, held on a complex protected tenure, invented by Parliament in 1886, and found only in the north of Scotland.

In Lewis and Harris a croft generally, although not necessarily, consists of four distinct elements.

First, the crofter's house, which he provides himself, but does not own. In law the house is regarded as an improvement on the agricultural land, for which the crofter is entitled to claim compensation from his landlord, if he gives up the tenancy of the croft. Parliament has thus created the fiscal absurdity that a house costing £30,000 or more has to be valued as if it were a permanent improvement on an agricultural holding, rented at £10 a year or less. As an escape from this predicament, in which an outgoing crofter could suffer serious loss, Parliament, in 1976, gave the crofter the right to acquire the ownership of the essential parts of his croft on very reasonable terms, with or without the landlord's consent.

The second element in the croft is the inbye land: the arable land round the house, which the crofter cultivates (or neglects) at his own hand. The inbye land is now generally fenced and is entirely under the crofter's control. Until well after the second world war, however, most crofts were unfenced, and, in an open township, it was customary to remove all stock, during the growing season, to land held in common by all the crofters in the township, where the animals were herded, to prevent them wandering back.

This land held in common is the third element in a croft. The common land is generally regulated by a committee, elected by all the crofters in the township. In Lewis there are 111 such Grazings Committees and in Harris 38. The number of cattle and sheep a crofter can put on the common is regulated (in theory at least) by the 'souming', which is related to the croft rent and the carrying capacity of the land.

These three elements make up the croft for most crofters but, in some areas, notably Point, there is a fourth element – a General Common or hill pasture, shared by a group of townships and used only in the height of summer. Until comparatively recently, when the cattle were on the hill, the young women of the village accompanied them, living in temporary summer houses called sheilings, or airidhs, so that they were on hand for the milking and other chores.

Nowhere in the Highlands was the communal element in crofting demonstrated more dramatically than in Point. The grazings for all the Point villages lie on the far side of Stornoway. On a day in May, decided by a joint committee of the different villages, a mass movement from the crofts to the hill pasture would begin. Men, women and children with their cattle, sheep and dogs marched in a loose, unregulated but orderly procession, from the furthest end of the peninsula, through the town of Stornoway, and several miles beyond, along the road to Uig, where each family had its own airidh, at that time generally built of dry stone with two openings but no door. According to the wind direction, one opening was closed with turf to provide shelter, the other was open for ventilation.

On the long march to the sheilings, the women carried food and household utensils piled high in creels on their backs. Many of them knitted incessantly as they marched. The men and the boys – and the dogs – were equally busy, trying to keep the animals from invading the gardens, or even the houses, of Stornoway, as they passed. Nowadays the people of Point, for good economic and social reasons, have given up keeping cows. The sheep are transported to the hill pasture unobtrusively by lorry. The sheilings are abandoned, except in so far as they have been replaced by modest chalets, purely as holiday homes.

As in the rest of Lewis and Harris, life in the villages of Point is changing rapidly under the pressure of television, computers and a rising standard of living, but a visit to Point takes us through a swatch of island history, both recent and remote, which we must understand before we can address ourselves to the present or the future.

Before we actually reach the Ui peninsula, we should pause at one of the most significant memorials in the island – a simple slab erected, belatedly, in 1969, to mark the scene of the *Iolaire* disaster in 1919. It stands some distance from the side-road which leads to Holm Farm.

Even at this remove in time I find it impossible to write of the *Iolaire* without emotion, or to tell the story more effectively than it was told by my father, reporting for the *Stornoway*

Gazette, within hours of the disaster.

Hundreds of servicemen were travelling home, on New Year's Eve, by way of Kyle of Lochalsh (then the mainland terminal for Stornoway). No adequate provision was made for their conveyance across the Minch, by the Admiralty or the War Office they had served so well.

Between forty and fifty of those who reached Kyle on December 30th failed to get a passage to Stornoway and were stranded in Kyle overnight. Another five hundred came on by train on the following day. Altogether nearly six hundred people, soldiers, sailors and civilians, were at Kyle on the last day of the year.

That was beyond the capacity of the mail steamer *Sheila*, and H.M. Yacht *Iolaire* – parent ship of the Stornoway base – was sent to Kyle to assist. The soldiers and civilians, and a few of the sailors, were put on board the *Sheila*. Some 260, all naval ratings, were assigned to the *Iolaire* which, in addition, carried a crew of 23.

'The company included many boys in their teens coming home on their first leave since enlistment. There were also there many veterans who had been mobilised in August, 1914, and were coming home from the ends of the earth, on their first leave since the outbreak of hostilities.

'On the deck of the *Iolaire* men met with schoolmates whom they had not seen since together they rushed to the Colours, four and a half years ago. The older men were glad to meet with relatives whom they had left behind as pupils in the village school, now striplings in naval uniform.

'Two hours' steaming from Stornoway, the New Year was welcomed in, in time-honoured fashion. All were in high spirits.

'As the light on Arnish point drew near, many began getting their kit together, expecting in a very short time to be safely moored at the well-known wharf.

'Suddenly there was a crash, and the ship heeled over to starboard. When she listed, huge waves came breaking over her, and 50 or 60 men jumped into the sea. All of them perished.

'It was impossible in the pitch blackness to see the land, which, as it transpired, was less than 20 yards distant. When

Ui church sketched around 1900 by a Stornoway artist, Malcolm Macdonald, who like many of his contemporaries had to emigrate to Canada to find an appropriate outlet for his skill.

rocket lights were fired, the landscape was lit up, and it was found that the stern of the vessel was only half a dozen yards from a ledge of rocks connecting with the shore. There was a tremendous rush of water between the stern and the rocks, but many men were tempted to try to reach the shore there, and scores of them were drowned or killed by being dashed on the rocks.

'As the ship settled down, she turned broadside on to the shore, thus breaking the force of the seas amidships, and it was at this point all who were saved got off.

'Several swam ashore, and one man, John F. Macleod, Port of Ness, took with him a life-line by means of which a hawser was pulled ashore and made fast between the beach and the ship.

'About 30 or 40 men got ashore by hanging on to the rope and altogether 75 men were saved from the wreck.

'About 3 o'clock in the morning, one of the survivors, in a dazed condition, made his way, he cannot tell how, to Stoneyfield farmhouse.

'Soon the town was ringing with news of the frightful disaster, and many made their way to the scene.

'Taking the shorter way by Sandwick Beach, evidence of the terrible happening was soon found, for along the shore portions of the wreckage were strewn, and here and there a body which had been cast up on the tide was found and carried beyond reach of the sea.

All that remains of the ill-fated *Iolaire* — the ship's bell preserved in the Lewis museum in Stornoway Town Hall. Another memorial is to be found in the poems of Iain Crichton Smith who, more than half a century after the event, has grappled with some of the profound philosophical and religious questions such a disaster, at such a time, raises for a community which sees the hand of God in everything.

'It was still dark when the first of the townsfolk reached Holm, and there was a high sea running. The wreck was found lying between the Beasts of Holm and the shore. She had disappeared all but her masts, one of which was broken. Perched on the top of the remaining mast was one of the survivors, clinging in a most precarious position. Other two men had been on the mast with him, but they had become numb, fell off, and were drowned.

'On the grass were laid out the bodies that had been recovered from the sea, and below the crews of eight row-boats proceeded in silence with their work of dragging round the wreck. At very short intervals the grappling irons brought another and another of the bodies to the surface, and the crews proceeded with them to the ledge where they were being landed. Here they were placed on stretchers, and slowly and laboriously the bearers clambered up with them to be laid out reverently on the grass lands above. Scarce a word was spoken, and the eyes of strong men filled with tears as the wan faces were scrutinised with mingled hope and fear of identification.'

In many cases the relatives were not advised by the men to

expect them and people, who had gone to express sympathy with neighbours, learned that their own sons or brothers were on board and had perished in the great catastrophe.

'The remains, as they were recovered, were brought to a temporary mortuary at the Naval Barracks, where relatives of the missing men from all parts of the island gathered. As the bodies were identified, they were handed over to the friends, and the little processions of carts, in groups of two and three, each with its coffin, passed through the Barrack gates on their way to some mourning village for interment.'

More than two hundred perished. Every village in the island, almost every home, was affected. The disaster, together with the war which preceded it, and the mass emigration which followed, affected the lifestyle of a whole generation. Its influence can still be traced, although now fortunately in the relief that a shadow has passed rather than the gloom occasioned by its presence.

The nearby village of Holm takes us into a very different area of island history. While the *Iolaire* memorial reminds us of the contribution the island made to the defence of Britain and the price it paid, at Holm, once a busy little fishing village, we are reminded of a period before the Long Island became part of Britain or even effectively part of Scotland.

As late as the reign of Elizabeth, the English court maintained agents in Lewis, stirring up trouble for the Scottish Crown. The cover for the operation was an international organisation of carpenters bearing some resemblance to Freemasonry.

The organisation still exists in Sweden, purely as a social club, or existed as late as 1954, when a Swedish professor visited Lewis to try to find a place, referred to as Nuan in the society's records, where a number of Swedish carpenters were engaged in shipbuilding – and espionage.

The likeliest location is Holm where the bay is protected by Eilean nan Uan – the lambs' island – which on the old Blaeu map appears as 'Ylen na Nuan'.

The same theme of conflict with the Scottish Crown confronts us at the old church of St Columba at Ui which was, in its day, the Westminster Abbey of Lewis.

The church, now a ruin, is believed to have been built in the fourteenth century but it stands on the site of a very much earlier chapel dedicated to St Catan. Nineteen Macleod chiefs are reputed to be buried at Ui. The number seems excessive, even allowing for the fact that, in a turbulent age, tenure of the chiefship may frequently have been short. Even if we trim the tally somewhat, Ui was clearly the principal ecclesiastic site in Lewis for several centuries and the burial place of the rulers of the island.

The effigy of a warrior which survives at Ui is believed to be that of Ruaraidh (Roderick), generally referred to as the seventh chief of Lewis, although William Matheson's hypothesis about the origin of the clan would alter the numeration somewhat.

Ruaraidh's daughter is also buried at Ui and commemorated by an inscribed stone. His son Torquil was the subject of an anonymous panegyric recorded, with an English translation, in W.J. Watson's edition of *Scottish Verse from the Book of the Dean of Lismore*.

The recurring theme is that Torquil is a worthy son of his father so in effect the poem becomes a panegyric for Ruaraidh, who is praised for his looks, his hospitality 'in the house of feasting', his prowess on the field of battle, his patronage of poets and of the arts in general.

While the poem is full of allusions drawn from Irish history and mythology it asserts the Macleods' Viking origin 'from the rock of Bergen'.

With unintended irony, the poet declares that young Torquil 'is a key that unlocketh the hearts of ladies' and wins victories 'over every land'.

The lady whose hand he won was Catriona, daughter of the Earl of Argyll, which gives us some measure of the status of the Macleods of Lewis at the time. Unfortunately, her sister was married to Angus Og, the son of the last of the Lords of the Isles: a turbulent fellow, often at odds even with his own father, whom he predeceased, allegedly assassinated by an Irish harper, bribed by the chief of the Mackenzies, and others, who wanted to be rid of him.

The Macleods of Lewis had been loyal to the Lords of the Isles during their long resistance to the centralising power of the Scottish kings but, when the Lordship was forfeited,

Ruaraidh quickly made his peace with James IV.

Torquil, because of the family tie, was less prudent. Angus Og's son, Donald Dubh (Black Donald), was kept a prisoner from his infancy in a castle in Loch Awe. He escaped as a grown man to take up the struggle for the forfeited Lordship. Whether or not Torquil was involved in the escape (as he may have been), Donald made straight for his uncle in Lewis.

According to contemporary accounts, the Macleods of Lewis at that time could muster seven hundred armed men. In Dr I.F. Grant's phrase James IV had to call out 'the whole array of the Kingdom north of the Forth and Clyde' to suppress the rebellion. In face of the King's decisive action Donald Dubh's supporters melted away. By 1506 Torquil was the sole substantial ally left in the field, and the whole might of the Crown was directed against Lewis.

Guns and gunners were taken from Edinburgh and Stornoway Castle was bombarded. A royal army, led by the Earl of Huntly, marched across Lewis into Uig, laying waste with fire and sword the homesteads of the Macleods' loyal allies and subordinates, the Macaulays. In this task they were assisted, quisling fashion, by the Morrisons of Ness, who aligned themselves with the invaders, to wipe off old scores against their hereditary enemies.

At this point Torquil – bracketed with the great Cu Chulainn by the anonymous bard – disappears from the pages of history. Surprisingly enough, a few years after this punitive expedition against the rebellious Macleods, Torquil's younger brother, Malcolm, held a Royal Charter for Lewis and Raasay. The Macleods were clearly too powerful for the Crown to disregard.

Even more surprisingly, Malcolm made the same mistake as Torquil. When Scotland was reeling from the shock of Flodden, Sir Donald Macdonald of Lochalsh, who had been knighted on the field shortly before his King was killed, rose against the Crown, in an attempt to re-establish the Lordship of the Isles and secure it for himself. He went to Lewis seeking support and got it, but the revolt quickly fizzled out and no punitive measures were taken by a weak government.

It was Malcolm's successor, another Ruaraidh, who was abducted by James V on his visit to Lewis, but later restored to the Royal favour. Despite that experience – perhaps because of

Muirneag — the last herring drifter in the Scottish fleet to use sail — putting out to sea around the start of the Second World War. The skippers at that time were known by the names of their vessels as farmers are known by the names of their farms.

it – Ruaraidh joined in still another attempt to restore the Lordship of the Isles: led once again by Donald Dubh, who had escaped from prison, for the second time, after nearly 40 years' incarceration.

On this occasion the island rebels were used by the Earl of Lennox to assist his personal ambition to be made Regent of Scotland with the help of Henry VIII. An extraordinary meeting of the Council of the Islands, which had existed under the old Lordship, appointed Commissioners to enter into a treaty with the King of England, accepting him as their overlord instead of the infant Mary Queen of Scots. Against this background, it is not surprising that Henry's daughter still had emissaries in Lewis, posing as Swedish shipbuilders!

Against nineteen Macleod chiefs reputedly buried at Ui, there was only one Mackenzie. That fact shows the change which took place in the status of Lewis when the Mackenzies took over. Lewis was now an appendage of a mainland earldom with its family burial ground in Fortrose and, more importantly, its seat of power at Brahan Castle, also in Easter Ross.

This point is reinforced by the fact that the solitary Mackenzie chief laid to rest in Lewis soil was William, the 5th Earl, who was involved in the abortive Jacobite Rebellion of 1719 with the two Keiths. After some years in exile, Earl William returned to Scotland but he was still an attainted rebel. Presumably he was buried in Ui, rather than Fortrose, for reasons of discretion, not as an indication of the place that Lewis held in the affections of the family. As W.C. Mackenzie says in the *Book of the Lews* in a memorable phrase, Earl William 'was a faithful servant of the interest of the Stewarts, but it cannot be said that he was a faithful steward of the interests of his servants'. Lewis paid dearly for his Jacobite views.

To balance this picture of rebellious island leaders it should be added that one of the two Lewis naval officers who took part in the battle of Trafalgar is also buried at Ui – Lieut. John Morison, tacksman of Aignish. His descendants still own the walking stick Nelson presented to him as a token of his regard. The other Lewis naval officer at Trafalgar was James Robertson of Stornoway who was a young midshipman at the time of the battle. In *The Memoirs of a Highland Gentleman* his nephew, Evander Maciver, says he was standing close to Nelson when he fell.

Lewis has a very long history of resistance to central government, but an equally long history of quite exceptional service to the Crown. There is perhaps a little unintentional symbolism in the fact that it was in the Point district of Lewis – guarded by the burial place of many unruly Macleods and at least one rebellious Mackenzie – that Prince Charles performed his first official function as heir to the throne.

In 1955, when he was only six years old, he inaugurated a new foghorn at Tiumpan Head lighthouse, at the end of the Point road. It was a glorious task for a small boy, blasting off a horn that could be heard many miles away! Although official, the inauguration was private. The whole attention of Lewis was focused on the public engagements of the Queen and Prince Philip, making the first Royal visit to the island for more than half a century.

Prince Charles has been back to Lewis on several occasions since. As a schoolboy at Gordonstoun, getting up to boyish pranks, and as Prince of Wales, deeply conscious of the fact that he is also Lord of the Isles and showing a lively interest in the problems of the crofters.

There are other symbols of significance in island history along the road to Point. The fields beyond the cemetery, for instance, were the scene of a riot in 1888 when the poverty-stricken crofters drove the cattle off Aignish farm in the hope that it would be divided into holdings.

The crofters, from their point of view, were not attempting to seize another man's property. They were trying to recover land from which an earlier generation of crofters had been driven, half a century before, to create the farm. Whatever the law might say, they felt that right was on their side.

They acted openly. They told the Estate Office in Stornoway, well in advance, the precise day and hour at which they would move in, and, when it came, four hundred men and women were gathered round a flag on a hill overlooking the farm, ready to march.

Opposing the raiders was a posse of policemen, under the command of an aged Sheriff, whose voice quavered as he read the Riot Act, and warned the people in Gaelic of the dangers they incurred if they broke the law.

Behind the Sheriff and police there was a company of Marines, fully armed, hiding in the steading of the farm, to which they had crept, secretly as they thought, through the night but tailed, as they discovered to their chagrin, from the moment they landed at Sandwick Bay from H.M.S. *Seahorse*.

Also closing in on the crofters was a detachment of the Royal

C

Scots, marching from Melbost farm nearby, each soldier armed with rifle and bayonet and ten rounds of ammunition. The situation had the makings of a Peterloo or Amritsar massacre.

The danger was averted by the tact of the Gaelic-speaking Sheriff, and, even more, by the restraint of the crofters themselves. A long period of agrarian unrest in Lewis and Harris, precipitated by gross injustice and inflamed by the pangs of hunger, produced no serious act of violence. Property was invaded, but people – even the most hated factor in the island's history – were unmolested. The contrast with what was happening in Ireland, at the same time, and for the same reasons, is startling.

There were one or two critical moments during the Aignish Riot. When a minor official stupidly brandished a revolver, a spokesman for the crofters gave a warning that, if a shot was fired, the troops would be disarmed and stripped of their uniforms. Given the force mobilised by the authorities, the threat could clearly not be carried out but, if the occasion had arisen, it would have been attempted.

There was a scuffle but no gunfire. Thirteen men were arrested but the raiders achieved their symbolic objective: the cattle were driven from the farm.

In the High Court in Edinburgh those who were arrested were given sentences of up to fifteen months, which was grossly excessive in the circumstances.

Their womenfolk, struggling to keep their families alive on rotting potatoes and shellfish from the shore, consoled themselves with the thought that their husbands were better fed in Calton gaol than they would have been in their own homes, in that bitter island winter.

In the end of the day, when the British government belatedly got round to a policy of land settlement, Aignish farm was broken up and divided into crofts, just as the raiders had wished, but much too late to relieve the poverty of those who participated in the raid.

Another monument to official procrastination can be found at Portnaguran Pier. The creation of a harbour at Portnaguran was recommended by a government committee in the 1880s, when Point had a flourishing fishing industry. No harbour was ever built, but a pier, which dries out at low tide, was eventually provided, seventy years after the report, when fishing at Portnaguran had all but ceased. Small piers are of some value to crofting communities but, if harbours had been provided when they were essential, the economic and social history of the island would have been very different.

Some of the essential strands in that history can be found in the lives of a number of men and women who spent their childhood in the villages of Bayble and Garrabost in the centre of the Ui peninsula.

John Macleod of Garrabost sailed from Stornoway in July 1811 to enter the service of the Hudson Bay Company. Apart from the notable work he did for the company in opening up the west, he helped to save the Selkirk settlement, when it was attacked by Indians and halfbreeds. In this way he made a material contribution to the early history of the city of Winnipeg.

Macleod's defence of the Selkirk settlement, on the Assiniboine River, is the central incident in a novel entitled *Mine Inheritance,* by the Scottish Canadian author Frederick Niven.

Macleod belonged to the tacksman class, who held land from the proprietor, farmed it in part, and in part sublet it to smaller tenants. The tacksmen stood in a rather ambivalent love-hate relationship with the crofters below them, especially at times of social change, but they provided essential leadership in their communities.

This important middle class was eliminated, in the late eighteenth and early nineteenth centuries. Many of them emigrated, like John Macleod, taking with them talents which were sorely needed in the island from which they were driven.

Surprisingly, the crofters were able to generate a new class of leader for themselves: not differentiated by wealth or status; resting solely on the recognition by their fellow islanders of outstanding qualities of intellect and character.

They were known as the 'Men'. Basically they were active figures in the Presbyterian Church. Eloquent lay-preachers, concerned with a kingdom of the mind and spirit, as an escape from the misery of the world around them.

Outstanding among them was Roderick Macleod, Upper Bayble, known as 'The Pope' and revered all over the

Highlands as an eloquent man of prayer.

Later he became equally well known for his eloquence on behalf of the crofters' campaign for the return of the farms taken from them during the Clearances. This, however, brought criticism from many of his fellow churchmen, who thought he should not be involved in secular affairs. His status was such that he was invited, in his eighties, to meet Joseph Chamberlain when the great radical visited Lewis, advocating his simplistic remedy for the Highland problem – 'three acres and a cow'.

Island radicalism found another voice in 1935 when Malcolm K. Macmillan, whose people belonged to Garrabost, won the Western Isles from the Liberals, who had hitherto always held it, becoming simultaneously the youngest member of the House of Commons and the first Labour M.P. to sit for a Highland constituency.

When he lost the seat, nearly forty years later, it was because of another convulsion in Hebridean radicalism, returning another islander, Donald Stewart, as the first Scottish Nationalist to represent the Western Isles, and the first Scottish Nationalist to be made a Privy Councillor.

While Macmillan and Stewart are both, in different ways, products of the island's social and economic history on the political side, another Bayble-Garrabost group are products of the island reaction to nearly four centuries of government neglect, and sometimes outright repression, of the Gaelic language.

Professor Derick Thomson of Glasgow University – poet, scholar and propagandist; and Iain Crichton Smith – poet, novelist and dramatist in Gaelic and English, represent two related but somewhat different responses to the Gaelic-English dichotomy. They however belong to the present and the future and must be looked at more closely in my concluding chapters.

Sheila Macleod, the London writer of science fiction and literary criticism, may serve as something of a foil to them. She too has close connections with the area. She moved out of the Gaelic milieu as a child but has not perhaps escaped the Gaelic influence entirely. That too is something to explore.

CHAPTER 6
A Bridge That Leads Nowhere

At the end of the Tolsta road there is a magnificent concrete bridge across a gorge. A little way beyond it, the road peters out unfinished, in the moor. The bridge leads nowhere.

It was even more impressive when it was built, in the early twenties, than it is today; it wasn't dwarfed in our mind's eye by the concrete monsters of the motorways. It was the first stage in a road Lord Leverhulme planned to construct along the east side of Lewis from Stornoway to Ness.

The engineers mapped a line across the moor by the easiest route, as they were trained to do. Leverhulme said, 'No!' He wanted to follow the coast: hacking what would have been one of the most spectacular roads in Europe out of the hard Lewisian gneiss, dropping sheer to the sea, hundreds of feet below.

That certainly was the story circulating in Lewis while the work was in progress. When Leverhulme abruptly abandoned his schemes, many people saw the bridge that had no purpose as an appropriate memorial for the dream that failed.

The reasons for Leverhulme's failure confront us in the villages of Coll and Gress, which we pass on the way to Tolsta; each of them, like the bridge itself, looking out on a sandy beach. Three beaches: all lovely; all different; all peaceful; very unlike the bloodless but hard-fought battlefields they were at a critical point in the history of Lewis.

The best account of the Leverhulme 'affaire' is to be found in Nigel Nicolson's *Lord of the Isles*. It is well researched, eminently readable and completely accurate on all the major questions of fact.

His touch is not so sure, however, when he analyses the islanders' character and motives. Coming from a wealthy, aristocratic, English public school environment, Nicolson had no key to the egalitarian island mind. I will take up some of his errors as we go, but for the substance of the story Nicolson can be recommended with confidence to anyone who wants a fuller account than mine.

Garry Bridge beyond the village of Tolsta on what was to have been Lord Leverhulme's new route to Ness. It spans a deep gorge and overlooks one of the loveliest beaches in the Western Isles but it leads precisely nowhere. A few yards beyond the bridge the road peters out in the moor.

When Leverhulme came to Lewis, what are now the villages of Coll and Gress were farms. Modest farms. If they survived today they would not be viable agricultural units, but Leverhulme attached great importance to them: he regarded them as essential for the milk supply of what he saw as the growing industrial town of Stornoway.

The farms were raided by landless ex-servicemen from the neighbouring villages, who wanted to stake out crofts and build homes for their families. The post-war government was committed to a programme of land settlement but events were moving too slowly for impatient young men, after four long years of war. Men, moreover, who had been tutored, by the vacillations of government, to believe that the only way to get land was to seize it. Across the bay they could see the village of Aignish where a raid on a farm eventually led to a programme of land settlement.

It was not a simple confrontation between Leverhulme and

the raiders, as it is often represented to be. There were two other active parties: the vast majority of the people of Lewis, who were not involved in raiding, and central government. There was also a Greek chorus, several choruses in fact, not involved in the dispute but vocal on the periphery, and often ill-informed.

One chorus was provided by émigré Lewismen. I can think of no other way to describe them. Living comfortably on the mainland, generally in professional posts, with a romantic attachment to the island they now visited, only on holiday, or in their dreams. Free from the urgent need of the raiders for homes. Free from the urgent need of all islanders, whether raiders or not, for the employment Lord Leverhulme promised them.

Then there were the ideologues, the political activists, like the communist folk-hero John Maclean, who accused the Lewismen of cowardice for accepting work from a capitalist.

And there were the Highland lairds, resenting the appearance on the scene of an upstart Englishman, who despised the shooting and fishing for which, or by which, they lived. Who also threatened to introduce a new style of progressive estate management which they would find it equally difficult to imitate or ignore.

In a sort of harmonious cacophony the three choruses sang the same song, although they had irreconcilable views on almost everything that had a bearing on the situation in Lewis. They did nothing to affect the outcome, but they helped to perpetuate the myth, evolved by the national press, in its simplistic way: that the raiders were humble crofters defending an ancient freedom against the machinations of an English interloper who wanted to enslave them in his factories.

The media myth is almost a complete reversal of the truth. The crazy paradox of the Leverhulme 'affaire' is that the great majority of the Lewis crofters supported the laird against the raiders. Support for the raiders, in their illegal seizure of the land, came from Ministers of the Crown, in a Coalition government dominated by the Tories.

At one stage large numbers of crofters pled with Leverhulme to have the raiders imprisoned, for breach of the interdict he had obtained against them, while the Scottish Office was hinting to him privately that, if the raiders were imprisoned, the government would release them.

In every area of the island, meetings were held calling for a ten years' abstention from land raiding to give Leverhulme's schemes a chance to prove themselves. Even in Back, the area which includes Coll and Gress, only nine people, in a crowded schoolroom, voted for the raiders against the laird.

It was an astonishing situation in an island notorious – or famous, according to one's point of view – for its long history of land raiding, of which the Aignish Riot was merely an example.

Feeling in Lewis in support of Leverhulme ran so high the government was forced to change its stance. He was promised ten years of freedom from land settlement, on the farms round Stornoway. At that point fate intervened. The post-war economic depression set in. Leverhulme found himself temporarily short of cash. He had to halt his Lewis schemes until the economic blizzard passed.

As soon as Leverhulme announced the stoppage, the Scottish Office withdrew the guarantee of immunity from raiding. And that, despite the fact that the government had been compelled to curtail its own programme of public works, at the same time, and for the same reason.

Leverhulme thereupon abandoned his Lewis schemes and concentrated his attention on Harris.

The immediate sequel was the mass emigration from Lewis of many hundreds of young men. Ostensibly they went to work on the land in Canada, but a considerable proportion slipped across the frontier into the States, often illegally, looking for industrial employment.

When Leverhulme died in 1925, the *Times*, still cherishing the media myth, said the crofter population at first welcomed Leverhulme's schemes for the island, 'but when they realised they would have to pay for their prosperity by being, as it seemed to them, industrialised, they rebelled, and, ultimately, after four years' struggle, Lord Leverhulme had to accept defeat'.

It is difficult to understand how a reputable newspaper could perpetuate so gross a falsehood.

It was not Lord Leverhulme who was defeated: it was the

In an island with a hundred crofting villages the identification marks on the sheep are of the utmost importance. Many crofters are skilled in identifying the multitude of ear marks used by different owners. Horn brands are also used. This Stornoway blacksmith used his door for checking new brands as he made them until eventually it became almost a crofting directory. Courtesy Acair Ltd.

people of Lewis. It was not the crofters who inflicted the defeat: it was the government. When the *Times* published its fatuous and misleading comment, hundreds of the crofters, who were supposed to have resisted industrialisation, were working contentedly in the motor industry in Detroit.

There is another twist to the story. The raiders, in resisting

the pleading and the pressure of their fellow islanders to give
Lord Leverhulme's schemes a chance, displayed an indomitable
determination to go their own way, regardless of the
consequences, which is at the same time one of the strengths,
and one of the weaknesses, of the island character. A rugged
individualism which seems at variance with the strong tradition
of communal solidarity, but which is just as surely part of the
mix.

And in one sense the raiders were right, although for
reasons which they did not know, and could not have foreseen.
The conflict Leverhulme saw between crofting and
industrialisation was rapidly being resolved by the motor car,
which eventually made possible a marriage of the two. And
although industrial employment was essential, the croft still
had a value. In the great depression of the thirties, survival was
easier on a Lewis croft than in an urban breadline in the USA,
as the return of many emigrants dramatically proved.

While the depression confirmed the value of the croft, it was
the experience of earlier years which imbued the Lewisman
with the passion for a piece of land. It was just as strong among
those who opposed raiding as among the raiders; just as strong
possibly, among those who emigrated as among those who
stayed.

We can pick up much of the history which conditioned the
island in the village of Tong.

Tong is a lively village with a good community spirit, and the
local Historical Society has gathered all the information
available about it, in an excellent publication, *Tong: the Story of a
Lewis Village*.

Among the social and economic forces which produced the
present settlement pattern in Tong were the forced migrations
of the early part of the nineteenth century, when Park and
Harris were cleared to make sheep farms, and the displaced
crofters were settled near the shore, in locations like Tong, to
provide cheap labour for kelp-gathering or the fishing
industry.

There was some land raiding in Tong in 1919, at the same
time as the raids in Coll and Gress, but with a rather different
result. Lord Leverhulme did not attach the same importance to
the small farm of Tong (formerly a minister's glebe) as to the

One of the first commercial flights to Lewis brought a party of fisher
girls home from Orkney. The journey took less than an hour. By
surface transport it would have taken several days — by sea to
Scrabster, by train from Thurso to Inverness, another train from
Inverness to Kyle of Lochalsh, and then a sea voyage of more than
four hours to Stornoway. The coming of the plane altered the
relationship of the islands to each other and brought them closer to
Glasgow, London and New York than many mainland cities.

larger farms of Coll and Gress. He granted the raiders' wishes
almost immediately.

In the island-wide context this was no doubt intended as a
conciliatory gesture, a sign that he was not inflexible. It must,
however, have helped to harden attitudes in Coll and Gress.
The raiders there, from their point of view, now appeared to
be discriminated against. Others got land from Leverhulme:
they did not.

The Tong book highlights the emigration which resulted
from the collapse of Lord Leverhulme's schemes, and which
affected Tong like other places, despite the additional holdings

created. There was no way the Lewis problem of the 1920s
could have been resolved by a redistribution of land, in spite of
the obsession of the Scottish Office.

All these movements, in and out of Tong, are documented
by individual family histories. It is a record of the village very
much more detailed than William the Conqueror's famous
Domesday Book, but compiled to serve the purposes of local
people, interested in their antecedents, rather than a
conqueror's tax collectors.

The Tong book also gives an insight into the life of a crofting
township, both in the present day and in the past; illustrating
the seasonal rhythm associated with the ritual – it is a ritual! –
of peat cutting, and the communal activities, such as dipping
and clipping the sheep, or improving the township pasture by
surface seeding. These activities give cohesion to crofting
communities in which the skilled, the semi-skilled, the
professional man, the employer of labour, and the employed
labourer, all meet on the level and share the same agricultural
tasks, whatever their main wage-earning occupation might be.

It also charts the changes which have taken place in the
fishing industry in Broad Bay, and describes the life of the
fisher girls who travelled annually in hundreds to fishing ports
from Shetland to Yarmouth, performing, with remarkable
dexterity and cheerfulness, the cold, dirty, disagreeable,
repetitive and wearisome task of gutting thousands of herring
every day with a sharp little knife, known in Gaelic as a 'cutag'.
They generally worked in the open air, exposed to rain, wind
or sun, according to the season; bloodied to the elbows with
herring gut, their fingers swathed in bandages to cover the cuts
they had already received or protect the fingers which had so
far escaped.

The seasonal migration of the fisher girls was an event of
social and economic importance in every Lewis village up to the
second world war, and it still bulks large in the folk-memory of
the island. When the Queen visited Lewis in 1956, the official
gift from Stornoway Town Council was a golden replica of a
cutag.

Only an island like Lewis, devoid of any sense of class or
status – ministers of religion apart! – could have thought of
presenting a Queen with a gutting girl's knife, as the symbol by

Bosun Kenneth Stewart of Tong was the artist's model for this statue forming part of the Merchant Navy Memorial on Tower Hill, London.

which the community wished to be remembered.

The Tong book also highlights the importance of education, and the central place of the Free Church in the life of the community. Island Sabbatarianism can be irksome at times. It is so all-pervasive it represents a considerable diminution of individual freedom, but those who are inclined to rebel are still likely to be churchgoers and to appreciate the Sabbath calm, even when they are tempted to break it.

The genealogical information and the precise detail in the Tong book are specific to the village, but, in broad terms, it is relevant to every crofting village in the island, especially in the questions it raises about future trends.

Being within easy reach of Stornoway, Tong has become a
commuting village. Council houses and some private building
have been superimposed on the crofting infrastructure.
Crofters in fact are now outnumbered two to one.

Tong is thriving, says the Historical Society, but whether as a
crofting community or a dormitory suburb of Stornoway, they
add, is open to question.

Tolsta, at the end of the road, has also been documented in a
book published by the local Community Association although,
in this case, the compilation is the work of an individual:
Donald Macdonald, a Tolsta man, who was headmaster for
many years of an Edinburgh school.

His spare time in winter was spent in the Scottish Record
Office, unearthing the hidden history of his native village from
Estate papers, recording the views and decisions of remote
landlords and their minions, which bore upon the crofters'
welfare, although the crofters were never consulted, and
seldom informed, until the blow fell.

His summer holidays were spent at home, in Lewis, in a very
different atmosphere, compounded of Gaelic stories and peat
smoke: exploring the rich store of oral tradition which
enshrines the crofters' perception of township history, and
records the havoc which remote officials wrought. The
bringing together of the oral and the documented makes *The
Tolsta Townships* an invaluable social record.

As well as recording the history of the townships, Donald
Macdonald describes the clothes, the food, the recreations, the
marriage and funeral customs, and the superstitions of a
community in transition.

In the process of transition Donald himself has been
something of an anchorman: not resistant to change, but aware
of the importance of getting on the record, before it was too
late, the things that were fast disappearing.

His cousin, George Morrison, also from Tolsta, and also a
city headmaster, played a rather different role as a sort of
licensed jester, commenting on all aspects of island life and
providing, by his humour, the lubrication a process of social
change inevitably requires.

These two cousins represent a very important class in Lewis
social history: those who have left the island for professional

reasons but still contribute, in a very real way, to its wellbeing. They must be distinguished from those I have mentioned earlier, who retain only a romantic affection for an island they have no intention of ever returning to.

Other representative figures from the area, who identify important threads in the island story, are Murdo Morrison, Alex Morrison, Isabella Thomson, Kenneth Stewart and Lewis Maciver.

Murdo Morrison was born in Tong in 1872, the year of the great Education Act which had such far-reaching effects mainly, but not wholly, for good in Lewis, as in other places. The Act had not effectively reached Tong when Murdo went to school: the time-lag itself is a recurring and important element in the island's social history. His education began in the Free Church school: a little thatched hut by the shore, which was eventually replaced by a public school when the Act caught up with Lewis.

When he left Tong, Murdo went to Aberdeen Grammar School. There was no Secondary School in Lewis then. Eventually he became an Inspector of Schools, and later Director of Education for Inverness-shire, a post he held until his retirement. He was back in Lewis in his 92nd year, to speak at the formal opening of a new and modern school in his native village.

He thus encapsulates, within his own lifespan, practically the whole history of education in the island, from the small struggling voluntary schools, providing a modest education eagerly sought by a minority avid for learning, to the era of universal state education, from infant-room to university, for anyone who wanted it. A high point in educational provision from which we now seem to be receding.

Alex Morrison, from the neighbouring village of Back, represents another aspect of the same story. A man of immense natural talent, Alex was one of the many in his generation who could not afford the education he could have assimilated. Economic pressures drove him to emigrate to America. Economic pressures drove him back to Lewis during the great depression. Educated, as the old saying puts it, 'in the school of hard knocks', he returned to Lewis, determined that later generations should have the opportunities his generation

A striking study by Murdo Macleod of the concentrated skill which goes into the making of a web of Harris tweed.

lacked. He devoted a fiery eloquence, and a sharp logical mind, to the cause he had espoused.

The third on my list takes us into very different territory. James and Isabella Thomson were married in Stornoway in 1877. She was a village girl with almost no English. He was a trapper with the Hudson Bay Company, stationed at Fort Chipewyan, in the remote fastnesses of Northern Canada.

She was unable to go with her husband, when his leave was over, because of the disturbed state of Canada around the time of the Riel Rebellion. Three years later she set out to follow him: the first white woman to settle in Athabasca. Alone, yet curiously not alone.

Throughout the whole journey she was under the care of what can only be described as a benign Mafia of Gaelic speakers, many in positions of authority, like the Captain of the vessel on which she crossed the Atlantic, who made a point of seeing her every day, and the Chief Deputy of the Hudson Bay Company, at Fort Charlton, who made every possible provision for her safety on the last 1500 miles of her hazardous journey, but added to her problems by asking her to take a crate of live hens to a friend of his at her journey's end.

Most of the 'mafiosi' were Lewismen. Some were relatives of her husband. At that time the frozen north-west of Canada was almost a suburb of Stornoway. Indeed, Fort Chipewyan, to which she was bound, had been established by a Lewisman – Sir Alexander Mackenzie, the great Canadian explorer.

Many of the trappers eventually returned to Lewis – including the Thomsons – and tales of the Talamh Fuar (the cold country) bulk large in the island's oral tradition. Many more remained in Canada, making a contribution to its development quite beyond computing.

Kenneth Stewart, whose home was just two doors from the Thomsons in Tong, was a humble bosun but his face and figure are seen by thousands of visitors to London. At the end of the second world war he was chosen, for his record as much as his physique, to be the model for the National War Memorial of the Merchant Navy on Tower Hill.

He served with the Royal Navy in the first world war and with the Merchant Navy in the second. He was awarded the Parchment of the Royal Humane Society for life-saving, and the BEM for his services when his ship was torpedoed off New Zealand and the crew were two days in an open boat before being rescued. The New Zealand Shipping Company endowed a prize in his memory as a model bosun.

Lewis Maciver takes us into a different era and a different class. In the early years of last century he was the leading businessman in the island. He lived in the farmhouse at Gress, which still survives, and which was the eye of the storm in Leverhulme's day. He was a notable land-improver, importing cargoes of lime and shell sand to reclaim the peat bogs, but he also had business interests in Stornoway as a fishcurer, shipowner, and general merchant. He helped to improve the mail service, handled a large part of the island's import and export trade, and was sometimes resorted to by crofters in trouble as a 'legal' adviser. He was reputed to be as kind as his ancestor William Maciver, also of Gress, whose hospitality is celebrated by one of the greatest of Gaelic poets, Rob Donn. When the crofters from the villages along Loch Shell were evicted, it was to Lewis Maciver they turned for help. He negotiated with the Estate in their name, and committed himself to a considerable financial risk on their behalf. Yet, in

his history of Lewis, Donald Macdonald describes Lewis
Maciver as an arrogant man, whose tenants 'led an unenviable
uncertain existence'.

The explanation is simple. It anticipates, and roughly
parallels, the Leverhulme situation, which arose a century later
in the same area. Lewis Maciver and the crofters in his vicinity
were competitors for what little land there was. The local
crofters saw him, correctly, as a grasping man and an
oppressor. The rest of the island, having no conflict with him,
saw him, also correctly, as an able man of business and a friend
in need. Both his virtues and his faults were compounded by
the fact that he was a choleric little man with a very short fuse.

He appears to have fought at least two duels. Around 1820,
there was a quarrel about a shipload of coal the Chamberlain
was discharging at Maciver's private pier. In the heat of the
argument, the Chamberlain, a much taller man, put his hand
on Maciver's top hat and thrust it down to his chin. A duel
followed at Tong sands, with pistols. Maciver fired impetuously
and missed. The Chamberlain, a crack shot, took his time and
blew Maciver's whiskers off.

That story rests on hearsay. The other is better authenticated
because it was reported to the Crown Office in Edinburgh. In
1844 Alexander Macleay, Collector of Customs in Stornoway,
accused Maciver of smuggling, probably with truth. Maciver
'called him out'. Together they repaired to a field on Goathill
Farm, not far from Tong sands, the scene of the first affair.

A Stornoway tailor named Mackenzie, the tenant of the field,
was the only witness, and the unwilling umpire. The duellists
had no seconds. They fired simultaneously and missed; shook
hands, and went off together for a dram: no doubt of
smuggled schnapps.

Lewis Maciver might have been involved in a third duel
when he quarrelled with Sir Thomas Johnstone, a rather
pompous gentleman who had a sporting let of Gress from
Seaforth.

Sir Thomas, in a lordly manner, commanded Maciver to see
him on Sunday to discuss the arrangements. Maciver replied,
in an equally lordly way, 'We are not in the habit of making
bargains on Sunday in this country'.

Johnstone called him a humbug.

That 'raised my Highland blood', commented Lewis to Seaforth, but unfortunately the record does not tell us what he said when his blood was up.

Weeks later, he was still complaining to Seaforth about Sir Thomas' 'absurd aristocratic notions', which would have amused his tenants, had they known, because he was not without some aristocratic notions of his own.

There is a story that, when King William died in 1837, two Lewis crofters were discussing the news.

'Who will be King now?' asked one.

'Who but Lewis?' was the answer.

The story is generally told to illustrate the naiveté of the island crofter. Actually it illustrates his propensity for the barbed comment that cuts the lordly down to size. The oral tradition of the island is studded with examples.

An island peat bank. For centuries peat was a product of prime importance both to the economic and the social life of the island.

CHAPTER 7
One of Britain's Major Landmarks

Standing at the Butt of Lewis, even on a summer day with no wind, you can feel the restless power and surge of the sea. In winter, when the waves are driven by a hurricane, blowing uninhibited across three thousand miles of open ocean, the scene at the Butt is awe-inspiring – if you can keep your feet for long enough to see it.

The force of the wind, however, is puny compared with the other forces which have made these contorted and tormented rocks.

The message comes over vividly, even in the cautious, bureau–scientific prose of the Nature Conservancy Council, which has published a report entitled *Outer Hebrides*, identifying 'localities of Geological and Geomorphological Importance'. Several of them significant on a world scale.

'The Outer Hebrides consists almost entirely of a rock assemblage known as Lewisian gneiss, whose name derives from the Island of Lewis. Their history can be traced over more than half of geological time, as far back as 2800 million years, further than any other area of Britain,' writes the Council.

'These rocks, once sedimentary and igneous in character, have been altered on more than one occasion by exposure to high temperatures and pressures due to deep burial within the Earth's crust; during such periods of burial the rocks were recrystallised and new minerals and structures formed.'

'The geology of the Outer Hebrides is thus complex and its elucidation is of great importance in determining Earth's history.'

The Butt of Lewis, and the whole stretch of coast between Port of Ness and Skigersta, are among the sites of interest to geologists listed by the Conservancy.

For the specialist the interest lies in contrasting examples of 'Laxfordian folding', but even those of us to whom the technical terms mean nothing can feel that, at the Northern tip of Lewis, looking west to Labrador or north to the Pole, we are closer to the dawn of creation than anywhere else in Britain. It is for the poet rather than the scientist to define the experience.

The Butt of Lewis is one of Britain's major landmarks. The Romans knew it, and the Vikings. The Spanish Armada – what was left of it – passed this way.

In the American War of Independence French privateers haunted the area. In 1780 one of them, 'Luke Ryan', made a cheeky foray into Stornoway. They were back again during the Revolutionary and Napoleonic Wars. In 1793 the Hebridean cattle trade was disrupted because drovers were afraid to cross the Minch. The Royal Navy sent a frigate and a sloop to protect them and the fishermen. There are even tales, which may be true, of Ness fishermen carried into captivity by Barbary pirates.

In two world wars the Royal Navy, steaming west from Scapa, and the vast convoys of merchant ships assembled in Loch Ewe, saw the Butt of Lewis lighthouse as their last glimpse of Britain.

For thousands of emigrants, both from the islands and the mainland, the Butt of Lewis must also have been the last glimpse of the homeland from which they were being driven, or which they were leaving voluntarily, in the expectation of finding a better life elsewhere.

Although it has been an important milestone for many thousands of travellers, the Butt has not figured in the news except once, in May 1919, when a little Danish cargo vessel, the *Mary* of Copenhagen, which no one had ever heard of, hove to below the lighthouse and ran up a flag signal which sent Britain mad with joy.

In the International code the flags spelled out the message 'Saved hands!'

The *Daily Mail* had offered a prize of £10,000 for the first airmen to fly the Atlantic: something never attempted before. The American navy laid on a massive fail-safe expedition via the Azores, using seaplanes and with naval vessels stationed along the route. The prize money meant nothing to them – they had spent it ten times over – but they were determined to be first. Harry Hawker, an Australian, and Mackenzie Grieve, a Scot, set off from Newfoundland to beat them to it, with no

back-up, in a tiny aeroplane with a water-cooled engine, no
heating and a defective radio. They took off into a hurricane,
and disappeared.

Britain had given them up for lost when the *Mary*, one of the
last freighters on the Atlantic which had no radio, broke the
news that she had them safe on board.

A destroyer was sent from Scapa Flow to meet them. Hawker
and Grieve were fêted by the fleet. At every station, from
Scrabster to London, huge crowds greeted them, often with
bands playing. They were treated like conquerors in a Roman
triumph but, in a few weeks, their names had vanished from
the newspapers. Now they have disappeared from most of the
reference books as well.

The evanescent fame of the aviators contrasts strangely with
the brooding presence of one of Britain's most impressive
megaliths.

The Thrushel Stone – Clach an Thrusail – which lies not far
from the main road between Barvas and Ness speaks to us of a
civilisation which must have flourished here four thousand
years ago or so. It has aroused the wonder and whetted the
curiosity of every generation since.

The Thrushel Stone has given its name to the neighbouring
village of Ballantrushal; it was depicted by Daniell in his
famous series of Scottish prints; it is the theme of a Gaelic
poem written in the city of Niagara Falls; and it has featured as
one of the characters in a book: a sort of enigmatic, ogreish
chorus.

The book is not a novel, nor a biography, nor a sociological
study, but it contains some of the best elements of all three.

Devil in the Wind by Charles Macleod is based on fact. A
snowstorm which struck the Western Isles in 1955 and
immobilised all transport for more than a week.

The storm threatened to prevent a wedding, linking two
villages on the west coast of Lewis, some distance apart. Rather
than postpone the wedding, the villagers turned out en masse
and dug their way through miles of frozen snow, heaped high
between the roadside dykes.

Around this incident, Charles Macleod weaves a vivid
tapestry of the warm communal life of a Lewis village in the
fifties, before the onset of television and the relative prosperity

The Lewis white fishing industry died largely because of the lack of safe harbours from which modern boats could be operated with ease and safety. This photograph explains the problem graphically. In addition to manhandling a boat weighing many tons up and down the beach, the crew had to remove and replace the ballast each time they went to fish.

of the present day. He also explains the circumstances, and the motivation, for his own return to rural Lewis from a teaching job in Glasgow, which was itself something of a portent. A sign that Lewis, after years of decline, was beginning to attract young men back.

I can think of no better introduction for a non-Gaelic speaker, anxious to break through the language barrier, and catch the flavour of island village life: the humour, the characters, the customs, the memories, the problems, the little personal jealousies, the neighbourliness, and above all, the egalitarianism which enabled Charles Macleod to function simultaneously as a full and active member of the crofting township, standing level with everyone else, as the headmaster of a large junior secondary school, and as a respected member of official and unofficial bodies, ranging from the Highlands and Islands Advisory Panel and the Broadcasting Council for Scotland to a very combative Crofters Union, which stymied a government and altered significantly the terms of an Act of Parliament.

The Thrushel Stone belongs to a remote pre-Christian past although, as Charles Macleod suggests, it still broods over the village in an eerie questioning way. At Eoropie we are much closer to the present, but still in the debatable land between pagan superstition and Christian faith, conscious simultaneously of the continuities and the dichotomies which have made Lewis what it is.

The Teampull Mor – the big church – at Eoropie is a Catholic chapel, abandoned by the Presbyterians, restored by Episcopalians, and associated for many centuries with a pagan ritual which illuminates the agricultural practices of the past and shows how, in the Long Island, even the produce of the land depended on the bounty of the sea.

The Teampull Mor was dedicated to St Molua. Sometimes it is said to have been dedicated to St Olaf. W. C. Mackenzie, the Lewis historian, who earned his livelihood on the Baltic Exchange in London but lived in Lewis in spirit, suggests in *Book of the Lews* that Olaf is merely a corruption of Molua. He shows convincingly how the error could arise.

At the same time he does not rule out the possibility that there was a pre-Christian Viking shrine on the same spot, providing a more substantial base for the association with Olaf which persists in local tradition.

After the church at Ui, the Teampull Mor was the most important ecclesiastical building in Lewis and an object of special veneration.

Captain Dymes, an Englishman, visited Lewis in 1630, at the behest of Charles I, to report on the development of the fisheries for the Royal profit and as a nursery of seamen. He has left us one of the earliest accounts of the island. He seems to have been there long enough to experience both the iridescent summer evenings, when there is almost no night, and the short winter days which, rather surprisingly, he says are 'almost as long as ours here in England'.

In Dymes's day people visited the Teampull Mor in search of health. Those who could not go themselves sent replicas of injured or festering limbs to be laid on the altar. When he visited the temple he saw, as he puts it, 'lame arms or legges in wood with the forme of their sores and wounds'.

The local people held two great festivals in the year at

Candlemas and All Hallows when, according to Dymes, it was their custom 'to eat and drincke until they were druncke. And then, after much dancing and dalliance togeather, they entred the chappell at night with lights in their hands where they continued till nexte morninge in theire devotions'.

Which sounds not unlike a modern Christmas, except that we are more sparing with our devotions.

The worthy captain clearly disapproved. He thought the proceedings idolatrous. So did the minister, who came specially to Eoropie to stop it. Presumably he came from Ui because Dymes says Eoropie was 'farr from his abode and out of his cure'.

In spite of the minister a full generation later, according to Martin Martin, as soon as 'the natives came within sight of the church, although it might be four miles distant, they would kneel and repeat the Paternoster'.

Martin records that at All Hallows the inhabitants round about brewed ale, each family providing a peck of malt. A chosen representative then waded waist-deep into the sea and poured out a libation to a heathen god called Shony, accompanied by a prayer for a plentiful harvest of seaware to be used as manure, enriching the ground for the ensuing year.

W.C. Mackenzie makes the interesting suggestion that Shony is a corruption of the Cymric word for sound. Shony, he believes, was the god of noise: roaring along the Atlantic coast in the winter storms; heaping the beaches with the precious seaweed.

Just how important seaweed was to the life of the island communities is examined by Alexander Fenton in *The Shape of the Past 2*. He quotes, and does not dispute, a calculation, made in 1794, that it took 200 large creelfuls of seaweed to produce a boll of barley or fourteen barrels of potatoes. The seaweed had to be carried, dripping, from the beach to the crofts, however steep or long the climb. Its use involved an immense expenditure of labour for a meagre return.

In 1630 the minister told Dymes he had put an end to the idolatrous ritual of the Teampull Mor. Around 1700 two ministers assured Martin Martin they had stamped it out thirty years before his visit.

Alexander Carmichael, however, points out that the ritual of pouring out a libation 'of mead, ale or gruel', to ensure a good harvest of seaweed, continued for more than a century and a half after Martin Martin declared it dead, not only in Lewis but in Iona, where he knew a man who, as a boy, had seen his father perform the ceremony.

By that time seaweed was not only of value as a manure; it was an important article of commerce, and a destructive influence on the social life of the community, as James Hunter shows in his classic *The Making of the Crofting Community*.

The Teampull Mor, which tells us so much about the mechanism of social and cultural change, would probably be a ruin today if the Matheson family had not restored it, and placed it under the care of St Peter's Episcopal Church in Stornoway. Presbyterian and anti-landlord Lewis owes this treasure to an alien landlord and an alien church. No man is an island. No island either!

Ness at one time was an important judicial centre – the home of the Breves: hereditary judges named Morison, of whom there were reputed to have been twelve in succession, spanning several centuries, during the Lordship of the Isles.

The Lords of the Isles would appear to have dealt with criminal matters directly, or through the principal chiefs, among whom were the Macleods of both Lewis and Harris. The Breves were concerned with civil disputes as arbitrators or men of knowledge and skill.

The name Breve derives from the Gaelic 'Breitheamh', a judge. There was a Breve in each of the major islands but, according to some authorities, the Morisons of Ness had some sort of pre-eminence. Certainly the Morison Breves have left a more durable mark in Highland tradition than any of the others. So durable that more than three centuries after the death of the last to hold office, George Morrison, the Tolsta satirist, chose 'the Breve' as his *nom de plume*, when he began to castigate, in a gentle, humorous way, the foibles of his contemporaries, in the columns of the *Stornoway Gazette*. He had no need to explain the significance of the name to his readers: they were all familiar with the status of the Breve and the particular association with the name Morrison.

It has sometimes been objected that the northernmost tip of the northernmost isle was an unlikely location for a supremo among the judges, in a Lordship of which the power base lay in Islay, far to the south.

In a formally structured society, power, including the judiciary, would certainly be centralised, but the Lordship of the Isles was a looser organisation, on the Celtic model, and one family of judges or arbitrators could well have acquired a special reputation, because of the quality of their judgements, sustained over a period of time, or because of quite adventitious circumstances.

The oracle of Delphi was not located in Athens, and the function of the Breve seems to have been closer to that of an oracle than a modern law court even if, as seems probable, the Breves were guided in their judgements by an established legal code, whether written or orally transmitted.

The existence of the Breves reminds us that the Islands were not the barbarous fringe of a civilised Scottish kingdom, as they are often represented to have been.

The Lordship of the Isles was a viable Celtic alternative to the feudalism of lowland Scotland. As well as the chiefs and the judges, there were family groups devoted to medicine and the arts, to record-keeping and to the regulation of weights and measures, which implies a thriving trade.

'As distinct from feudalism with its well-nigh absolute property in land, and its absolute claim upon the service of the vassals', the Lordship of the Isles was 'a patriarchal system'. 'The chief who abused his power and became oppressive was apt to find himself in trouble with his clan,' writes D.J. Macdonald of Castleton, in his book *Clan Donald*.

It was as part of this alternative structure that the Morison Breves established the reputation as lawmen which echoes down to the present day. It is, however, a muted and distorted echo.

As D.J. Macdonald points out, the records of the Lordship of the Isles have suffered sadly as a result of wars and raids and, when the Campbells eventually ousted the Macdonalds from Islay, in the early seventeenth century, all traces of the Lordship were virtually obliterated. There is no vandal like the 'civilised' conqueror, wiping out all trace of the 'barbarians' he claims to have destroyed.

As a result we know of the Breves mainly through the oral

tradition, which has come down to us from the time when the Lordship of the Isles was in dissolution, and the Morison Breves were caught up in the power struggle of the Macleods, and their allies the Macaulays, against the Mackenzies who, as I have already related, took over Lewis from the Macleods with the connivance of the Morisons, much as the Campbells took over Islay from the Macdonalds.

We know the bloody and untidy end of the Breves. We do not know them in their finest hour.

William Matheson, in the *Proceedings of the Gaelic Society of Inverness*, suggests that the Breves were resented by the Macleods and the Macaulays for two reasons.

They were placed in Ness as representatives of a higher power than the Macleods – the Lords of the Isles – and they were of a different racial origin.

Matheson believes that the Morisons were originally Celts, while the Macleods and Macaulays were indubitably Norse and inordinately proud of their ancestry.

By the time the clan feuds broke out, the different groups were so mixed and intermarried they were genetically indistinguishable but, in a society which placed great store on genealogy and emphasised only the male line, differences in allegiance could survive long after all rational basis for them had disappeared.

The Breves' house has completely vanished. It is said to have stood on Habost machair between the two cemeteries. The Breves themselves, however, have left something of an afterglow which is richly displayed in the appendices to William Matheson's book *The Blind Harper*.

Roderick Morison, the celebrated blind harper and poet of Dunvegan, was a descendant of the last of the Breves. His father John Morison, the Breve's great grandson, was also something of a poet. He wrote the first extant account of the island by a native, and was one of Martin Martin's principal sources of information about Lewis.

Surprisingly and significantly, Matheson makes the comment, 'John Morison ... seems not to have attended a university'. Several of his contemporary tacksmen were university educated and some of the Breves, even from the period of their notorious feud with the Macaulays, were also

Ness Football Team with their supporters and an array of trophies. To anyone who has watched the rapidly changing social scene in Lewis the sponsorship by a local garage is a significant pointer. Whereas Lewis used to be two distinct entities — Stornoway and the crofting villages — it is now one large commuting community: Los Angeles without the smog! Courtesy of *Stornoway Gazette*.

university men. I wonder how many lowland or English farmers of the sixteenth and seventeenth centuries held university degrees?

The tradition of respect for learning for its own sake persists in Ness (and in the islands generally) down to the present day, but it is as seamen that the people of Ness really excelled.

There are few more inhospitable coasts in the world than the stretch from Barvas north to the Butt of Lewis: without safe harbours, open to the fury of the Western Ocean, and lashed by winds which frequently reach storm or hurricane force.

On January 31st 1953 the 7000-ton CPR vessel *Clan MacQuarrie* was driven ashore near Borve in one of the worst gales of the century – the storm which, a few hours later, sank the ferry *Princess Victoria*, in the Irish channel, with the loss of over 130 lives.

At Borve, despite a wind gusting over 100 miles an hour, the seamen from the coastal villages assisted the Lifesaving crew from Stornoway in effecting what was then, and may still be, the greatest rescue by breeches buoy in the history of the sea. The whole crew of sixty-five, and the ship's cat, were taken safely ashore without even wetting their feet.

The story of the rescue, which is told in Lennox Kerr's book *The Great Storm,* had a fairytale ending: the first officer of the stricken ship married the local postmaster's daughter.

There are, however, more disasters than rescues in the history of that bleak coast. Perhaps the worst of them occurred in December, 1862, when five boats were lost with thirty-one able-bodied men on board leaving, in a few small villages, twenty-four widows, seventy orphans and twenty-eight other dependent relatives.

One woman, who lost her only son and a son-in-law in the 1862 disaster, had lost her husband, son and son-in-law in a similar disaster a few years earlier. As a result, there were three destitute widows and five orphans in one home with no able-bodied man to support them.

A relief fund was generously supported. Queen Victoria was among the contributors. But it was harshly administered. Donald Munro, the most hated factor in Lewis history, was treasurer and used the fund as a guarantee for the landlord's rents. Disbursements were made on rent day and most of the money was swept back across the table into the coffers of the Estate.

The situation was exposed in a pamphlet written and published in London, by a Lewisman, who gave his address as the Oriental Club in Hanover Square. To cover his tracks, Munro set off for Ness on horseback with a bag of coins for the widows. He also carried two pistols. He had just heard that the Swainbost crofters were marching to Stornoway to protest about an unrelated grievance of their own. Munro was not molested by the crofters and, when he got to Ness, he distributed the whole remaining fund in one irresponsible bonanza, to a group of bewildered women who had never seen so much money in their lives before.

Much of the history of Lewis in the last century is encapsulated in that single paragraph. The poverty of the people; the lack of safe harbours; the oppression by factors – even the factors of a magnanimous proprietor; the docility of the people in face of that oppression; and the overseas element – the islanders who had left but had not disengaged themselves.

When my father came to Lewis in the 1890s it was said that no Nessman of working age had ever died in bed: if a Nessman survived his childhood, he lived to a great age or he was drowned at sea. It was an overstatement but contained an element of truth.

Parallel with their skill in handling boats, the Nessmen developed a skill in building them. There were several local families involved in boatbuilding. The representative of one, John Macleod, Port of Ness, told the Napier Commission in 1884 that he built six boats a year. He was in communication then with Gladstone about the need for a deepwater harbour so that the fishermen could have bigger boats, as they had in other places.

A harbour was being built, he said, at Port of Ness but it was too small, and the outer wall was insufficient to withstand the winter storms. The sweep of the sea, he said, was stronger there, according to the Stevensons – the great lighthouse builders – than at any other place they had encountered.

The silted-up harbour at Port of Ness today bears testimony to the accuracy of his observation.

Best known of the boatbuilders were another family of Macleods with a tradition extending over nearly two hundred years. The first boatbuilder in the family, Finlay Macleod, was born at Fivepenny in 1805, and his great-grandson, John M. Macleod, is still in business as a consultant in Stornoway: probably the last custodian of the traditional skills employed in building the distinctive boats used in the great years of the ling fishing – the 'sgoth Niseach'.

The family illustrates another trait in the Ness, and Lewis, character – versatility. John M. Macleod, who learned his trade from his father at Port of Ness, became a lecturer in Lews Castle College when it opened in 1953.

His father, John F. Macleod, was highly regarded in Lewis as the man who got a line ashore from the *Iolaire*, saving more than forty lives. As a young man he worked around Saskatoon in Canada. On his return to Lewis he broadened the base of the business to include general carpentry and joinery, because the fishing was in decline. He also built the bodies of many of the buses which revolutionised the island's transport in the twenties.

The decline in the ling fishing, which forced the Macleods to diversify from boatbuilding into coachbuilding, turned the attention of the fishermen from home waters to the Merchant Navy. In the period between the wars there were so many Lewismen at sea, the *Stornoway Gazette* devoted two columns each week to the latest news from Lloyds about the vessels on which they were sailing. That employment vanished with the decline in the British merchant fleet.

Thus, twice within a lifetime the villages of Ness have lost their employment base, as completely as any worked-out mining town, but, in defiance of logic and economics and the inhospitable terrain, they continue to survive.

And more than survive. A period which should, by all the precedents from urban areas, have been marked by a loss of morale and a breakdown of community life has been distinguished by a vast improvement in housing and a remarkable display of communal enterprise.

Undoubtedly, Ness has economic problems. There is probably no area of Britain where the cards are stacked so heavily against a community's survival. Yet Ness has taken the lead in many of the communal movements of recent years which set an example not only to Lewis but to Britain, because they are not rooted in greed and motivated by personal gain, but rest on a tradition of service and a desire to enrich the lives of others.

CHAPTER 8

Structures That Span 4000 Years

There are three major monuments on the west side of Lewis now under the care of the state: the standing stones at Callanish; the broch at Dun Carloway; and the black house at Arnol. Between them they encompass four thousand years of island history.

Magnus Magnusson has described Callanish as 'one of the greatest prehistoric monuments in Europe'.

The joint authors of *Symbols of Power at the time of Stonehenge* – a recent massive and authoritative work – write of 'the astonishing circle and complex of stone alignments at Callanish'.

They believe the stones represent a re-writing of history: 'the same sort of deliberate manipulation that we see in the renaming of towns and cities – (St Petersburg-Petrograd-Leningrad; Salisbury-Harare)'.

It will surprise many people to think that the Outer Hebrides had a history to rewrite, four thousand years ago. It is still a popular fallacy that the Hebrides were discovered by Dr Johnson two centuries after Columbus discovered America!

Aubrey Burl in *The Stone Circles of the British Isles* describes Callanish as 'famous'. A prehistoric monument 'which has long excited the imagination'. 'Archaeologists,' he adds, 'have been taciturn about Callanish, seeing in it an enigma not easily solved by traditional methods.'

It is not necessary to be an expert to feel the power of the Callanish Stones or be confronted by the questions they raise.

The stones are magnificently sited on a hilltop overlooking what Burl has called 'a rare and magnificent bay sheltered from the Atlantic gales by the island of Great Bernera'.

We see them in the distance like a group of mourners: a funeral procession straggling across the skyline. It is only when we get among them we realise the size of the stones – the tallest is nearly sixteen feet; and the complexity of the layout, with avenues and arms superimposed on a circle, almost in the form of a Celtic cross. It is difficult to repel the illusion that a pagan

91

The Callanish Stones are older than the blanket of peat which covers the island of Lewis. This sketch was made 130 years ago by the Clerk of Works on the Lewis Estate when five feet of peat was removed to restore the stones to the state they had been in when first erected.

monument four thousand years old is a Christian sanctuary.

It is even more difficult, in some ways, to attune one's mind to the fact that the Callanish Stones are older than the Lewis peat.

The all-pervasive blanket bog is the most obvious characteristic of the landscape. Lewis was described by John Bright as a peat floating in the Atlantic. A Lewis poet, Donald Morrison from Bragar, recalling the same aspect of the island, in what he regarded as his exile in Duluth, sang of 'Eilean beag donn a' chuain' – the little brown isle of the waves.

When the Callanish Stones were erected, Lewis was a relatively wooded island, with a drier and more favourable climate, and no peat. In fact, five feet of peat had to be dug away in the middle of last century to reveal the stones as they were when they were first erected.

The sea level was lower than it is now. There were areas of fertile land around Callanish where now there is sea. At the same time, I believe – although none of the authorities I have read has made the point – that the produce of the sea was just as important, when the Callanish Stones were erected, as the produce of the land.

The waters of Loch Roag have always been rich in fish of many species. Oysters flourished naturally at Gisla even in my own boyhood, and the eminence on which the Callanish Stones were erected commands the estuary of several prolific salmon rivers.

Cecil Braithwaite in *Fishing Here and There* records that, on one of them, the Grimersta, fifty-four salmon were caught, by one rod in one day in 1888. On another occasion an angler lost his wager when he landed thirty-six fish in a single day. His rival had thirty-seven.

Victorian fishing stories are not a reliable guide to conditions in prehistoric Callanish, but the proximity of the Grimersta is, I believe, one of the key elements in the Callanish enigma.

It is not the existence of one spectacular circle which has to be explained at Callanish, but the existence of a complex of megalithic monuments in close proximity to each other, nearly twenty in all, which seems to imply that Callanish, in prehistoric times, was a regional centre of considerable significance.

Gerald and Margaret Ponting, who spent some years in Lewis and made a special study of the subject, have gathered the essential information conveniently in their booklet *New Light on the Stones of Callanish*.

The Pontings have added considerably to our knowledge of prehistoric Lewis. In addition to their detailed observations at Callanish, they have located important archaeological remains at Dalmore beach and have discovered a large but hitherto unrecorded circle at Achmore.

Although much has been written about Callanish, the archaeology of Lewis has not yet been systematically explored. The Pontings made a brave beginning and now Edinburgh University has established a field centre in Lewis from which much may be expected in future.

Professor Harding and his Edinburgh team have already begun the excavation of an island dun at Loch Bharabhat in west Uig, using underwater techniques for the first time in the Outer Hebrides.

Stone circles like that at Callanish have been described as Druid temples, Christian sanctuaries, astronomical observatories, symbols of power, and trading posts where primitive men met for great fairs in which the buying and selling of goods, religious observances and recreation were all inextricably mixed together.

These explanations are not mutually exclusive although some of them are untenable. It is unlikely that Callanish was a Druid temple. It is certain that it was not a Christian sanctuary.

An old Lewis 'black' house and the Carloway dun: two remarkable examples of Hebridean drystone construction.

We are perhaps not much further forward in a precise understanding of the function of the stones than the first writer who is known to have described them.

Three hundred years ago my great-grandfather's great-grandfather's grandfather, John Morison of Bragar, set it on the record that the megalithic circles of Lewis, according to tradition, 'were a sort of men converted into stones by an enchanter, others affirm that they were set up in place for devotion'.

We claim to be too sophisticated to credit the traditional story of an enchanter, but not long ago it was seriously suggested that the Callanish Stones were erected by 'Martians arriving in a flying saucer', which, so far as I am concerned, imposes quite as great a strain on one's credulity.

Personally I don't think we can do better than stick with a 'place for devotion', although what constituted devotion four thousand years ago is still beyond our ken.

The broch at Dun Carloway is approximately half the age of the Callanish Stones but almost as great a rarity.

Brochs were built only during a short span of time around

the beginning of the Christian era, and in a restricted geographical area – the north of Scotland.

Apart from the broch of Mousa, in Shetland, Dun Carloway is the best preserved: a great circular tower still standing thirty feet high, and located on a hilltop commanding a wide view of the approaches to Loch Roag.

A section has been gouged out of the wall on the landward side, presumably to provide stones for domestic use. References to 'stone thieves' which occur in some descriptions of the broch are, however, misplaced. Considering the poverty of the people who lived around the broch over the centuries, and the absence over much of the period of any system of law-enforcement or any law protecting ancient monuments, the wonder is that anything has survived.

It would be more relevant to say the Lewis crofters had an instinctive respect for the memorials of the past which wealthier individuals, communities and governments have often lacked.

In so far as the broch has been despoiled, it has not been wholly loss. In effect we now have a cross-section which enables us to examine the structure and admire the skill with which the inner and the outer skins were bonded together by the large slabs of which the stairs and corridors are built.

It is remarkable that a tall drystone structure, without mortar or buttress, on an exposed hilltop, on the Atlantic coast of the Hebrides, should have withstood the hurricanes of two thousand years, especially in the period since the wall was breached and the integrity of the circular structure impaired.

To the layman, Dun Carloway would appear to be a watchtower, or fortress, designed to guard against a seaborne invasion. The experts think differently. In his excellent little *Guide to Prehistoric Scotland* Richard Feacham makes the point in a picturesque phrase: 'Despite its striking appearance, the broch is no more than an extreme form of defended home-stead, the occupants of which may be likened to the tender meat of the crustacean secure within the hard shell'.

Not always secure, according to tradition! Long after the broch had ceased to serve its original purpose, a party of Morisons, sheltering there for the night, were murdered by their traditional enemies, the Macaulays, who scaled the outer

This 'Norse' mill at Bragar was in use up to the start of the Second World War. There were several mills at that time still in use in Lewis or recently abandoned. They were of very simple construction, built on a slope so that there were two storeys. In the lower storey there was a verticle paddle wheel driving directly the millstone in the upper storey.

wall, using dirks as pitons, and smothered them with burning heather. As the Morisons were returning from a raid on Macaulay territory in Uig, it was no doubt a reasonable tit for tat.

Feacham draws a sharp distinction between brochs and duns, although there were similarities in design and purpose, and the precise points of difference elude the layman. If he is correct, Dun Carloway is a misnomer, but it is too well established now to be changed.

What is more relevant is that the dun or the broch, whatever we call it, provides evidence that two thousand years ago there was a settled agricultural community on the west of Lewis, with the technological skill to build a structure strong enough to defy the centuries; and the ability to innovate, creating a new design appropriate to their particular needs.

A few miles along the road there is another broch on a little promontory on the shore of a loch at Bragar, right beside the road. It is not so well preserved but the wall still reaches a height of fourteen feet.

The third in this trio of significant structures protected by the state – the Black House at Arnol – is almost as far removed in time from the broch at Carloway as the broch is from the Callanish Stones. The Arnol house was occupied, as a functioning croft house, well into the sixties of this century. It brings us down almost, but not quite, to the present day. Up to the end of the second world war, more than 40% of the croft houses in Lewis were of similar design.

By any standard the black house was a remarkable architectural achievement.

The island is – or was – completely devoid of trees so the black house was designed to use the minimum of timber. The rooftrees for a house could often be found as driftwood on the shore. When people were moved from site to site, or village to village, at the whim of a factor, as they often were, they carried the precious timbers with them.

The islands lie in one of the windiest regions of the world, so the black house was designed low and snug, like a sheltering animal. The thatched roof, and even the corners of the stone walls, were rounded, denying a fingerhold to the wind. The black house was streamlined before the word was invented or the concept known. When they moved into the new, and modestly elegant, houses we see today, islanders became conscious of the wind in a quite new and sometimes terrifying way.

Rain falls on more than two hundred days each year in the Western Isles so, in the old black house, the manure, on which the crops depended, was kept indoors: protected from the leaching rain. Not because people were indifferent to dirt or smells, but because they knew the price of survival.

They even put the rain to use. The black house was designed, as a general rule, with double walls, the cavity between being packed with earth. The thatched roof rested on the inner wall, decanting the roofwater into the cavity, where a blanket of moist earth effectively sealed out the draughts, which otherwise would have blown through the chinks in the drystone walls.

The upper storey of the Bragar mill showing the simple device of a piece of stick rattling on the moving millstone which was used to shake the grain into the central hole.

Long before ecology was invented, or people began talking of conservation and self-sustaining systems, the island crofters used or recycled everything they could. The water in which fish was boiled, for instance, was used as a soup or drink. (No liquor ever invented was tastier or more health-giving.) The thatch, saturated with soot, was spread on the crofts each spring to fertilise the potatoes.

Alexander Fenton, in his book *The Shape of the Past 1*, suggests that, when the pressure of population made the food supply critical in the middle years of last century, the design of the black house changed: the chimney holes which had previously existed were stopped up to conserve the smoke. The value of soot was rising: not in money terms but as an imperative of existence.

Considerable ingenuity was also shown in the labour-saving features of the design. Bringing the thatch to the inner rather than the outer wall not only disposed of the roofwater advantageously and denied the winds a purchase on the eaves, it provided a broad walk around the house at roof level, facilitating the regular removal and replacement of the fertilising thatch. Steps, after the manner of a stile, were often built into the wall to make the roof walk (or 'tobhta') more accessible.

'In suitable summer weather,' writes Alexander Carmichael, 'the women of the family take possession of these grassy wall-tops, and sew, spin or knit, and look about them, while the household dogs sleep beside them in the sun.'

Fenton points out that older black houses had a feature which is missing from the one preserved at Arnol. Part of the gable wall was built with turf instead of stone. This section was known as the horsehole because, in spring, the turf was removed, giving the crofter direct access with his horse for the conveyance of the winter's accumulated manure to feed the hungry soil.

The Arnol house lacks that feature because it was built after the imposition of bye-laws by the Estate and the local authority, banishing the midden from the homestead: thus ensuring that a good deal of the value was washed away by the winter rain.

That brings one to the nub of the predicament in which island crofters were trapped. The old black house had many deficiencies: it was dark, smoke-filled and in some ways insanitary.

Improvers, looking in from the outside, saw only the deficiencies and tried to eradicate them by the standard stick-and-carrot procedure. Bye-laws and penalties on the one hand, modest inducements on the other, such as the offer of internal doors and window frames free, if crofters would instal them.

These measures were well-intentioned and, when crofters did not respond as quickly as they were expected to, cries went up about laziness and resistance to change.

The reformers made the mistake of assuming that the black house was capable of piecemeal improvement, and that only ignorance and conservatism held the crofter back. In fact, the black house was an integrated functional system; every change had disadvantages as well as benefits, and the crofter had to weigh the one against the other.

It would be true to say that the availability of artificial manures and baker's bread had as much to do with the improvement of housing in rural Lewis as any bye-laws

This photograph of a funeral at Dalmore on the Atlantic coast of Lewis says all that need be said about the relationship between Lewis and the sea and the effect of that relationship on the islanders' fatalism. It is one of a remarkable series of photographs taken by Murdo Macleod, Shawbost, on behalf of the Harris Tweed Association.

imposed in the hundred years from 1830, when Seaforth issued his ukase that tenants must admit more light 'to the dark recesses of their habitations'. Artificial manures and baker's bread at least did something to reduce the crofter's dependence on the grudging crops his land would yield, and the sooty thatch with which he fed them.

The real instruments of the crofter's escape from the black house were the Crofters Act of 1886, which freed him from the risk of being rented more heavily if he built a better house; the availability of wage-earning employment, which released him from the treadmill of subsistence agriculture; and the offer of government grants and loans for the building of new houses to overcome the difficulty that the crofter could neither qualify for a council house, nor raise a mortgage to build his own, because of the complexity of the tenure Parliament had invented for him.

The government assistance is often represented as exceptionally generous because the crofter, for purely legal reasons, had to get a special package of aid which no one else enjoys. Actually, it was considerably less than the state was giving, at the same time, to people of the same economic status, through local authority housing schemes, in every town and city in the land, and very considerably less than the government gave, and continues to give, through mortgage interest relief, to people who are immensely rich by traditional crofting standards. The crofter was treated differently, it is true, but he was certainly not pampered.

Even when the crofter was able to break out of the black house, it was not all gain. He (and his animals!) lost the benefit of central heating and moved into a much colder environment than they had previously known. It is only within very recent years that working-class families in the islands (or anywhere in Britain, for that matter) have been able to afford the modern heating systems which have brought that element of domestic comfort back to the level of the old black house.

Even more remarkable than the architecture of the black house was the life sustained within it.

One of the first to make a study of the black house was Colin Sinclair, a Glasgow architect, whose book, *The Thatched Houses of the Old Highlands,* contains drawings and photographs to illustrate the different architectural styles in the different islands.

Describing a visit to a typical Lewis thatched house, Sinclair writes: 'With the customary salutation expressed in the language of the people, I sought admission to the house, and was received with cordiality as a matter of course.

'The doorway led directly into the end part of the house, where a cow was placidly reclining on a bed of straw. Proceeding through a door in a thick partition wall of stone, I found myself 'aig cois an teine', beside the fire, which was heaped with glowing peats, set on a slab in the middle of the floor. The usual 'seise' or bench invitingly occupied a side wall, and a dresser, scrupulously scrubbed, displayed rows of plates which glinted in the light of the flickering flames . . . There was nothing to offend; the inhibitions and prejudices of an outside world were spirited away in the smoke of the peat fire.'

Peat is a remarkable fuel. It is clean to handle. The smoke is aromatic and inoffensive; indeed, medical men have claimed for it valuable antiseptic properties. Life in Lewis would have been very bleak had there not been an abundant supply of such a pleasant and versatile fuel.

The life of the household – domestic, religious, social and cultural – revolved round the central peat fire. It was seldom if ever allowed to die out. At night the embers were covered with ash. In the morning, when the ash was removed, they were still glowing, and the addition of a few fresh peats brought the fire to life again.

In the evening, neighbours would gather round the central fire, in some favoured house, to discuss the affairs of the village or the world outside, reminisce, swop anecdotes, listen to the old traditional tales handed down orally across the centuries, sing or perhaps even hold a religious service. The fire was almost a symbol of the close domestic and communal life. It is significant that, when crofters gave evidence before the Napier Commission about the evictions, they were less likely to speak of the loss of land than to complain of the fires that had been 'quenched'. They were less concerned with the loss of property than the destruction of communities.

The decay of the clan system over a long period of time separated the landlords from the crofters. The landlords were absorbed into the social and political life of London; the crofters vanished behind a Gaelic curtain, seen from the outside as ignorant barbarians, except when they were romanticised in a manner that was even more revolting. The supreme irony is that they were considered ignorant only because those who so regarded them were unable to understand their language!

With the fragmentation of the community, the skill in the plastic arts evidenced by such artefacts as the Book of Kells (compiled in Iona, although now in Dublin), and the tomb of Alastair Crotach in Rodil, was lost. It could not possibly be sustained by an impoverished community of subsistence fishermen-farmers living in homes which had few adornments and little light.

On the other hand, the poetry and the great tradition of story-telling flourished around the central peat fire, and for several centuries an almost unlettered and deeply impoverished peasantry kept alive a rich and varied culture, despite a long-sustained official policy aimed deliberately at 'extirpating' the language and the treasures it contained. It is a remarkable conservationist achievement in the face of official vandalism, both Scottish and British.

Hector Maciver who, after serving in the Navy in the second world war, became head of the English Department at the Royal High School in Edinburgh, and was one of the formative influences on Karl Miller, used to tell of his delicious terror as a child, hurrying homewards through the dark from the ceilidh house in which an elderly crofter had told with dramatic skill a blood-curdling ghost story from the past.

A Hebridean ghost story might not be great literature, but let us just consider for a moment the intellectual content of the popular culture of today as represented by television, the tabloid press, and the top ten in the charts in any week you care to choose.

Moreover, it was not only popular tales which were kept alive in the old thatched house, but a vast repertoire of poems and songs which will bear comparison with any similar collection in the world.

When a rising standard of living and the extension of the state education system after the second world war provided the opportunity, the lost skill in the plastic arts resurfaced.

In the early fifties James Cumming, now one of Scotland's leading artists, elected, surprisingly, to use the travelling scholarship he won by visiting Lewis, instead of going to one of the great art centres of the world. He had had enough of travel in the RAF during the war, and wanted to work out his own ideas in the quiet of a crofting community.

He produced a remarkable series of paintings on island themes. 'Cerebral yet poetic' in the words of Sidney Goodsir Smith, hovering between direct representation and formalised symbolism, on subjects like 'The Quarrymen of Shawbost', 'Hebridean Boatmen', 'Winter Poacher by the Harris Hills', 'Tinker and Owlet', 'The Grazings Committee', and 'Woman with Second Sight'.

He was quickly drawn into the work then starting in the rural Lewis schools under the direction of Iain Campbell, the Organiser of Art for the area. His influence was marginal, because his stay was relatively short, but he was impressed by the talent he found, and gave things a considerable nudge in the right direction. In a short time paintings by Lewis children were attracting attention in national exhibitions and finding their way to Paris, the USA and Japan under the auspices of UNESCO. The old skills had been dormant, not dead.

Even at the most difficult period, before the Education Act of 1872, or the Crofters Act of 1886, had reached the statute book and become fully operative, crofters' sons occasionally broke out of the social and economic bonds which restrained them. The autobiography of Norman Morrison from Shawbost, who was born in 1869, gives an insight into the sort of struggle they had.

Morrison's father could 'read a little and with an effort write his name' but had no sympathy with his son's scholastic ambitions. People in their humble station, he thought, had no need of schooling. Morrison's mother was more sympathetic. She 'had no English education, but was a fairly good Gaelic scholar and spoke with a sonorous fluency'.

Morrison was ten before he saw the inside of a school – a thatched building with an earthen floor, no map, diagram or wall card of any kind; and benches made of roughly planed planks – even the ink was a home-brew made by mixing soot and water, which he says was 'quite indelible but lighter than ordinary ink'.

The school 'bell' was a gigantic conch with the end chipped off. 'By blowing hard through the aperture one could produce an ear-splitting eerie sound which had a carrying capacity almost equal to a full blast from a ship's siren.' The curriculum was 'a smattering of the three Rs, Latin, Bible instruction and an overdose of the Shorter Catechism'.

Morrison joined the police force in Glasgow and became one of the pioneers of the Police Federation. At one stage he was given five minutes, standing at attention before a senior officer, to decide whether to give up his work for the Federation or be dismissed from the force. Although he was then a married man, supporting a daughter at university, he chose dismissal. The people of Oban, where he was stationed, held a protest meeting and he was reinstated.

While earning his living as a policeman, Morrison devoted his spare time to the study of natural history and earned a

Doctorate of Science from a French university for a treatise on the common eel.

He was not an isolated phenomenon. He points out that the little school in Shawbost, despite its limited resources, produced clergymen and doctors. Even in the period when the island was most depressed, it was a net contributor to, rather than a drain upon, the nation's wealth, especially if one takes into account the quite disproportionate contribution the crofting population made to the defence of Britain through the Royal Naval Reserve and the army.

The transformation of Lewis in little more than a generation from an island predominantly of thatched houses to the island we know today involved a tremendous amount of initiative, hard work and self-sacrifice on the part of those who achieved it – the three qualities in which, in the well-established mythology of the English-speaking south, the Gael is supposed to be deficient.

When they were struggling to escape from the black house islanders were sensitive to the gibes of ignorant critics – of whom there were many. Now they look back on the black house with a certain affection and pride. Life was poor in material resources but rich in spiritual values and in the difficult art of neighbourly, compassionate living. During their sojourn in the black house the people of the islands learned to do without their natural leaders and evolved an egalitarian society from which Britain has much to learn.

With this in mind, Shawbost School, under the headmastership of Charles Macleod, author of *Devil in the Wind,* created, some years ago, a pioneer folk museum which preserves at least the outward features of the old crofting life.

Charles Macleod, however, was not an antiquarian delving into the past. He was concerned with the future. The museum was established, by the pupils in the school, to raise their morale and create a datum line from which progress could be measured.

From the local point of view, however, the most important structure on the west side of Lewis is not the Callanish circle or the Carloway broch, the black house at Arnol or the museum at Shawbost. It is the spinning mill of Kenneth Macleod (Shawbost), Ltd. which shows that industry can flourish efficiently and successfully in the remotest corner of 'Ultima Thule', and that native enterprise is more likely to thrive than exotic transplants, which require hothouse treatment to establish, and which perish quickly in the cold reality of Hebridean geography.

The Thrushel stone – ancient monument and character in a modern book!

CHAPTER 9

Chessmen, Statesmen, Nuns and Ships

Scenically, West Uig is the jewel of Lewis. One of the jewels of Scotland! The mountains are modest as mountains go, but they are shapely; they change colour almost by the minute in the furtive Lewis sunshine, and they provide a backdrop for some of the loveliest beaches in Europe.

All the Lewis parishes, except Lochs, have accessible sandy beaches, but the concentration and variety in Uig is unequalled, except perhaps on the west coast of Harris.

Berie sands is probably the favourite, with its delicate pink shells and its view of the islands at the mouth of Loch Roag, but Mangursta, where the Atlantic roars in, even on the calmest day in high summer, is surely the most impressive.

The cliffs round Mangursta are equally impressive, and the Nature Conservancy regards the whole area as important for both teaching and research.

At the 1985 Edinburgh International Festival, Mangursta beach – and the Callanish Stones – featured in an interesting experiment in time-lapse photography by a young Inverness artist, Stephen Lawson, who has recently returned to Scotland after a sojourn in the United States.

His photographic collage of Mangursta shows the beach at five-minute intervals from dawn to dusk, illustrating the effect of changing light as the sun strengthens; or clouds, hurrying in from the Atlantic, weave their own patterns on the sea and sand. It also arrests the movement of the sea, showing us flood tide and ebb tide simultaneously.

It is not just a gimmick. It is a genuine attempt to achieve the impossible: to record an experience which must be lived through; each moment savoured as the scene unfolds.

One doesn't go to Mangursta for 'a day at the beach'. One goes to see, to hear, and indeed to feel, the beauty and the power of the Western Ocean; and to fill one's lungs with the purest air in the world.

The poet saw Mangursta rather differently. Donald Maciver, a native of Uig, was a headmaster successively in Lemreway,

Breasclete and Bayble. He visited Mangursta on one occasion with an Uig friend home from Canada. They were saddened to see the village they had known as children cleared of its inhabitants to make a farm. Nothing remained unchanged except the sea.

He enshrined the experience in a song – 'An Ataireachd Ard' – in which both words and music reproduce the restless, unending surge of the sea.

The village of Mangursta was later recreated, as part of the land settlement policy after the first world war, but the song is still popular and there are several recordings available. The Gaelic words, and the music, are included in *Eilean Fraoich,* a collection of Lewis Gaelic Songs and Melodies, published by Comunn Gaidhealach Leodhais (The Gaelic Society of Lewis).

The flora and fauna of Uig are also of interest. The golden eagle nests in the hills and, on some of the machairs – the sandy grassland by the sea – one can find, in July, the rare Hebridean orchid: 'a wine-dark beauty' in a phrase of Peter Cunningham's, which, not inappropriately, links the Hebrides with the islands of Homer's Greece.

For those who wish to study the flowers systematically the standard work is M.S. Campbell's *The Flora of Uig.*

There is much more, however, in Uig than scenery and natural history. The ghosts of a thousand years still haunt the villages around the great bay of Uig, described by William Black, a Victorian bestseller who knew it well, as 'a strange and impressive scene'.

At the eastern end of the bay, at Baile-na-cille, which means 'the village of the church', there is a tiny graveyard on a little promontory, which links this crofting parish on the edge of the Atlantic with some of the major institutions and events in British history.

The Viking invasions. The Jacobite rebellions. The battle of Hastings. The conquest of India. The abolition of the slave trade. The founding of the Cunard Line. The Highland Clearances. The Disruption which shook the Church of Scotland in the 1840s. The British Museum, Westminster Abbey and the Houses of Parliament. All have links with the close neighbourhood of Baile-na-cille.

But first – a mystery. There are many traditions in the

SEAFORTH'S
HIGHLANDERS

To be forthwith raifed for the DEFENCE of His Glorious Majefty KING GEORGE the Third, and the Prefervation of our Happy Conftitution in Church and State.

All LADS of *TRUE HIGHLAND BLOOD*, willing to fhew their Loyalty and Spirit, may repair to *SEAFORTH*, or the Major, *ALEXANDER MACKENZIE* of *Belmaduthy;* Or, the other Commanding Officers at Head Quarters, at where they will receive HIGH BOUNTIES, and *SOLDIER-LIKE ENTERTAINMENT.*

The LADS of this Regiment will LIVE *and* DIE *together :— as they cannot be DRAUGHTED into other Regiments, and muft be reduced in a BODY in their OWN COUNTRY.*

Now for a Stroke at the Monfieurs my Boys! KING George for ever!

H U Z Z A!

The notice displayed by Seaforth throughout his domains in 1793. It is perhaps not surprising that the Gaelic-speaking crofters of Uig took to the hills, especially as there was a threat hanging over them that the whole parish might be sold as a sheep-farm in their absence.

Highlands, especially in Lewis and mainland Ross-shire, about Coinneach Odhar (Sallow Kenneth), the famous Brahan Seer who is said to have foretold many historical events, including the doom of the Seaforths: a highly dramatic story, used with great effect by Sir Walter Scott.

According to tradition, Coinneach had a stone with a hole in it through which he saw the future. He was given the stone by a Norwegian princess, or rather by the ghost of a Norwegian princess, buried in the little graveyard at Baile-na-cille. The ghost had gone on a midnight visit to her old home in Norway, but Kenneth intercepted her return at dawn, and the magic stone was the price of her readmittance to the open grave.

Many of those who find the ghost of a Norwegian princess too much for their credulity, still accept the rest of the story, including some of the prophecies even now being invented for the long-dead seer.

William Matheson examined the legend of Coinneach Odhar in a paper read to the Gaelic Society of Inverness in 1968. It is a fascinating and convincing piece of historical detective work. He concludes that Coinneach Odhar really did exist, and was probably burnt in a barrel of tar, for witchcraft, at Chanory Point in Ross-shire, as tradition says.

He goes on, however, to show that the historical seer existed a century earlier than the traditional accounts of Coinneach Odhar would suggest; that many of the prophecies attributed to him were invented after the events to which they refer; that unfulfilled prophecies now in circulation can generally be shown to be somewhat garbled accounts of events that have already happened; and that the Uig connection is an illusion or rather a reflection.

The real Coinneach Odhar flourished in Easter Ross, as his alternative name, the Brahan Seer, suggests, but the Easter Ross stories were brought into Lewis by the Mackenzies when they ousted the Macleods. One of the first Mackenzies to settle in the island made his home at Baile-na-cille, so the Lewis tradition focused on that spot and spun its myths around the old historic churchyard there.

Matheson remarks in passing that when the Mackenzies took over Lewis the incoming families generally located themselves 'in places where a pre-Reformation chapel, or the ruins of one,

During the Riel rebellion in Canada in 1885 this troop of Canadian Mounties, commanded by Charles Dickens' son, Capt Frederick Dickens — the bearded figure at the right — was saved from annihilation by a Lewis trapper, William McLean from Gisla, who surrendered with his family as hostages to the Indians who had surrounded the fort the Mounties were defending. Courtesy of Saskatchewan Archives Board/RA1083.

gave them the benefit of sanctuary'. They couldn't have been too sure of the vanquished Macleods! There is more to it than that, however.

It was half a century after the Reformation in Scotland before the Mackenzies obtained possession of Lewis, which suggests that pre-Reformation beliefs must have lingered, and lingered effectively, for a long time after the nominal change.

The Catholic twilight was particularly long in Uig. Humorous Gaelic sayings about the different Lewis villages, which were still in circulation, up to the second world war, refer to 'the Catholics of Islivig' and describe Mangursta as 'the village without a Sabbath'.

At the end of the Uig road beyond Mangursta, Islivig and Brenish are the very fragmentary remains of a pre-Reformation chapel, and a nunnery, referred to in the Lewis tradition as 'tigh nan cailleachan dubha', which is generally translated as 'the house of the black old women', but could

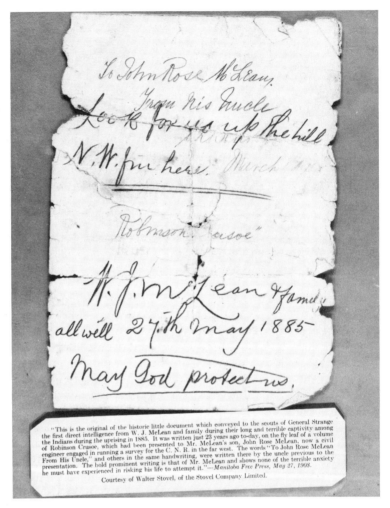

"This is the original of the historic little document which conveyed to the scouts of General Strange the first direct intelligence from W. J. McLean and family during their long and terrible captivity among the Indians during the uprising in 1885. It was written just 23 years ago to-day, on the fly leaf of a volume of Robinson Crusoe, which had been presented to Mr. McLean's son, John Rose McLean, now a civil engineer engaged in running a survey for the C. N. R. in the far west. The words "To John Rose McLean From His Uncle," and others in the same handwriting, were written there by the uncle previous to the presentation. The bold prominent writing is that of Mr. McLean and shows none of the terrible anxiety he must have experienced in risking his life to attempt it."—*Manitoba Free Press, May 27, 1908.*

Courtesy of Walter Stovel, of the Stovel Company Limited.

When McLean and his family were led off by the Indians they left this note nailed to a tree as a guide to their whereabouts. It was written on the flyleaf of a copy of *Robinson Crusoe* sent to William's son, John Rose, by his uncle in Lewis. The father's frantic SOS and the uncle's inscription to his nephew are strangely intertwined. Courtesy Manitoba Archives N7315.

equally well be translated 'the house of the black-veiled women'.

Unfortunately we know nothing about the nunnery. The Keeper of the Scottish Catholic Archives assures me there is 'no medieval mention whatsoever'.

On the subject of the lingering Catholic twilight in Lewis, however, he draws attention to the presence in the island, as late as 1690, of an Irish Catholic priest, Fr. Cornelius Con, who received forty converts (or reconverts) in twenty days, and blotted his copybook by seducing the daughter of one of the Catholic tacksmen. He finally abandoned Catholicism but his presence, and his affaire, show that the old religion still had a considerable grip in Lewis into the early eighteenth century.

The Macaulays of Uig and the Morisons of Ness – the old warring rivals – both took to the church, when they lost their secular power, and both were active in the eventual conversion of Lewis and Harris to the Presbyterianism which prevails today.

According to tradition, one of the early Morison converts, Kenneth, who was minister of Stornoway parish around the end of the seventeenth century, had to carry a sword when he walked to church, and to post two men, with drawn swords, at the church door when he preached. Despite his precautions one of the Catholic tacksmen attempted to abduct him.

The Macaulay ministers came into prominence when two of them, father and son – Rev. Aulay in Harris and Rev. John in Uist – attempted to seize Bonnie Prince Charlie when he was in hiding in the Western Isles. One can only hope that they were actuated by their religious and political principles rather than the £30,000 on the Prince's head.

While we can only speculate about their motives, there is little doubt about their convictions. The Macaulays by that time were perfervid Whigs, already on the way to becoming one of the leading families of the British, and indeed the narrower English, establishment. Their extraordinary contribution to public life in England is examined by Noel Annan in his book *The Intellectual Aristocracy*.

The Rev. Kenneth Macaulay, a brother of John, gave the first hint of literary aspirations with a book about St Kilda, and a generation later the Macaulays crossed the border in force.

Four of Rev. John's family stormed the bastions of influence and power.

Aulay entered the Church of England, contributed to the *Gentleman's Magazine*, spent some time at the Court of the Duke of Brunswick and taught English to the young lady who became known to history as Queen Caroline.

Jean married Thomas Babington of Rothley Temple and ruled over his household with dignity and decision, despite the 'alarm and disapproval' with which her arrival was greeted by the petty gentry of Leicestershire. Her grandniece, Viscountess Knutsford, says the news that Babington was engaged to the daughter of a Highland clergyman was received with 'the same feelings of astonishment and dismay with which the family of an Arctic explorer might hear of his intention to return home with an Esquimaux bride'.

Colin went into the army and became a General. He was a close friend of Wellington and was one of his advisers at the Congress of Vienna. He knew most of the leading figures of his day from Blucher to Madame de Stael, and appears to have been unaffected by four years in captivity during the Second Mysore War, under the none too tender care of the notorious Hyder Ali.

The fourth of Rev. John's family was Zachary, one of the leaders of the anti-slavery movement, of whom the *Dictionary of National Biography* writes: 'Macaulay's services towards abolishing the greatest wrong existing in his time can hardly be overpraised. Few men have devoted themselves so entirely and unselfishly to a noble cause'. After his death a memorial to him was erected in Westminster Abbey, to be joined in due course by a second memorial to his even more illustrious son, Lord Macaulay, the historian.

The Macivers of Uig made a somewhat similar progress. They had established themselves as shipowners working out of Loch Roag. The centripetal pull of the industrial south drew them first to the Clyde and then to the Mersey, where David and Charles MacIver were associated with Samuel Cunard in establishing the Cunard Line.

Although the first and most famous company to maintain a regular service by steamship on the Atlantic bears the name of the American who peddled the idea, it remains an open question, according to Clement Jones, in his book *Pioneer Shipowners,* whether he or Charles MacIver was the real architect of the Cunard Line.

Appropriately, the first Cunard liner to enter New York harbour was commanded by a Lewisman who had close associations with Uig – Capt. Alex Ryrie. He was feasted on his arrival by the leading merchants and businessmen of the city. One of the last Commodores of the Cunard fleet was also a Lewisman, Capt. D.M. Maclean of Stornoway.

While the Macaulays and the Macivers were making the transition, over several generations, from Uig to the industrial south, with considerable benefit to both sides, the ordinary people of the parish were making an even longer journey for purposes which were not their own. It was in Uig that the Lewismen who fought at Assaye and Maida were recruited: a remarkable contribution by one small parish to the British army at a critical point in the nation's history.

The survivors of these hard campaigns in the Low Countries, Italy, South Africa, Egypt, India and Java returned to Lewis with a rich store of adventures, recounted in eloquent Gaelic round the peat fires of the parish until the last of them died, and reverberating down the years since then in the oral tradition of Uig.

The remnants of the tradition still surviving were recorded, between the wars, by Col. A.J. Mackenzie who, as a native of Uig, had been familiar in his youth with the Gaelic tales handed down by the old soldiers and later, as a chaplain in the Seaforth Highlanders, had the opportunity of comparing the oral tradition with the official record. His account has recently been published by Comunn Eachdraidh Uig – the Historical Society of Uig.

The old soldiers of Uig, as they are still generally called, were the Hebridean counterpart of the 'soldier-husbandmen' described by Balzac in *The Country Doctor:* the veterans of Napoleon's Grand Army, 'covered with wounds and decorations . . . after twenty years of fighting in all parts of the world' who later 'were listened to greedily at evening gatherings in the villages'.

Despite the 'Auld Alliance' between Scotland and France, the Hebridean crofters and the French peasants had been ranged

An unusually calm day at Mangursta, one of the scores of lovely beaches which the visitor has almost entirely to himself on most days of the year. Courtesy Acair Ltd.

against each other in a titanic struggle which concerned them little, but in which they shared a common experience of the comradeship, the glory, the squalor and the futility of war.

Many of the Uig veterans were blind. They had contracted ophthalmia in Egypt. Others had been captured by the Turks and sold into slavery: an indignity that was burned into the souls of those who were subsequently released and returned to their native island.

Although the old soldiers seem to have gloried in their great achievements, they were unwilling recruits to begin with. There was a notable confrontation between them and Seaforth on a hilltop not far from Baile-na-cille, which thereafter became known as 'the hill of the camp'. The spot is still clearly identified in local tradition, about three hundred yards south of the second house in Ardroil, as you approach from Stornoway.

During the Reign of Terror, when war between Britain and France was imminent, Seaforth visited Uig to recruit. The people of Uig sent a boat with six women at the oars to meet him in Callanish. The men took to the hill.

Seaforth was furious. He stormed into the manse at Baile-na-cille to complain to the minister of the insult. The minister soothed him and together they went to speak to the wary Uigeachs.

According to local tradition, Seaforth and the minister quickly calmed the fears of the people and, in a short time, more recruits came forward than Seaforth required. A good deal must have depended on the minister's eloquence because Seaforth was deaf and almost mute. In fact the recruits he raised in Uig are known in the local tradition as 'Saighdearan MhicChoinnich Bodhair' – 'the soldiers of the deaf Mackenzie'.

There was rather more to it, however, than the local tradition suggests. Kenneth Logue, in his book *Popular Disturbances in Scotland, 1780-1815*, quotes correspondence between Seaforth and the Home Office, implying that the resistance to recruitment was a Jacobin conspiracy, fomented by men who had returned home after service in the American War of Independence. The fears of the authorities of a rising in the north were increased by the report that copies of Paine's *Rights of Man* were circulating in Lewis and a French privateer was cruising down the coast.

There may have been Jacobins in Lewis. The island has never been insulated from the outside world. But there is another and simpler explanation of the Uigeachs' disaffection. In 1793 Seaforth advertised the whole parish of Uig for sale as a sheep farm which, in effect, put the whole community under notice to quit! Colin Mackenzie, the Stornoway man who became the first Surveyor General of India, wrote to the Factor from Hyderabad asking, 'What is to be done with the inhabitants?' If Mackenzie, then a young lieutenant pursuing his own career in India, was worried by the proposal, what was the state of public opinion in Uig itself? Is it possible that that was the matter discussed at the hill of the camp and that the flow of willing recruits was a *quid pro quo* for some assurance that the sale would not proceed?

If assurances were given, they were of little long-term value. The conversion of the whole parish into a sheep farm was not proceeded with but, over the years, successive proprietors, factors or trustees carried out individual evictions and sometimes cleared whole villages.

Donald Macdonald, in *Lewis*, lists thirty-nine villages in Uig which disappeared from the map, although many were later resurrected, nearly a century later, when the government at last got round to a policy of land settlement.

Most of these Lewis evictions involved resettlement in another area and possibly another job, rather than an outright clearance, but they were completely arbitrary and bitterly resented. The memory influences attitudes down to the present day.

The manse at Baile-na-cille is now a small hotel. The fact that it is a listed building reflects the poverty of Lewis in eighteenth-century structures rather than any architectural merit, but there are other good reasons why it should be preserved. It links together many of the major strands in island history.

The recruitment of the Uig soldiers during the Revolutionary and Napoleonic wars was the last anachronistic flicker of the old clan spirit. A few years after the end of the Napoleonic war, the manse at Baile-na-cille was the starting point of a religious revival with profound social, cultural and political implications, setting the island on a new course. The effects are still evident in Lewis down to the present day.

The Lewis revival was part of an evangelical movement affecting the whole of Scotland, but there are specific and significant deviations from the national pattern.

The key event in the national movement was the Disruption of 1843, when 470 ministers dramatically walked out of the General Assembly of the Church of Scotland, abandoning their churches, their manses and their stipends, on a point of principle. They formed the Free Church of Scotland and, despite the fact that times were hard, they raised, within a year, by voluntary subscription, half a million pounds – an immense sum by the standards of the day – and organised a national system of churches, schools and colleges rivalling that of the state church which they had left.

The central issue was the continued imposition on the Scottish Church, by the UK Parliament, of an alien system of patronage, under which the laird, or the Crown, could settle a minister in a parish in defiance of the wishes of the congregation.

The Disruption was 'a real stand for real freedom carried out with as great generosity as courage . . . an outstanding event of its century', in the words of Agnes Mure Mackenzie, the Scottish historian, who was born in Stornoway but could take a dispassionate view of the conflict, being herself an Episcopalian.

Within three months of the Disruption, Parliament, aware at last of the strength of feeling in Scotland, abandoned its stance on one of the major issues, and a long slow process of change began within the sundered church, which led eventually to a modified but reunited Church of Scotland, recognised by the state but not subservient to it. A considerable minority, however, refused, for doctrinal reasons, to re-enter the Church of Scotland, and the Free Church remains strong.

The evangelical revival in Lewis is often dated from 1824 when Rev. Alexander Macleod was inducted at Baile-na-cille. But it had its roots much earlier, as Rev. Murdo Macaulay points out in *Aspects of the Religious History of Lewis,* which is an excellent source of information about the numerous pre-Reformation ecclesiastical buildings in Lewis of which traces remain, and other aspects of the island's religious life.

Rev. Alexander Macleod was already well known throughout the Highlands before he came to Uig, both for the fervour of his preaching, and for his elopement with the daughter of a Skye farmer to whose family he had been tutor.

The appointment was not immediately welcomed by his congregation. They saw the newcomer as a hard taskmaster – imposed on them by the very patronage which twenty years later he helped to destroy. Their opposition was intensified by the fact that the village of Timsgarry had been cleared to enlarge the Uig glebe.

Rev. Alexander Macleod is now one of the major figures in a rich hagiography of preachers and lay evangelists, both men and women, held in great esteem by all the Presbyterian churches in the island but especially by those who remained outside the reunited Church of Scotland.

Although there are congregations of the Free Church in cities, it is now pre-eminently a Highland church and its heartland is in Lewis and Harris. Apart from the questions of principle – somewhat abstruse to the outsider – which separate the Free Church from the reunited Church of Scotland, there is also a difference of mood, and it is significant that the congregations of the Church of Scotland in rural Lewis and Harris are in many ways closer to the Free Church congregations in the same areas than they are to city congregations of their own denomination.

The Presbyterian Church is a major fact of life in Lewis and Harris where mainland patterns are almost completely reversed. In a city church most people who attend services take Communion, and many who take Communion are infrequent attenders. In the island churches only a minority of those who consider themselves as part of the congregation take Communion, but the great majority are regular churchgoers, whether communicants or not. All share the basic aspiration, but the final commitment is regarded as an act of high seriousness involving the renunciation of a great many worldly activities.

One can feel the deep pervasive spirituality of the islanders in the unaccompanied singing of the Gaelic psalms. It is unique and characteristic: a survival from a period when people could not read, and depended on the precentor to lead them line by line. The School of Scottish Studies of Edinburgh University has made it accessible, up to a point, to non-Gaelic speakers in an album of recordings with an excellent explanatory leaflet.

There is of course another side to the island's religious life. An all-pervasive church exerts its own pressures, against which many Lewismen have rebelled. Hector Maciver used to boast that he smuggled a copy of Joyce's *Ulysses* into Free Church Lewis while it was still banned throughout mainland Britain. Although a rebel, perhaps because he was a rebel, he was in many ways the quintessential Lewisman.

It has been argued that the predominance of evangelical religion in Lewis and Harris, and the Highlands generally, anaesthetised the people during the bitter years of the Clearances and delayed the rebellion against oppressive landlords which eventually led to the Crofters Act of 1886.

That, I think, is a misreading of history. Minorities cannot impose their will on insensitive majorities by direct action. An earlier revolt might have retarded, rather than accelerated, change. If the people were, in a sense, anaesthetised by their preoccupation with the hereafter, it was probably that fact which enabled them to endure the unendurable and re-emerge as the lively confident communities of the present day.

The relationship between Lewis and the rest of Britain is also illustrated by the history of the famous Uig chessmen, which must be the most frequently reproduced and best-loved artefacts in either of the National collections, British or Scottish.

The chessmen were found in 1831 just across the bay from Baile-na-cille. Rev. Alexander Macleod, the revivalist preacher, was one of the first to set eyes on a treasure which had been hidden for centuries in the sand. He is alleged to have confiscated them from the finder as Popish relics, but that I think is an anti-clerical canard. Although Lewismen have accepted the dominance of the church, they have never relinquished the right to make fun of their ministers.

O.M. Dalton of the British Museum has described the Uig chessmen as 'the outstanding ancient chessmen of the world'. Macbeth-Beeson in his book *Chessmen* described them as 'the earliest authentic European pieces'. 'Drawn up in full array they look like a summit conference of medieval monarchs and their advisers', according to Stephen Hudson in *A History of the Enchanted Chessmen*.

They date from the twelfth century and are of Scandinavian origin. Michael Taylor, who has written the official British Museum account of them, asks a revealing question: 'How the chessmen got to the remote Isle of Lewis in the Outer Hebrides?'

The answer is obvious to anyone who does not suffer from London blindness.

The Hebrides were under Scandinavian domination before they came under the domination of London, and for a longer period. Around 1150, when the chessmen found their way to Uig, Lewis was Norwegian, not British, or even Scottish. It was, moreover, a staging post on the busy trade routes between Scandinavia and the Viking city of Dublin.

According to the Orkneyinga Saga there was a Lewis contingent at the battle of Stamford Bridge in 1066. They were on the losing side but, if the battle of Stamford Bridge had not been fought, the outcome of the battle of Hastings (and English history) might well have been different.

So far from being remote, when the chessmen came to Uig, Lewis was exercising an influence on affairs in England which England, at that time, was not capable of exercising on affairs in Lewis.

The-so called remoteness of the Hebrides is not a fact of geography but an artefact of history. A man-made result of the political dominance of Britain by the south-east of England.

CHAPTER 10

The Last Stand of the Macleods

When Donald Macaulay, a lecturer in the University of Aberdeen and a Gaelic poet, sat down to study the place names of his native Bernera, he found a complex and revealing pattern. In his list of 600 names 460 were Gaelic, 150 were Norse and one was English. Much the same, I suspect, would be found in any area of Lewis or Harris subjected to the same analysis.

The significant point in Macaulay's study is that all the main topographical features had Norse names, including all the villages in Bernera itself and all the villages which existed on the offshore islands no longer inhabited. This shows how complete the Norse domination of the Hebrides was, but it also suggests that, when it ended, there was no general massacre or even exodus of the Norse inhabitants. There is no evidence of Gaelic incomers, or an oppressed but resurgent Gaelic community, trying to obliterate the traces of vanquished overlords. The peaceful fusion of Viking and Gael must surely have begun when the Norse were still in control.

This ability to live in harmony with other people is one of the Gael's most important attributes. It can be seen today in the ease with which a number of Pakistani families have been accepted into the Lewis community.

Macaulay was not working from the Ordnance Survey map which would have shown a much higher incidence of Norse names, perhaps as high as 80%. He compiled his own list of names locally in use, many of them too insignificant to find a place on any map. Some of them are rapidly going out of use because young folk growing up in Bernera now have no need to know them. Macaulay caught them just in time.

The Gaelic names in Macaulay's list, which he analysed in a paper for the Gaelic Society of Inverness, are generally of a domestic nature, relating to the use to which various places were put, rather than enshrining the names of those who owned them. A significant difference in itself.

He shows how much can be learned from place names at this

123

intensively local level. There are references to the keeping of
goats, long since abandoned in the isles; to the swimming of the
cattle across to the summer pasture on the mainland of Lewis;
to cairns built or used by those herding the cattle; to whale
hunts; the bleaching of linen; the enlistment of mercenaries;
the distilling of whisky; and many which relate to religious sites
which clearly date from a very early and possibly pre-Viking
period.

Macaulay found the Ordnance Survey unreliable for his
purpose. On the map we see the names 'through a glass
darkly'; perhaps through several glasses: Norse names orally
transmitted across the centuries by Gaelic speakers and then set
down, often by people who knew neither Gaelic nor Norse and
according to orthographic rules which apply to English but not
to the other languages. The process is well described in Friel's
play *Translations* which illustrates the disastrous effects of this
process in an Irish context. It is a recipe for confusion.
Sometimes, fortunately, a happy confusion.

It has given us this modest island off the west of Lewis,
swaggering across the map of Britain as Great Bernera.
Bernera claims no pre-eminence over the other islands of the
Hebrides. It was called Bearnaraidh Mor (Big Bernera) to
distinguish it from its even smaller neighbour, Bearnaraidh
Beag (Little Bernera), a sandy gem on the Atlantic seaboard,
once inhabited but latterly used only as a graveyard.

Bernera has, however, some claims to greatness in a Lewis,
and perhaps even a Highland, context. The bridge by which we
approach it was the first pre-stressed concrete bridge in
Europe. More importantly, Bernera witnessed the last stand of
the Macleods against the Mackenzies and the Crown. It also
staged the first successful revolt in the crofters' fight for
security of tenure. And it was for a time, under the alias of
Borva, the Ambridge of Victorian Britain.

The name of William Black is now almost forgotten but a
hundred years ago his books were read with a fervour the age
of television does not know.

Richard Garnett in the *Dictionary of National Biography* says
few men of letters were more widely known in literary circles
than Black and none 'more generally esteemed and beloved'.

Black got the background for the novel which first made his

I would far rather, as I am sure you know, sit for the Isles than any other constituency, but the necessity of earning a living makes it impossible. But

it isn't easy to see more than a few years ahead politically these days and maybe in time a reformed Conservative party and the Liberals will unite. I hope so. If the young men can capture the Tory party I don't think there is much between us.

Kind regards.

Yours sincerely —Iain Macl.

In a single sentence a future Chancellor of the Exchequer — Iain Macleod — sums up the Lewis problem: the ablest cannot afford to stay!

reputation when he was correspondent for the *Morning Star,* covering the Franco-Prussian war. He was suspected of spying and imprisoned in the Black Forest where his story is located.

He got the background for his most successful novel – *A Princess of Thule* – and found his best-loved heroine when, on a fishing holiday at Garynahine, he became familiar with Loch Roag and the island of Bernera.

Sheila Mackenzie is drawn from life. Black found the name among the daughters in a farmhouse at Miavaig in Uig, but he found the heroine herself in the home of John Macdonald, Tobson, Bernera. The fictitious Sheila Mackenzie was the real-life Isabella Macdonald, grandmother of Iain Macleod, Colonial Secretary and Chancellor of the Exchequer and, in the words of Harold Macmillan, 'the last of the orators in the Tory party'.

Iain Macleod was proud of the association. Although he was born in Yorkshire, he spent most of his holidays at Scaliscro in Lewis, where his father had a small shooting and fishing estate. His parents both came from Lewis and frequently spoke Gaelic in the home, although only when they didn't want the children to understand. That is the process by which Gaelic has died in many homes, to the subsequent regret of those who lost their second window on the world.

During the war Iain Macleod wrote a nostalgic little poem contrasting the Harris hills, which he saw from the windows at Scaliscro, with the hills of Yorkshire and Wales and the rolling casual Downs. The others have their moments, he concedes,

> But the Harris hills are elfin hills
> Blue-etched against the night;

and, even more importantly,

> The Harris hills stand sentinel
> Above my Lewis home.

The strength of his attachment to Lewis is underscored by the fact that his widow, who had no connection with the island, chose a Lewis title – Baroness Macleod of Borve – when she was made a life peeress following his untimely death.

There can be no doubt that Iain Macleod derived many of the qualities which distinguished his approach to politics, especially as Secretary of State for the Colonies, from the Lewis ambience in which he was brought up, with its complete disregard of class.

The island's lack of class consciousness is highlighted by Black in *A Princess of Thule*. His story turns on the inability of his hero, a wealthy London socialite, to understand Sheila's attitude to her cousin Mairi, who is simultaneously her maid and her companion. In the islands personal relations may be good or bad, they are often complex, but they are never hierarchical.

Despite his perceptiveness on this key issue, Black's romance skims the surface of life in Lewis, missing completely the social struggle and the drama which was erupting around him, even as he wrote.

In the year *A Princess of Thule* was published, Donald Munro, the tyrannical factor who terrorised the Lewis crofters for more than thirty years, served notices of eviction on fifty-six families in the island of Bernera.

The crofters accepted the summonses quietly enough but, in the gloaming, a number of young lads threw clods and stones at the Sheriff Officer who served them. The Sheriff Officer, an arrogant bully, well worthy of the factor who employed him, vowed vengeance on them, declaring that, if he had his rifle with him, some of the women of Bernera would mourn the loss of their sons.

News of the threat went quickly round the island and, in the morning, a group of angry youths barred the Sheriff Officer's path to the ferry. They demanded to know if he had really used the threat. There was a minor scuffle in which the Sheriff Officer's coat was slightly torn, but neither he nor anyone in his party was injured.

A few days later, when some Bernera men were in Stornoway, settling accounts with the fishcurer who employed them, one of them – Angus Macdonald of Tobson – was seized by the police. He did not know there was a warrant out for his arrest and he resisted. A violent struggle ensued. Bystanders came to his aid. When he lost his outer clothing in the mêlée, the crowd held back the police until fresh clothes were obtained. An excited Sheriff read the Riot Act. Later he sent an urgent message to the authorities in Edinburgh, asking them to have troops in readiness to quell a rebellion in Lewis.

In 1939 this beehive sheiling near Garynahine was described by a Swedish archaeologist as the only building he knew in Europe erected within living memory on Stone Age principles. Unfortunately it has since been destroyed by the unintentional vandalism of those who did not know its significance. Islanders are now much more aware of their heritage, and the same sort of loss is less likely to occur in future.

As soon as the people of Bernera heard that one of their number had been arrested, they marched on Stornoway led by a piper, and set up camp on the edge of the town. In a very peaceable and orderly way, they went to the Castle and asked to see the proprietor, Sir James Matheson, to lay their grievances before him.

An appointed spokesman set out the crofters' complaints with eloquence but also with dignity and restraint. Sir James listened attentively and promised them redress. Lady Matheson ordered tea, and served it in the great conservatory which was once the glory of the Castle. As they prepared to leave, she took the leaders aside and asked them to promise that they would not go into town. She was afraid they would get drunk! They had no intention of getting drunk, but they had difficulty in giving the undertaking asked for: they had to go to town – to pay for the modest dram they had already consumed, to refresh them at the end of their punishing march!

Despite the amicable meeting at the Castle, the legal process ground on. A few days later three of the Bernera men were summoned to Court, to answer charges of assaulting 'an officer of the law in revenge for his having executed his duty, and to the injury of his person', 'a crime of an heinous nature'.

They appeared before a Sheriff and jury in Stornoway at a memorable trial. Charles Innes, a young Inverness solicitor, turned it into the trial of Donald Munro. His clients were acquitted but the Sheriff Officer, who had accused them of assault, was convicted of kicking one of them when he was handcuffed and helpless in the hands of the police. Donald Munro was stripped of many of the thirty public offices he held; and left to end his days shuffling along the street, while the children of Stornoway danced round him, shouting in Gaelic, 'I'll take the land from you!' – the threat he had used for more than a quarter of a century against the crofters.

Twelve years later the first Crofters Act was on the Statute Book, giving the crofters security in their holdings and remedying, in small part, the injury inflicted on the Highlands by the British government after the 1745 Rebellion, when the clan system was broken and nothing effective put in its place. When, in fact, a society based on human relationships was replaced by one based on the sanctity of personal property.

While William Black, ignorant of this social drama, or indifferent to it, was spinning his romantic and irrelevant tale, a young medical student in Earshader, whose academic career was interrupted by tuberculosis, was writing deeply spiritual poems in Gaelic about the tribulations of his people and the greed of those who battened on their misery.

William Black was well known and made a fortune. Literary London worshipped at his feet. John Smith lived and died obscurely in the village where he was born.

Today William Black is forgotten, except in so far as his modest reputation has been mummified in literary books of reference, but the Earshader bard is remembered and revered and, for those who know the language, his verse is still alive.

The story of the last attempt by the Macleods of Lewis to defend their ancient patrimony also lives in the island folk memory.

It is a complex tale of violence, intrigue, treachery and

All in the day's fun! Three members of the Stornoway Sea Angling Club with four huge cod caught somewhere off Bernera — they won't say where. Lewis waters provide some of the best sea angling in Britain. The Stornoway Club has hosted international competitions and members of the club have figured prominently in Scottish international teams. Courtesy *Stornoway Gazette*.

stubborn courage, like something out of the Italian Renaissance, stripped of the glamour and the cloth of gold.

The disintegration of the power of the Macleods of Lewis began with Roderick, generally referred to as the 10th chief. He succeeded to the chiefship in 1532 and his love life appears to have been more than a little complicated. Apart from the families born to him in three successive marriages, he had numerous illegitimate children, five of them boys: a rare brood of claimants for a tottering throne. The succession was further complicated by the fact that Roderick was not the only philanderer in Lewis at that time.

His first wife was Janet Mackenzie, daughter of the chief of the Mackenzies of Kintail. She gave birth to a son who was christened Torquil – the favourite name for the heir to Macleod of Lewis. But was he a Macleod?

The evidence would suggest that Roderick's putative heir was an illegitimate son of Hugh Morison, the Brieve or lawman of Lewis. Janet and Roderick parted company. According to some historians he divorced her. According to others, she ran away with another admirer, John of the Axe, a brother of Macleod of Raasay. She might even have been abducted by John but, if so, there would appear to have been some connivance on the victim's part.

On whatever basis Roderick and Janet parted, Torquil was brought up by his mother's people in Mackenzie country in Strathconon, and is known to history, for that reason, as Torquil Conanach. The Mackenzies now had a foot in the Lewis door and the Morisons of Ness had an excellent reason for helping them to push it open.

Roderick's second marriage, however, raised a formidable barrier. The bride was Barbara Stuart, daughter of Lord Avondale, a family close to the Scottish throne. These two marriages of Roderick give some indication of the standing of the Macleods of Lewis in sixteenth-century Scotland. More importantly, they sharpened the interest of the Crown in Lewis.

When Barbara presented Roderick with a son he too was called Torquil. Pointedly, he was always referred to as Torcul Oighre – Torquil the heir. When he was old enough to think of matrimony, he received a letter from Mary Queen of Scots reminding him of his Stuart blood and warning him not to marry without the Queen's consent. The Stuarts clearly had their eye on the Lewis succession.

Not long after the letter was written, Torquil the heir was dead. Drowned at sea, according to the accepted account, although W.C. Mackenzie reminds us there is a tradition that he was killed in Assynt. However he died, the way was clear for Torquil Conanach. He swooped on Lewis, abducted his father and held him in captivity for four years, in the mountains and caves of Ross-shire.

Under duress, Roderick accepted the cuckoo as his heir but, when he regained his freedom, he married a third prestigious bride – a daughter of Maclean of Duart, who presented him with still another Torquil. The third Torquil was known as Black Torquil (Torcul Dubh). If Torquil Conanach was illegitimate and Torquil Oighre dead, little Torquil Dubh was now the heir.

The family didn't wait for the old man to die. Torquil Conanach, accompanied by his son John, raided Lewis once more. Roderick was kept a prisoner in Stornoway Castle, with John as his gaoler. Torquil returned to his mainland estates, taking the Lewis charters with him. As if anticipating later events, he handed them over to his mother's people: the Mackenzies of Kintail. The five illegitimate sons took sides in the feud. Two supported Torquil Conanach; three stood by Roderick and the infant heir.

The old man was tough. Despite the feuding all around him, he survived into his nineties. At times, in his old age, he sought sanctuary on the island of Pabbay, in Loch Roag, where there had been an ancient church. Clearly, the Scottish Reformation had not yet effectively reached out to Lewis.

When Roderick died, Black Torquil succeeded him, but not for long.

Torquil Conanach, as if confirming his own illegitimacy, appealed to the Brieve for help. The Brieve had captured a Dutch ship with a cargo of wine and brought her into Stornoway. The lawman of Lewis was a pirate, if you like, but so was his great contemporary, Sir Francis Drake!

The Brieve invited his friends aboard the captive Dutchman to sample the wine: among them Torquil Dubh. When Torquil was adequately drunk he was seized, bound and locked below hatches. The Dutchman set sail across the Minch and the captive was handed to Torquil Conanach.

If Torquil Conanach had any claim at all to Lewis, Torquil Dubh was his half brother. That didn't save him. He and his companions, in the vivid phrase quoted by Dr. I. F. Grant from contemporary documents, were made 'short of their heads without doom or law'.

However, the way was not yet clear for Torquil Conanach and Mackenzie of Kintail. It was at this moment that James VI, soon to be James I as well, played the joker in the pack. He gave a title to the lands round Stornoway to the Fife Adventurers whom I mentioned in an earlier chapter.

A scramble for the inheritance of Lewis, within the family, was transformed, in an instant, into a threatened conquest by aliens seeking to disinherit the lot. The Mackenzies, the Macleods and the Morisons all strove to resist the takeover in their own way and for their own advantage, but they didn't make peace with each other.

The Macleods went for their objective openly, as Lewismen tend to do, not counting the risk or the cost. The Mackenzies (astute survivors, like the Campbells to the south) played their cards with greater subtlety.

Neil Macleod, one of Roderick's illegitimate brood, emerged as the leader and the hero in the fight. Three successive attempts were made to plant the colony of Fifers in Lewis but, in the end, despite the support of the Scottish Crown, Neil drove them out.

On one occasion Neil, with 'two hundred barbarous bludie and wikit Hielandmen', attacked the colonists in their camp with claymores, arquebuses, pistols and bows. In the fight twenty-two of the colonists were killed and the Macleods drove off their cattle, their sheep and their horses.

When the colonists retaliated, by laying a trap for Neil on a dark winter night, he sprang it on themselves, cut them off from their base, and killed between fifty and sixty of them.

The family feud obtruded at times and dulled the lustre of Neil's resistance. He paid off old scores against one of his half brothers, Murdoch, by handing him over to the Fifers during a truce. Murdoch was taken to St Andrews, tried and executed.

Whatever blemish there may be on Neil's record as the William Tell of Lewis, he deserves the profound gratitude of posterity.

King James pretended – perhaps he honestly believed – he could 'civilise' the people of Lewis, whom he described as 'void of any religion', by planting among them impecunious and greedy Lowlanders whose morals, and whose education, were no better than their own.

If he had succeeded, Lewis would have become another Ulster. The enmity would still be rankling. Indeed there might be open conflict as there is in Ireland, and the people of Lewis might well have remained within the Catholic Church rather than accept a Protestantism force-fed to them by aliens.

Although Neil drove out the Fifers, he couldn't save Lewis for the Macleods. He merely created a situation which enabled the Mackenzies to take over Lewis with the approval of the angry and frustrated King.

Neil retired to the rocky island of Bearasay off the west of Bernera, with forty companions. For three years he defied the attempts of the Mackenzies to winkle him out.

At one point he tried to make his peace with the Crown. He captured, by rather devious means, a pirate ship, the *Priam,* which was prowling off the Lewis coast. According to Pitcairn's *Criminal Trials,* her cargo included silver plate, spices, sugar, cochineal, a box of diamonds and precious stones of great value. Neil handed the pirate captain, Peter Love, and the loot, to the Crown. Love was hanged on Leith sands.

That earned Neil a Privy Council pardon for his own offences, but it was of very temporary effect. When at last he wearied of his rocky hideout and made a deal with the Mackenzies, his fellow clansman, Sir Roderick Macleod of Harris, handed him over to the Crown. Under duress, rather than as an act of treachery, according to Dr. I.F. Grant.

In 1613 Neil was tried in Edinburgh, convicted of fire-raising, murder, theft and piracy and condemned to death. As I said in an earlier chapter, he died 'verie Christianlie', a tribute which, surprisingly, comes from his enemies: it is contained in the official report telling King James in London that the Macleods of Lewis had at last been subdued.

Not surprisingly, his fame lingered on in Lewis. Two hundred years after his death, Donald Morison, a Harris shoemaker, who had been brought up among the Macaulays of Uig, sat down to record the traditions of Lewis and Harris, especially of his own clan.

He is not the most reliable of chroniclers but he does tell us what the people believed. In his version, when Neil was being hurried out to his execution, he foretold a Royal pardon and composed an extempore poem, from the gallows, telling his gaolers what would happen to them if he had them on the deck of a ship. The pardon arrived the moment he was hanged.

Neil deserves to be remembered for his real achievement rather than for a fictitious act of defiance at the end.

The Mackenzies, according to the standards of the time, and certainly in comparison with many of their contemporaries, were reasonably good clan chiefs; and not too bad even when, after the Jacobite rebellion, they became landed proprietors, like the other Highland chiefs, absolved from the old reciprocal bond which tempered their dealings with their tenantry.

They were nevertheless resented; not unnaturally. As William Matheson puts it succinctly, 'The Macleods were reduced to the level of small tenantry, holding their lands on sufferance from an alien ascendancy'.

More than two and a half centuries after the Mackenzies acquired Lewis, in fact nearly half a century after they had sold it, the sense of grievance still found a voice. 'How did the Mackenzies of Seaforth acquire their right to the Lews?' Dr. Roderick Ross asked the Napier Commission when he appeared before them as a witness in 1886. Answering his own question, he added, 'We know they got it by a process that cannot bear investigation, and we know the right they got to the Lews is certainly more questionable than the right the Lewismen have to their share of it'.

A strange attack on private property in land for the grandfather of a Tory Chancellor of the Exchequer, but I suspect Iain Macleod might have endorsed it had the problem before the Napier Commission arisen in his own day.

The last stand of Neil Macleod at Bearasay, and his subsequent execution, cast a long shadow over the affairs of Lewis but we can see, with the hindsight of history, that he achieved more by his failure than he would had he succeeded.

The warring Macleods of Roderick's illegitimate progeny had reduced Lewis to anarchy but Neil, the best of them, saved the island from the even greater disaster which might have been inflicted by the stupidity of the man who was known to his contemporaries, and to history, as 'the wisest fool in Christendom'.

CHAPTER 11

Tierra del Fuego and the Great Deer Raid

I cannot understand why the Countryside Commission omitted the parish of Lochs when they included the whole of Harris and west Uig among their designated areas of great natural beauty.

It is true the main road from Stornoway to Tarbert lacks character for most of its length, but the coastal roads, winding along the shores of innumerable sea lochs, are sheer enchantment even on a day of driving rain.

It was the area chosen by Arthur Ransome for his novel *Great Northern* in which he tells how a group of children protected the eggs of a threatened species: the great northern diver.

Ransome spent a holiday fishing trout on the lochs behind the village of Grimshader, where the proliferation of reflecting surfaces, salt water and fresh, creates the illusion that the light is coming from the ground rather than the sky. While he was in Lewis a party of Esthonian refugees arrived in Stornoway, fleeing across the Atlantic in a small fishing boat, after the Russian occupation of their country. It was like an echo, or a haunting, from his own past.

Ransome helped to negotiate the peace treaty by which Esthonia got its freedom from the Soviet government, just after the Russian revolution. Thirty years later, in Stornoway, he was confronted with the next generation of Esthonians, fleeing from a new Russian tyranny.

When he heard of their arrival, he hurried to the quay. He met one of the women of the party and greeted her in Esthonian. She beamed. When his Esthonian was exhausted, he lapsed into Russian. She fled – afraid the secret police had caught up with her even in the Hebrides.

The Esthonians got across the Atlantic safely, despite the fact that it was late in the season, and their first act on reaching Newfoundland was to telegraph thanks to the people of Lewis for all they had done to fit them out for the voyage.

It is not only the great northern diver which nests in the lochs round Grimshader, Leurbost and Balallan. The heron is normally a tree-nesting bird but, in the isles, it has modified its habits. It is not unusual to find a small heronry on the treeless islands in the area.

Anyone interested in birds or flowers in Lewis and Harris should consult Peter Cunningham's book *A Hebridean Naturalist*. Peter – although that, incidentally, is not his baptismal name! – gives an added dimension to birdwatching in the isles. Perhaps several added dimensions.

He frequently gives the Gaelic names of the birds he mentions, and he devotes a chapter to Gaelic imitations of bird song. One Gaelic song he quotes imitates the thrush, and at the same time satirises the moderates, who are neither hot nor cold and do not match up to the rigorous standards demanded by the Free Church.

Normally the Free Church frowns on secular or frivolous songs. Perhaps this one has got by because it is on the censors' side of the argument.

Although he does not make the point specifically, Peter Cunningham provides some evidence that island birds display the same slightly perverse individualism as island people. They are not resistant to change but they can't be hurried into it.

He records that, when Sir James Matheson tried to establish a rookery in the Castle grounds at Stornoway, he failed. But the rooks came in unbidden when it suited them to do so. Now there are about two hundred nests around Stornoway, despite the fact that a great gale in 1955, assisted by the excessive windage the huge nests caused, felled the trees and practically exterminated the colony.

Cunningham's book does not provide a systematic list of the birds to be found in Lewis and Harris. He records his personal discoveries which should whet the addict's appetite. He reckons that, in favourable conditions in April, he could run up a count of nearly sixty species in a three-hour stint round Stornoway, given a car to take him quickly to the loch at Branahuie and the saltings at Tong, for the birds which favour these conditions. And he records the triumph of his occasional bonanza, such as the clear sighting of a flamingo on the beach at Bragar, or the arrival of a water rail – rare in the Hebrides – at a friend's house. It walked in the back door and gave itself up, exhausted by the unusual exertion for a 'walking' bird of having flown the Minch.

Rested and refreshed, it took off after a good night's sleep

The harvesting of seaweed for the production of alginates is an important island industry which blends well with crofting. When it came under pressure from cheaper foreign sources of raw material and Alginate Industries Ltd pulled out, the workers at Keose formed a co-operative. They not only saved their jobs, they branched into fish-farming.

on Peter's table where it aroused, as he puts it, both 'wonder and amusement'.

Seabirds, of course, are the island's speciality. Seabirds – and the golden eagle, which can be seen quite frequently among the hills of Park, Uig and Harris.

Much more important than the eagle in the history and economy of Lewis, is the stag. Red deer have influenced the life of the community for hundreds of years and at times have dominated it.

When the Mackenzies of Kintail were given an earldom in 1623 they took their title, surprisingly, from a Lewis sea loch, although they were a mainland clan and were anything but secure in possession of their recently acquired island territory.

One can only assume that they made the choice because the jewel in their crown was the great deer forest of Park, lying between Loch Seaforth and the Minch, and extending to nearly a hundred and fifty square miles, given over to sport. A forest of mountains with no trees.

When the Seaforths acquired Lewis a deer hunt was a communal activity, not unattended with danger, as readers of Walter Scott's *Waverley* may recall. The deer were driven as grouse are now. A good marksman could bring down a running stag with a bow and arrow. If he couldn't, his own life might be at risk from the stampeding herd. The chief kept the deer for his own sport but the ordinary clansmen joined in the chase, and shared in the venison.

John Buchan, in his splendid life of Montrose, makes the point that, in the seventeenth century, 'the Highlander, accustomed to full meals of meat from the chase, was physically far superior to the bannock-fed Lowland peasant or the apprentice from the foul vennels of the little cities'.

When deerstalking became a private pursuit, confined to the wealthy, the life of the ordinary people of the Highlands was gravely diminished. They lost a recurring social and recreational occasion which added excitement to their lives. They also lost an important source of food. Few things have rankled more with islanders than this expropriation of these ancient rights.

A belated attempt to exercise them was made in 1887 during the Crofters War. On a November morning, at a pre-arranged signal, hundreds of impoverished crofters from all the villages between Crossbost and Marvaig marched into the Park deer forest, armed with every weapon they could lay their hands on, and began to drive the deer as their ancestors had done in the early seventeenth century.

Estimates of the kill range from fifteen to two hundred. The truth is probably nearer the lower than the higher figure. Most of the fowling pieces available were less effective against deer than the bows and arrows of the past. Even so, the slaughter was considerable.

For some it was a political demonstration to bring their grievances to the notice of a remote, uncaring and somewhat hostile government. Some had the wild idea that, if they drove the whole herd of six hundred deer into the sea, the sporting tenants would go away and they would have the forest for themselves to graze their sheep. Most were interested simply in getting venison to feed their hungry families.

The Deer Raid lasted for two days. At the end of the first

day the raiders built a huge rectangular tent with sails and spars from their boats, to give shelter from the night wind. In front of it was a row of camp fires, some as big as a hayrick, with the carcase of a deer being roasted or boiled on each, or made into a succulent stew.

Before they ate, a grey-haired patriarch, silhouetted in the light of the fires, delivered a grace in rich and sonorous Gaelic, asking for the blessing of 'God the Father and God the Son' on their holy crusade, and expressing the hope that a church would one day be built on the spot to commemorate the great event.

After grace and food, the men sat round the fires talking and singing, entertaining visitors and giving interviews to journalists. In the eyes of the government and most of the outside world, they were ignorant and dangerous savages, defying the law and setting the kingdom at risk. The truth is very different.

One of the journalists who visited the camp said their favourite choruses were from the works of Donnachadh Ban nan Oran: fàir Duncan of the songs. An Argyllshire poet of the eighteenth century, Duncan Ban Macintyre, has been compared with Wordsworth (rather to Wordsworth's disadvantage) by one of the few people I know competent to pass judgment in the matter: the poet Sorley Maclean, who adds that Macintyre's magnificent song in praise of Ben Dobhrain is 'the greatest example of naturalistic realism in the poetry of Europe'.

People who had access to such a repertoire were certainly not ignorant, even if some of them could not read, write or speak English. The fact that they cherished a literature of such quality is all the more remarkable in face of the efforts of central government to destroy the language – and the efforts of the Presbyterian church to eliminate secular poetry, in so far as the language did survive.

Equally, they were not lawless. The Park Deer Raid was one of the most remarkable examples of peaceful protest in British history.

The raid was immaculately planned and coordinated. The men from Crossbost came to Marvaig by sea. The Crossbost and Marvaig men then marched in military formation to the dyke at Seaforth Head to rendezvous with the men from

Balallan. The dyke itself was symbolic. As pointed out later, in the High Court of Justiciary in Edinburgh, it was high enough to keep the crofters' sheep out of the deer forest but not high enough to keep the deer out of the crofters' little patches of arable.

There was no act of violence associated with the raid. No high words were spoken. The raiders fraternised with the keepers, even shared their food and exchanged tobacco; the men spoke reasonably with the Sheriff when he checked them, and when some of them later faced criminal charges they surrendered without demur to a single unarmed policeman and provided a fishing boat to convey themselves to gaol.

The sporting tenant whose land they raided harboured no grudge against the people of Park, nor the people of Park against her. A fact which reflects great credit on both sides.

Two English families, the Platts and Thorneycrofts, united by marriage and equally well known in engineering and politics, tenanted Park Deer Forest for one hundred years from some time before the raid down almost to the present day. When the raid took place, Mrs Platt with her gamekeepers met the crofters and invited them to Eishken Lodge, where she promised them food and drink. The men replied respectfully that they had no English, fanned out across the forest and commenced the drive.

Fifty years after the event I was told by one of the ringleaders, 'Mrs Platt was a young woman then, and a nice young woman she was. There was never the like of her on this side of the border'. Although Mrs Platt maintained good relations with the invaders of her land, a stupid and oppressive government acted very differently. A large contingent of mainland police was sent hurriedly to Lewis. Sheriff Fraser led them to Park and read the Riot Act, although there had been no riot; in fact nothing remotely resembling a riot.

The only untoward incident occurred when a crofter named Mackinnon, who had been very busy urging the others on, further perhaps than they were prepared to go, found himself confronted by a small group of policemen. Unlike the others, who replied to the police with dignity and respect when they were spoken to, he turned and fled. The police gave chase. When they were overtaking him he lost his head and aimed his rifle at the Superintendent in charge.

He fired no shot. Committed no physical assault. But clearly he laid himself open to serious charges. A few days later he was arrested and locked up in Stornoway gaol. What happened there no one knows but, at the end of two days' incarceration, he emerged as the principal witness for the prosecution! And so the Crown created the anomaly that the only person who had committed a criminal offence faced no charge, while six innocent people, including the schoolmaster of Balallan, faced the risk of long terms of imprisonment on trumped-up charges of mobbing and rioting.

Donald Macrae, the schoolmaster at Balallan, was one of the most eloquent leaders of the Land League. Clearly the authorities were out to get him. There was ample evidence that he had not taken part in the raid, but he was privy to the arrangements, and alerted sympathetic journalists in Glasgow with the three-word telegram 'Hunt is up'.

In the High Court of Justiciary in Edinburgh, at the end of a two-day trial, the crofters' advocate, who afterwards became a judge himself, asked the jury not to put a criminal construction on anything that could be explained as the exposure of a social wrong.

The accused, he said, were charged with mobbing and rioting, one of the most serious crimes known to the law of Scotland. There was no mob, however: the raiders were spread out over 144 square miles of moor and mountain! And there was no riot. In fact, when Sheriff Fraser arrived, the men sat down and listened to him. He went through the farce of reading the Riot Act and told the raiders to go home. They went home.

He added that he had tried to cite the Sheriff as a witness for the defence – a piquant situation – but the Crown would not pay his expenses and the crofters couldn't afford to.

The judge's summing-up was very hostile. Even so, he made it clear there was no crime in taking the deer. They were wild animals, belonging to no one. So far as the deer were concerned, the remedy against the raiders was a civil action for trespass. The question before the jury was whether there had been mobbing and rioting. He indicated pretty clearly that he thought there had been. The jury differed. Unanimously, they acquitted all six accused.

The verdict was greeted with cheers which the court officials found it impossible to quell. Macrae was carried shoulder high through the streets of Edinburgh and at night the raiders were entertained in the Prince of Wales Hotel.

Seven years later the crofters of Lochs were lighting bonfires to welcome the Report of the Deer Forest Commissioners recommending a great reduction in the area of the Highlands under deer.

Despite the report and the jubilation, Park has remained a deer forest and the laws against poaching have been immeasurably tightened up. Yet relations between the Platt/ Thorneycroft family and the crofters continued to be friendly. One incident told heavily in the crofters' favour at the trial. Mrs Platt's brother, Douglas Thorneycroft, came out with food for the gamekeepers, who were maintaining a watch on the raiders from a discreet distance. Getting into conversation with one of the raiders, Thorneycroft gave him some of the food he was carrying. That made nonsense of the prosecution claim that there was a riot in progress. Later the raider became a keeper with the Estate, and Thorneycroft, when they were on the hill together, used to chaff him, saying, 'If I hadn't fed you that day in the forest you would still be in gaol as a rioter'.

The surprising thing is, not that the Deer Raid took place, but that it was so long in coming, was attended by so little violence, and left no permanent bitterness behind.

Within a few weeks of the trial the Crofters Commission began fixing fair rents in Lewis. In their first 150 cases, rents were reduced by nearly 50%, and more than 80% of the arrears standing against tenants were written off. Even those who had land were being grossly overcharged for it.

Around the same time four women from Ness were fined – because they had gathered heather to make ropes for holding down the thatch on their homes! It was held that, as they pulled the heather, they had also taken some wisps of grass belonging to Galson Farm. No one actually saw the grass. It was said to have been shaken out from among the heather!

When two young men from the village of Bayble were accused of maliciously damaging the fences of Aignish Farm, an elaborate encircling movement was launched against the village by the police and the navy. HMS *Seahorse,* with armed marines on board, closed in on the village from the sea while Sheriff Fraser and a posse of police approached by land.

Despite the elaborate arrangements, the police failed to arrest either of the accused, although they gave themselves up voluntarily at a later date.

The whole operation was so ludicrously mismanaged that it probably aroused more laughter than resentment, but it is all part of a pattern of bumbling oppression by central government which has burnt itself into the folk memory of islanders although, paradoxically, it has not diminished in any

This strange figure in a Lewis home symbolises the long connection with Easter Island, one of the remotest islands in the world. One day Lewis might get around to creating a museum of exotic gifts brought home by island seamen from the far corners of the world.

way the service they gave to the Crown, out of all proportion to the population, in a succession of bloody wars, from the French Revolution down to the present day, as I have tried to show in my books *Surprise Island* and *The Gaelic Vikings*.

In 1842, nearly half a century before the Deer Raid, the people of Park had resisted eviction from the villages of Lemreway, Orinsay and Eishken. On that occasion, when a posse of ground officers, constables and others arrived, led by the Sheriff, and began to unroof the houses, the women rebelled and, in the words of a contemporary press report, 'drove them from the field'.

The victory of the Amazons was short-lived. The villages were cleared in the following year. Even when many of the Park villages were resettled by a 'benevolent' government after the first world war, the whole area south of Loch Erisort was still without a road linking it with the rest of the island. Park was, in effect, an island communicating with Stornoway only by sea.

In the middle thirties of this century, when roads were eventually provided, the crofters were obliged to give a proportion of the labour free. The result was that, whenever a difficult patch of rock was struck, the wages fell to something like 2½d. an hour for hard manual work without the aid of modern earth-moving equipment.

As a result of these conditions there was heavy and sustained emigration from Lochs. While Canada, the USA and Australia were the usual destinations for Lewis emigrants, many of the Lochsmen went to South America.

Just ten years after the Deer Raid, the first group from Balallan and Arivruaich set off for Tierra del Fuego. Many others followed. In the first half of this century, Lochs had closer ties with Punta Arenas than with Birmingham.

The Falklands became known to Gaelic-speaking Lewismen as 'Eilein nan Caorach' – the Sheep Islands – just as the Hudson Bay Territory became known as the 'Talamh Fuar' – the Cold Country – and the campaign against Napoleon in Egypt as 'Cogadh nan Turc' – the War with the Turks. They were all nearer, more real, than England.

Even Easter Island was a 'colony' of Lochs. For more than a quarter of a century a succession of Lewismen, mainly from

Lochs, managed the sheep farms on this lonely outpost 2400 miles from the nearest city – Valparaiso. At times they were the only Europeans there.

And *Tschiffeley's Ride*, the travel classic by the Swiss schoolteacher who rode on horseback from Buenos Aires to Washington, had its Lochs connection. Before the journey began, when Tschiffeley was buying the horses which carried him over the Andes and the Mexican plateau on the longest horseback ride in history (10,000 miles), he spent a week with a friend from Balallan, Murdo Macleod, who managed a sheep farm in the Argentine.

That these facts are known is significant. They were recorded, not long before he died, by Murdo Macleod of Keose, who made a list of the Lewismen who had gone to South America, with interesting details about many of them. This was not the result of arid research about people who existed, for the researcher, only as names on a sheet of paper. It was a reminiscence about friends, drawn from the fireside conversations of a community which embraced Easter Island and Tierra del Fuego, just as surely as it embraced the villages along the fiords which indent the coast of Lochs.

Despite the disruption caused by a long continued process of eviction and resettlement; despite the leaching away of so many able-bodied and enterprising people, the villages of Lochs still show a surprisingly strong sense of community, and have responded to every little glimmer of opportunity which has come their way, on conditions relevant to the area's need.

In the late fifties when the Crofters Commission and the North of Scotland College of Agriculture were promoting land improvement by the method of surface seeding, there was an excellent response from the crofters of Lochs, despite the extreme difficulties of the terrain in which they had to work.

In the same way, Lochs has responded to the EEC's Integrated Development Programme for the Hebrides, and the HIDB's encouragement of multi-purpose cooperatives.

When Alginate Industries decided to close their seaweed-drying factory at Keose, six of the workers took it over as a cooperative on their own initiative, not under the HIDB scheme. In this way they preserved their own jobs and indirectly provided work for another ten crofters who cut seaweed and sell it to the factory.

After four years' operation, they were able to buy the factory and the jetty, and diversify into fish farming, producing something like 10,000 salmon a year.

The people of Lochs have always been distinguished by their versatility, their willingness to tackle anything that offered, and their ability to survive, however harsh the conditions. Without these qualities, most of the island would have become a desert long ago.

The good green grass snaking up the precipitous hillsides of Lochs and penetrating into the all-pervasive brown of the moorland, and the fish-rearing cages in so many of the lochs, are the symbols of villages which refuse to die and in which, despite the frictions inevitable in small close societies, the spirit of neighbourliness and communal self-help are still stronger than the desire for a fast buck at someone else's expense.

CHAPTER 12

The Golden Road

From Tarbert to Rodil we journey back through time: from a pleasant little village with a modern car ferry to an ancient church and the ghosts that inhabit it.

Part of our journey is by the Golden Road.

Not to Samarkand and the gorgeous east: a tortuous switchback substandard track winding like a rollercoaster round the Bays of Harris.

The name is ironical. Given by the locals to mark the anguish of a remote and grudging authority over the cost of providing a road – three quarters of a century after the local minister had told a Royal Commission: 'The want of a road and bridges on the rivers is an unspeakable hardship. There have been many narrow escapes crossing swollen rivers. Lives have been lost'.

Having waited so patiently, the people were due their jibe.

It is a Golden Road, however, in quite another sense, winding through one of the areas distinguished by the Countryside Commission as part of Scotland's Scenic Heritage. 'A small-scale landscape of detailed variety and visual pleasure that contrasts strongly with the softer wider landscapes of the island's west coast,' says the Commission.

As one drives along in wonder looking at the 'feannags' – miscalled 'lazybeds' – like little graves among the rocks, won from the bare moonscape of ice-scored gneiss with infinite labour; at the well-built homes scattered here and there at the water's edge; at the blue, brown, silver, jet-black lochans gleaming with water lilies, and changing colour with the changing light; or at the distant Cuillins marching majestically across the southern horizon, two questions reverberate in the mind like a drum-beat.

Beautiful though it be, how does anyone earn a living in this desert of tumbled stone? Why did anyone choose to come here in the first place?

The scattered residents live meagrely from fishing, labouring, the making of Harris tweed, tourism, the newly developed fish farming and other service industries. There has been a long tradition of mobility from job to job as opportunity offers. Joining the merchant navy or taking other seasonal work away from home. There has been a long secular decline in numbers as the young have left. Many of those who remain are pensioners, keeping a holiday base to which families come home seasonally, perhaps permanently, but sometimes not at all.

They have even lost a large part of the industry they helped to create – Harris tweed. The economist would say they made the wrong choice. The sociologist – the realist! – would say they were compelled to make it. The fish farm at Geocrab illustrates the point.

It was built more than sixty years ago by Lord Leverhulme as a carding and spinning mill to release the women of Harris from the burden of hand carding and hand spinning. To remove a bottleneck in their expanding industry. Later he complained, 'I have never been asked for one single pound of wool to be spun'. The people of Harris refused to use it.

Nigel Nicolson tells the story in *The Lord of the Isles* and sums it up in one pejorative phrase: 'The old prejudices returned'. A very superficial assessment loaded with the 'old prejudices' by which the wealthy judge the motives of the poor.

Any advance in technology is purchased at a price. The old firm goes bankrupt. The new one leapfrogs over it. The Harris people could only make the change by rendering their skill in hand spinning redundant. In the long term that would have paid them. Living from hand to mouth in the bitter twenties the option was not open to them. They had, besides, a legitimate pride in their traditional craftsmanship, pockets of which survive to the present day.

The change was easier in Lewis where new people were coming into the industry who hadn't to sacrifice an old skill to profit by a new one.

The relative size and compactness of the villages was also important. Numbers were essential for the emergence of the small indigenous entrepreneurial middlemen, buying yarn and hiring weavers, who were important for the evolution of the industry as we know it today.

Despite that lost opportunity the people of the Bays have clung like limpets to the rocks, defying the forces that would wash them off.

Whenever I look at this miracle of man's endurance, four images float into my mind.

I see a battered merchant vessel steaming into Valletta at the height of the war in the Mediterranean with a Harris captain – Angus Campbell – placid on the bridge. A Harris piper playing defiantly on the f'c'sle as his ancestors did throughout the centuries on many a bloody field.

I see Donald MacCuish, Scotland's leading authority on crofting law, sitting at the conference table, patiently drawing on a reservoir of knowledge both practical and academic to illumine the darkness for civil servants to whom crofting was a mystery at best, and at worst an unmitigated nuisance.

I hear a preacher, Rev. Murdo Ewan Macdonald, in one of the wealthiest of Edinburgh churches, boldly tell his congregation of advocates, bankers, heads of departments, and their comfortable fur-coated wives, 'We are waxing fat at the expense of hungry people . . . To glory in the affluent society . . . and preach Christianity to the hungry millions . . . is practical atheism at its very ugliest'.

I hear thousands of listeners chuckling around their radios as they listen to a Harris crofter's son, Finlay J. Macdonald, embellish the simple incidents of his growing up with a storyteller's gift for the dramatic or absurd.

How does such a barren countryside produce so rich a crop? – seamanship, courage, intellectual ability, resolute crusading faith, lighthearted self-mocking laughter?

The people of these remote townships are often regarded as an incubus, living parasitically on grants and doles from wealthier parts of the country. The truth is that historically they have greatly enriched the life of the nation, by a steady tribute of men and women of outstanding ability, paid to ravenous cities at home and abroad.

As for the question why people ever settled in such an agriculturally uninviting area as the Bays of Harris, the answer is, it was no choice of theirs. They came unwillingly for the profit of others: under duress and without redress.

James Hunter puts the story in a single sentence in his classic study *The Making of the Crofting Community:* 'In the 1820s and 1830s the relatively fertile machair lands on the Atlantic coast of Harris were completely cleared and the evicted population settled on the island's bare and rocky east coast'.

Half a century later, when the government appointed the Napier Commission to enquire into the condition of the crofters, a witness from Harris told them: 'Before my father's time there were no people in Geocrab at all. No person can conceive what kind of a place it is without seeing it'.

As a crofter he might have been biased but the next witness, the minister, Rev. Alexander Davidson, was an incomer, and his view was the same: 'It is most unnatural that a man should be chased away to make room for sheep and deer: that land should be left uncultivated, when men are perishing for lack of food'. Asked whether the crofters who remained on the good land in the west had benefited from the thinning out of the population, he replied drily, 'There were no crofters left!'

The last of them were driven out in 1839 from Borve, which a neighbouring farmer coveted.

As Eric Richards points out in *A History of the Highland Clearances*, 'It was a time when sheep farmers could dictate terms to landlords in the north'.

The proprietor, the Earl of Dunmore, did not want to lose a good tenant. His crofters were given the choice: Canada or the Bays. They refused to go to either. The army was summoned to shift them. At the point of the bayonet, so to speak, they opted for the Bays. After fifteen years of misery many of them decided that emigration was the lesser evil. In 1854 more than six hundred – men, women and children – sailed for Canada from Harris.

When they were cleared from the fertile west, they were expected to live by fishing. Many of them did. As they put it: 'We turned our faces to the sea'. Even there they were handicapped by lack of capital for boats and gear. Davidson put it starkly: 'If a man loses a cow he may not be able to buy another in his lifetime'.

Distance from markets was an even greater handicap, especially for the lobster fishermen. Transport was slow, and when the lobsters finally got to Billingsgate, only the buyer was there to say how many had survived the journey.

It would be wrong to assume that the privations suffered by the Harris crofters in the hungry forties and fifties of last

The highway authority showed unusual imagination in using the slightly satirical name — the Golden Road — for the winding track to Scadabay. The name, however, may vanish if the new Islands Council insists on having Gaelic-only names on its signposts.

century were due entirely to evil landlords. I will have occasion later to look at the credit side of the Dunmore account.

It would be even further from the truth to say the problems arose when incomers like the Dunmores took over from the native Macleods.

The change in relationship between chief and clansmen took place when the Macleods still owned Harris, and the reasons for it are very relevant to the problems of the western world today.

The Macleods were riding high both in Rodil and Dunvegan when the placid little village of Finsbay became the scene of one of the most discreditable incidents in the history of

Hebridean landlordism.

On a November night in 1739 a sailing vessel, the *William*, from Donaghadee in Ireland, came nosing into the bay as if she were a smuggler. In the darkness, men, women and children were dragged from their beds and carried prisoner on board. In daylight, subterfuges were used to entice others into the trap. One man was asked to help in rounding up some sheep. When he was beyond reach of neighbours, he was seized and bundled on to the *William*. A boy was decoyed on board by a man who asked him to deliver a message to the ship.

When the cargo was complete, the *William* set sail for Donaghadee to take on supplies for a voyage to the Indies, where the prisoners were to be sold as indentured labour on the plantations.

The *William* left a trail of derelicts on her way to Ireland. At Rum, a party of children were dumped ashore: they were too young to sell. They were left to make their own way home – if they could and if they still had homes or parents to go to.

At Canna the *William* paused to offload the corpse of a young woman who had died, possibly from terror at what had befallen her.

At Jura the *William* offloaded two pregnant women, whether for humanitarian reasons or because pregnant women were a nuisance is not clear.

While the ship was being refitted at Donaghadee the prisoners were secured in two barns: the men in one, the women and children in the other. In the night they escaped.

To cover their activities, the master of the *William* and his accomplices had represented their prisoners as convicted felons. They had provided themselves with forged documents to support that tale.

There was panic in Ulster when it became known that a large number of criminals, bound for the plantations, were at large.

While the crew of the *William* scoured the countryside to recover their valuable cargo, the magistrates searched, with even greater diligence, for the mythical felons.

Those who were caught by the *William's* crew were bound and driven back to the vessel with cudgels. They were flung into the hold where they were beaten with an iron bar.

By this time the magistrates realised that the ninety

Rodil church sketched around 1900 by Malcolm Macdonald, Stornoway.

'dangerous criminals' were mainly women and children, harmless and illegally abducted. They issued warrants for the arrest of the master of the *William* and his supercargo, but they fled.

What happened to those tossed ashore on the voyage to Ireland is not known. Some of those who escaped in Ulster made their way back to the Hebrides. Others, presumably, settled in Ireland. As least it is known that after the magistrates' inquiry many of the unfortunate prisoners were given work by Ulster farmers.

The most horrifying feature of the incident is that the supercargo, who masterminded it, was a son of a respected Hebridean family, the Macleods of Berneray, whom we will meet later in very different circumstances.

Lurking in the background were his fellow conspirators: Sir Alexander Macdonald of Sleat, 14th chief of clan Donald, and Norman Macleod, the 22nd chief of the Macleods of Dunvegan.

Other Highland chiefs have been known to send genuine criminals to the plantations but, so far as I know, this is the only instance in which Highland chiefs conspired to sell innocent women and children from their own estates into slavery for personal gain.

The incident had a sequel and may in fact have changed the

course of history. W.C. Mackenzie, the Lewis historian, whose papers relating to the affair are now in the custody of the Library in Stornoway, has suggested that Forbes of Culloden, Lord President of the Court of Session, hushed up the affair to protect his friends and avoid a scandal. But that put them in his power. As a result, six years later, in 1745, he was able to dissuade some of the leading Jacobite clans from taking up arms for the Prince.

If the Macleods of Dunvegan and Macdonalds of Sleat had been out with Prince Charlie, their support would not have been sufficient to win him a crown, but the 1745 rebellion might have run a different course and had an even bloodier end.

We move back into an earlier and happier phase in the history of the clans when we reach the church of St Clements in Rodil with the magnificent tomb of Alasdair Crotach, the 8th chief of the Macleods of Dunvegan and Harris, who flourished in the late fifteenth and early sixteenth centuries.

It is one of the finest tombs of the period in Scotland, with vivid portrayals of subjects both sacred and secular, including a galley, a stag hunt, and St Michael and Satan at the weighing of souls.

The twelve apostles, with the religious artist's customary disregard of both history and geography, wear typical West Highland quilted coats of the sixteenth century.

Alasdair is Gaelic for Alexander. The nickname 'Crotach' implies that he had a stoop. According to tradition it was the result of a sword wound received in the battle of Bloody Bay, resisting an invasion by his hereditary enemies the Macdonalds.

Alasdair is described as 'devout' by Dr. I.F. Grant in her impressive and authoritative history of the Clan Macleod.

He built the church at Rodil, including his own tomb 'with its reverent symbolism'. He built two other churches, one on Scarp and the other near Toe Head. 'He is said to have translated some psalms into Gaelic and gone to Rodil in his old age to end his days in religious retirement'.

Devout he may have been. He was also more certainly a patron of the arts, martial and otherwise. He trained his young kinsmen in sword play, rewarding the best of them with suits of armour.

F

The misnamed 'lazy-beds' of Harris. This photograph by Dr A. Fenton gives an idea of the infinite toil that went into the creation of the small plots of land from which crofters raised their crops in the Bays district of Harris and elsewhere.

He maintained, as was the custom of Highland chiefs in his day, harpers, bards and seanachaidhs (storytellers) to entertain his guests and perpetuate the history of the clan.

He was a notable patron of piping. Family tradition says it was he who founded the famous College of Piping at Boreraig in Skye, presided over by the most famous of all piping families, the MacCrimmons. The same source says that the MacCrimmons were natives of South Harris, which is less picturesque but more probable than the alternative tradition that they came from Cremona in Italy, in the wake of a remote ancestor of Alasdair Crotach returning from the Crusades.

The MacCrimmons are supposed to have got their great gift for music from a fairy, but in my experience fairies are scarce on the Harris hills. What is clear, and what is more significant, is that, even in the bloodiest period of internecine strife between the Highland clans, Rodil in Harris was a cultural centre where the arts were nourished.

An idea of the lifestyle of those days can be gathered from the poems of Mary Macleod, the Gaelic bardess who is buried, according to tradition, in the south transept of St Clements.

Mary is reputed to have been 105 when she died, which may not be true but should not surprise us if it were.

Captain Dymes, the rather gullible Englishman who visited the islands during her lifetime, has set it solemnly on the record that the 'air is very wholesome' 'as doth appear by the healthful bodies and long lives of the inhabitants'. There were 'divers yet living' when he was there, a hundred years, some of six score and one of 'a hundred and four score years'.

Many of Mary Macleod's poems are laments for her patrons and friends. The qualities she praises in them were kindness, patience, nobility, mirth, modesty, physical beauty, prowess on the battlefield or in the chase, scholarship and eloquence: 'the speech of thy mouth was worthy to hear'.

Even if we assume cynically that those she praises were not the paragons she makes them out to be, her catalogue of virtues gives us an idea of the qualities that were aspired to in the islands in the seventeenth century.

There is great insistence on music as an essential element in life, on unstinted entertainment, generosity, even chess playing. No evidence anywhere of so-called Celtic gloom. Mary herself enjoyed life: she is reputed to have relished both whisky and snuff.

The bards maintained by the Highland chiefs of the period were elaborately trained and the rules of their art were strict. Mary was a new phenomenon – a gifted amateur, singing the praises of the family in which she had been a governess or a nannie. She was, it has been said, the first to write court poetry in popular diction.

Many of her poems have been lost but those which can be ascribed to her with reasonable certainty have been published with an English prose translation by J. Carmichael Watson in *Gaelic Songs of Mary Macleod.*

The prose translation gives no hint of the flow and rhythm of the originals, which were intended to be sung, but Watson makes the point that, when Mary wrote, Gaelic had 'a perfection of harmony, flexibility and copiousness, along with a richness and purity of idiom, such as some languages never attain and few retain for a prolonged period'.

Even in Mary's day, however, the old Gaelic community was

A fish farm in the Bays of Harris — a very new but very common sight. The development of fish-farming has brought the islands into sharp conflict with the Crown Estate Commissioners who levy a charge on every pound of fish produced. Islanders see this impost as a tax on enterprise in an area where enterprise should be encouraged. It is a new and unpleasant reminder of the islands' quasi-colonial status within the British economy.

disintegrating. The chiefs were turning to London and Paris for their pleasures. Mary, in her Lament for Roderick the 17th chief and his brother, pointedly express her grief that an heir 'styled upon Harris' will not be laid in the tomb of his grandsire.

Her younger contemporary, the Blind Harper, whom we met briefly at Habost, the home of the Brieves, takes up the same theme in a poem which depicts Echo wandering disconsolate through the halls where music is no longer heard. The poem is 'strongly political', says Professor Derick Thomson, 'with its satire of the spendthrift absentee chief'. In *An Introduction to Gaelic Poetry* Professor Thomson, with a justifiable flurry of pride in a fellow islander, suggests that the Blind Harper's barbed verse is 'the independent and fearless voice of the Lewisman'.

Clearly the poets had already discerned the radical change taking place in the relationship between chieftain and clansmen, which presaged the kidnapping at Finsbay and eventually gave the fertile land to alien tacksmen and their sheep, while the erstwhile clansmen, on whom the chief's power had rested in the grand days of the clan, were driven into poverty and destitution in the Bays.

Astonishingly, the spirit of the people was not broken. In the cemetery at Rodil there is another poet buried, John Morrison, the Harris blacksmith, who lived through the traumatic years of the Clearances. He sang as joyously as Mary Macleod but with a very different theme.

Deserted by their natural and hereditary leaders, betrayed by them in fact, with the old close-knit society of the clans in ruins around them, the Gaels turned for solace to religion.

Thomson writes of Morrison's freshness, robustness of language and dramatic power. A poet himself, he illustrates his point by translating a verse from a poem in which the converted blacksmith has a dialogue with his unregenerate self:

> I am drowned in the 'old' man's sea,
> in sharp cold clear and winter coldness,
> the glorious 'new' man comes to the temple
> and he sets my feet a-dancing.
> It is the 'old' man who made me gloomy,
> the 'new' man is my blazing lantern.

The lantern of poetry still burns in Harris a century and a half after the blacksmith's death. There has been a long slow debilitating decline in the population under economic pressure. Many of the ablest in each generation have been forced to leave. But the language and the poetry are still cherished.

In 1985, a young German physicist published a Gaelic poem in Heidelberg, with translations into English and German. Behind this unusual publishing venture are an 84-year old seaman from Plockropool, and a Lewisman who worked for thirty years with the Ordnance Survey. Peter Campbell, the seaman, and Alasdair Macdonald introduced Gisela Vogler-Fiesser, a regular visitor to Harris, to the beauties of Gaelic poetry.

'Many a night we sat near the fire reading poems and translating them', she writes in the preface to her little book. The poem chosen for publication was 'Eilean na h-Oige'

('Island of Youth' or, in German, 'Insel der Jugend'). It was written by Fr. Allan McDonald in Eriskay around 1901 and gives a vivid picture of life in the Hebrides a century ago. The book is dedicated to 'the folk of a lively modern Gaelic community'.

A community which, despite the vicissitudes of four hundred years of disintegration and decline, still has the heart to sing.

A pupil at Lews Castle College, Stewart Graham, won Shell U.K.'s 'Livewire' Award in 1983 for his project to make lobster and prawn creels locally instead of importing them. He is now – at the age of 22 – the biggest manufacturer of creels in the U.K. and is breaking into the export market in Sweden. He is seen at the opening of his new factory, employing 40 people, with the Rt. Hon. Donald Stewart, P.C., Member of Parliament for the Western Isles. Courtesy *Stornoway Gazette*

CHAPTER 13

The Great Days of Berneray

Towering over Rodil is the rounded hump of Roneval. Modest as mountains go – a mere 1500 feet – it is of immense interest to geologists. It brings us back to the time when there was no Atlantic, and the Hebrides and Canada were locked in a close and fiery embrace.

The Nature Conservancy Council has identified it as one of two sites in Harris given the top grading as being 'of the highest international importance'. The interest of the site lies in an exposure of anorthosite which is 'unique in Britain'. 'It has been considered part of the belt of similar intrusions extending across the Pre-Cambrian areas of North-Western Europe and North America, and cited in studies of plate tectonics and continental drift.'

The anorthosite intrusion can be identified by the pinky-white colour of the outcrops which contrast with the dark grey of the surrounding gneiss. Those who are interested can reach excellent exposures of anorthosite conveniently from the Finsbay-Rodil road.

Those of us for whom geology is a closed book may prefer to climb to the summit of Roneval, on a clear day, for the magnificent view over Skye and the Uists, and the island-strewn Sound of Harris, which is regarded as a peaceful backwater today but which has been much closer to the centre of British power in the past.

The largest of the islands is Berneray which provides a key to much that is significant in the relationship between the islands and the rest of Britain. Berneray is readily accessible from North Uist, which it closely adjoins, but there is also a ferry service from Leverburgh, which is the more appropriate approach, as the island's historical links are with Harris.

In the churchyard at Rodil there is a tombstone to one of the many notable men Berneray produced. It has given rise to a number of rather ribald stories and has been read by generations of visitors with a snigger.

It was erected to Donald Macleod of Berneray, known as the

'Old Trojan', who had been out in the '45 and hid in a cave in the south of Harris while Cumberland 'pacified' the Highlands, in one of the most disgraceful acts of brutality and oppression in British military history. While the memorial is chiefly concerned with the family's record as Jacobites, what catches the visitor's eye is the statement that 'in his 75th year he married his third wife by whom he had nine children'.

I have heard it suggested that Donald had 'considerable assistance' in this unusual achievement. That, I think, is a modern invention of a prurient mind.

There is a much older tradition that Donald was so spry that, despite his age, he celebrated his third marriage by performing the salmon leap; bounding into his new bride's bed from a crouching position on all fours on the floor.

That story was given to Dr. I.F. Grant by Alick Morrison, a schoolmaster from Berneray, who has done more probably than anyone else to retrieve, as far as that can be done, the fast-vanishing history and traditions of a remarkable island.

Salmon leap or no, two of the sons of that late marriage rose to the rank of Lieutenant-General and were knighted for their services to Britain.

Donald's eldest son by his first marriage, Captain Norman Macleod, was involved in the discreditable episode of 'Long nan Daoine': the abduction of innocent men, women and children at Finsbay for sale to the plantations which I referred to in a previous chapter.

The significance of 'Long nan Daoine' is that it marks one of the first ominous results of the breach in the reciprocal relationship between chief and retainers, which was brought about in part by the deliberate policies of successive Scottish and British governments, and in part by the determination of the chiefs to pursue their fortunes (or squander their resources) in the capital cities of Edinburgh and London.

Despite the early blemish on Norman's reputation, Mr Morrison records that when he succeeded to his father's estates he became a notable improver, introducing better breeding animals and new meal mills, and extending the area under cultivation. Unlike many of the improving lairds of the period, he was still part of the local community and was accepted as such in spite of his past.

Another strand in the evolution of the chieftains from clan leaders to landed proprietors, from an economy based on people to an economy based on money, is represented by the Old Trojan's second son Alexander, who became captain of an East Indiaman, the *Mansfield,* amassed a fortune, and ploughed a good deal of it back into the development of his native Harris.

Captain Alexander Macleod bought Harris from the Macleods of Dunvegan, when their absorption into London society and the extravagance that entailed had almost beggared them. He appears to have driven a shrewd, perhaps even a hard, bargain.

Once in possession, he undertook the renovation and development of Rodil harbour, building quays, boat houses and stores; taking in fishermen from other areas to teach the locals new techniques; erecting a school, setting up a small factory for the spinning of woollen and linen threads and the making of twine for herring nets; planting trees; opening up south Harris with roads; and discovering new fishing grounds in a series of trials from the coast of Skye to St Kilda.

John Knox, whose report to the British Society for Extending the Fisheries, published in 1786, is still in print and still makes lively reading, records that the principal obstacle to Captain Macleod's success was the intolerable burden imposed upon him by the taxes on coal and salt, and the outrageous bureaucracy with which they were administered.

He tells the story of a shipload of coal taken by Captain Macleod from Greenock to Rodil. To save trouble he offered to pay the duty on the coal in Greenock in advance. That was against the rules! The boat sprang a leak so he made for Rodil instead of the Custom House at Stornoway. He asked the collector at Stornoway to send a man to Rodil to examine the coals and assess the duty. That too was against the rules!

In the end of the day, having loaded the cargo at Greenock and unloaded it at its destination, he had to reload the vessel for a second time, sail to Stornoway, unload for a second time, pay the duty, load the cargo for a third time and sail back to Rodil for a third unloading.

Knox believed that, despite the government, Captain Macleod would eventually 'line the coast with a numerous race

Although most of the very fine panels on Alasdair Crotach's tomb are devoted to religious themes, the galley is a key element. It was sea-power exercised through vessels like this which sustained the Macleods' modest empire.

of expert fishermen, comfortable in their circumstances'.

'It ought to be a model for some proprietors in the Highlands who, blinded by the representations of factors and misled by their influence, had never permitted their tenantry to raise their heads but are continually crushing them by new impositions on their industry and upon every appearance of improvement . . . Thus, each party impoverishes and distresses the other,' he wrote.

Knox meant the comment as a warning. Unfortunately it was a prophecy. Four years later Captain Macleod was dead; the factors were in control; the development of Harris was at an end, and the 'squeezing system', as Knox called it, to produce 'a fictitious instead of a real rent roll' was in full swing.

After the Clearances a relatively prosperous tenantry, with at least the prospect of rational economic evolution, was broken and dispirited, scattered overseas, or imprisoned in a poverty it was almost impossible to clamber out of.

Almost precisely a hundred years after Knox identified the disease, a crofter giving evidence before the Napier

Commission confirmed his diagnosis in a few stark phrases: 'Donald Stewart was factor under Macleod of Harris (the last of Captain Macleod's descendants to own the island). It was then our troubles commenced. He cleared seven townships at one stroke. His next move was to turn his attention to Macleod himself, and devise how he could manage to make a fool of him. He succeeded. Before the end came they used to call Macleod a beggar. I have seen him in the market, in this very place, leading a horse by the bridle and having no one that would wait upon him, while Donald Stewart was making his hundreds by his cattle on this man's lands'.

The power of the factors still fell heavily on the people of Harris when the Napier Commission sat. As another witness, Malcolm Macleod from Berneray, put it succinctly: 'If I tell the truth I shall risk the displeasure of those in authority over us. If I do not, my conscience will condemn me, and the people will stone me'.

Although it is the reference to the Old Trojan's virility which catches the eye on his tombstone, the inscription also records that his grandfather, Sir Norman Macleod of Berneray, fought at the battle of Worcester: a fact of which it is very easy to miss the significance.

Sir Norman was not a soldier of fortune, selling his sword to the best advantage, as so many Scotsmen of the period did. He was one of the leaders in King Charles' cause: a man of stature in the political life of his country, who was knighted by Charles II soon after the Restoration, in acknowledgement of his service to the House of Stuart.

Nor was he an alien laird, drawing rents from a Highland estate and spending them on luxurious living in the capital, as so many of his contemporaries were. He was a Highland chieftain living among his own people – except when he was in exile with the King he served! If he was at the battle of Worcester, so were his clansmen. Berneray was not then a remote and forgotten island 'at the back of beyond': it was playing an active role in the affairs of the kingdom.

Sir Norman Macleod of Berneray is celebrated in many Gaelic poems, especially in elegies which praise him, not only as an individual but as a representative of an old way of life which was rapidly changing.

J. Carmichael Watson's translation of one of Mary Macleod's dirges on the death of her beloved chieftain gives an indication (without the poetry) of the light in which he was seen by his clansmen and clanswomen.

'In thee would be found dignity and blitheness, in the hour of judgment thou wouldst solve the case, not with sullenness or anger, but courtly, orderly, with reason . . .

'Thou wast the tranquillity of friends at time of homecoming, when men drank deep without discord or quarrel, and thou didst love to have by thee tellers of a rare and pleasing tale . . .

'Often did friends wend to thy glorious fortress that was blithe and welcoming, festive and stately, without turbulence or arrogance, where the needy was not denied his due.'

English-speakers tend to discount the value of Gaelic culture because they have no access to it except in translation. Even if this position were tenable, it would be a mistake to think of Sir Norman Macleod of Berneray as an uncouth savage issuing from his Gaelic fastness to plunder the Lowland countryside.

He was equally at home in English. He maintained his Gaelic bards and storytellers but he had also studied at Glasgow University, and was at ease in the educated English society of his day. His vision was wider, not narrower, than that of his Lowland contemporaries who had no Gaelic. Even at this lapse of time the evidence of his scholarship peeps out from the scanty records that remain. William Matheson, for instance, points out that a correspondence between Sir Norman and Cathal MacVurich, the Gaelic poet and historian of Macdonald of Clanranald, deals not only with the genealogy of the Macleods, but refers to a new translation of Thomas a Kempis's *Imitation of Christ;* while Lord Tarbat quotes the views of Sir Norman in a letter to Samuel Pepys.

It was in Berneray with Sir Norman Macleod that General Middleton sought refuge in 1654 after the collapse of the Highland rising in support of Charles I, just as three hundred years earlier, according to local tradition, Robert Bruce found succour there when Edward's armies were rampaging through Scotland, hunting for the upstart who had the temerity to accept the crown at Scone.

Berneray is still a refuge, a quiet haven from the busy world. With fewer than 150 inhabitants it is one of the smallest inhabited islands in the Hebrides, and one of the loveliest.

The Gatliff Trust – founded in 1961 by a retired civil servant who had been a lifelong 'Youth' hosteller – maintains a chain of simple hostels in the Outer Hebrides in places the Scottish Youth Hostel Association does not serve. One of them is on Berneray to which, in the words of the Trustees, visitors are attracted for 'the peace, the quiet, the friendliness and community spirit of the people' as well as 'the flora and fauna' and 'the beauty of the island and its surroundings'.

A visitor from Tasmania has left a record in the log book of 'A concert like we had never seen before. Grown men and women singing unaccompanied by any music, their Gaelic songs. Scottish dancing and a bagpiper . . . It wasn't long until (thanks to local instruction) we were tripping the light fandango across the floor'.

The words used of Berneray by the Gatliff Trustees could be applied with equal truth to the whole of Harris, especially the superb Atlantic coast from Rodil to Luskentyre, which in recent years has attracted a growing number of artists, including two leading Scottish painters: John Houston and Elizabeth Blackadder, a husband and wife team who have produced sharply contrasting visions of the same landscape, both readily identifiable by those who know Harris in its changing moods.

Quite apart from the scenery and the magnificent beaches there are many places of interest. The varieties of rock types and structures round Toe Head are widely used by geologists for teaching purposes. In the same area there are natural arches and a small ruined chapel – one of those built by Alasdair Crotach.

There may also have been a nunnery there. Alick Morrison, who is better qualified than most to express a view, suggests that the name Nic Caparral, used on the Ordnance Survey maps, arose from a misunderstanding of a Gaelic phrase meaning 'the temple of the young women at Caipeval' – the hill overlooking the ruins.

So many of the Hebridean records have been lost – or wantonly destroyed to deprive the people of their history! – that the past has to be reconstructed by guesswork from oral tradition, and from place names which have gone through the distorting mirror of an alien language, as we saw in Bernera, Lewis.

Even for relatively recent events, such as the rise of the

Harris tweed industry, we are dependent on oral tradition as well as written records. We do know, however, that it was in this area the trade in Harris tweed began, in one of the happier conjunctions between native skill and proprietorial philanthropy.

Harris was owned by three successive Earls of Dunmore, the first of whom bought the island from the Macleods. The Dunmores maintained a private army for purposes of display as the Dukes of Atholl, a related family, do to the present day. In an old family scrapbook of the Dunmores there is an early photograph of the Harris army: men of magnificent physique wearing full Highland dress with sporrans so massive each looks like a complete lambskin.

When one thinks of the martial tradition of the old Macleods, the private army of the Dunmores was something of a grotesquerie. Their most elaborate 'campaign' of which I have knowledge was dragging an open carriage from Rodil to Luskentyre, like human horses, bringing a newly-married Dunmore couple to a wedding breakfast in a tent on the sands. The *Times* reported that the democratic Earl had invited his retainers to the feast, but made it clear that they were seated below the salt!

Requiring Murray tartan for his army's kilts, the Earl asked one of the Harris weavers, who were even then renowned for their skill, to copy it. The experiment was a success and from that small beginning the industry grew.

On the Harris side, the two pioneers are traditionally said to have been the 'Paisley' sisters, Marion and Christina Macleod from Strond, who came originally from Pabbay.

The delightful little island of Pabbay had been for centuries one of the minor seats of the Macleods of Dunvegan. It was evacuated early in the nineteenth century. According to one tradition, the evacuation took place because the tenants were caught distilling whisky, perhaps by the redoubtable Captain Oliver we met in Stornoway. In any event, the Paisley sisters moved to Strond, where their skill as weavers attracted the attention of the Dowager Countess of Dunmore: Catherine Herbert, a daughter of the Earl of Pembroke. She sent them to Paisley for training: hence the nickname.

The fact that in Harris weaving was predominantly women's

work, while in Lewis it was generally undertaken by men, may be part cause and part effect of the divergent courses on which the industry has developed.

Be that as it may, the name enshrines the fact that it was in Harris the industry had its beginning, and it was the native skill of the local people, trained with the help of the Dunmores to make their product marketable, which made 'Harris Tweed' one of the best-known brand names in the world.

The development of the Harris tweed industry from small beginnings is described by Francis Thomson in his book *Harris Tweed: the story of a Hebridean Industry*. Some of the waulking songs – 'Orain Luaidh' – associated with the making of tweed can be found in *Eilean Fraoich*, the collection published by An Comunn Gaidhealach; but the standard work on the waulking songs of the islands is Dr. J.L. Campbell's scholarly three-volume study – *Hebridean Songs* – published by the Oxford University Press. Dr. Campbell, however, is more directly concerned with the waulking songs of Uist, Eriskay and Barra than Harris, although many of them were known throughout the Hebrides.

There is a display on the history of the Harris tweed industry in An Clachan at Leverburgh, built by the Highlands and Islands Development Board in an effort to help one of the most difficult and economically underprivileged parts of Britain: an area in sad decline from the brave days when Sir Norman Macleod led his men to Worcester or the Old Trojan was out with Prince Charlie.

For a brief spell in the early twenties it looked as if the great days might be coming back.

The name Leverburgh recalls the whirlwind attempt of the first Viscount Leverhulme to achieve, at a stroke, the economic development the Highland Board and the people of Harris are still painstakingly seeking.

When Leverhulme descended on Harris, Leverburgh was the peaceful little village of Obbe, an economic backwater as it had been since the Clearances swept the west coast bare.

All that changed overnight. The name to begin with. Perhaps in response to a gentle hint from His Lordship, but certainly on the signed petition, and with the acclamation, of the people of Harris.

Lord Leverhulme's unusual Christmas Card for 1924 showing the curing of herring in progress in the open at Leverburgh when his Harris schemes were in full swing.

There was the same rush and flurry, social and commercial, as there had been in Lewis. Roads were built. Houses. Water towers. Piers. As well as beacons and other aids to navigation through the treacherous Sound of Harris. Leverhulme made frequent personal visits, travelling awkwardly through Skye to avoid the necessity of passing through Stornoway on which he had turned his back. For want of a frequent enough steamer service he sometimes crossed the Minch by fishing boat.

There was the same division of opinion over his schemes. The vast majority gave him enthusiastic, or at least tacit, support. A small minority defied him and raided Rodil farm.

The outcome of the raiding was very different from Lewis. The Scottish Office did nothing to encourage the raiders or dissuade Leverhulme from invoking the law. The first group of raiders were gaoled. A second group was chased from the scene by the people of Harris themselves.

The resolute intervention of the locals in support of the laird and against their fellow islanders is explained, in part, by the fact that the raiders had come from North Harris. They were not only threatening the jobs of the people in South Harris, they were encroaching on their land. In Lewis the raiders were not interlopers even to that modest degree: they were raiding farms in the immediate vicinity of their own homelessness, from which their forefathers had been evicted, and for which they had been actively petitioning the landlord, and the government, for more than thirty years.

That, of course, does not explain why the Scottish Office policy of land settlement was muted in Harris. Perhaps the bureaucrats had learned the lesson of Lewis but, if so, they had learned too late. The result of government ambivalence was that Leverhulme's plan to develop a modern fishery, based on one of the finest harbours in Britain, was frustrated, but no official obstacle was put in the way of his attempt to develop fishing in the rock-strewn Sound of Harris where all the cards were heavily stacked against him, and most experts declared he could not possibly succeed.

In spite of the difficulties, Leverhulme did succeed, at least to the extent that he reached first base. In 1924 he sent his friends a Christmas card with a photograph of fish-curing in progress at his new harbour in Leverburgh, and the caption 'The Birth of Commerce'.

Then fate once more took a hand. On a May afternoon in 1925, when work was proceeding busily on all his building projects, a prolonged blast on the factory hooter brought everything to a standstill. Lord Leverhulme was dead, and with him the dream.

His executors stopped everything immediately. They had no interest in the islands. One of them had earlier expressed regret that Lewis and Harris could not be towed into the Atlantic and sunk. Just for an hour or two to get rid of the encumbrance of people!

The building erected by Leverhulme as the Recreation Hall in a town he expected to have a population of 10,000 became a public school – in the Scottish sense – serving a countryside where the population was small and dwindling and getting proportionately older.

The roads he built were still of benefit. For one thing they gave access to the peat banks. The water supply was a boon and the houses were occupied. But the curing stations were deserted. The piers fell into decay, until finally some of them had to be demolished as a danger to shipping – if one can dignify with the term 'shipping' the few small infrequent vessels which now used the harbour.

The people of Harris tried from time to time to make something out of the wreckage. For some years they were led by an admirable Englishman, Col. Douglas Walker, who bought Borve Lodge when the Harris estate was broken up and sold. But the odds were against them. These were the years when Britain had no regional policy. No sharpened social conscience. Leverburgh was left to stagnate but refused to die.

The decline continued until the setting up of the Highland Board and the erection of An Clachan, which catches the eye as one comes through the village, a focus for visitors and the workshop of Co-Chomunn na Hearradh, the Harris community cooperative: one of the first signs of real hope in two hundred years, although whether it is the portent of a brighter future has still to be proved.

By every social indicator, except employment and the age structure of the population, Harris has made immense progress since the low point reached in the middle years of last century. It is a wonderful place to live in, if you have an income to live on.

During the potato famine of 1846 the *Inverness Courier*, reporting on the 'great destitution in Harris', wrote: 'They go to the shore and gather limpets, cockles and other shell fish and dig the sands at Scarista for sand eels. On these, and these only, do they subsist'.

Today, the old manse at Scarista is an hotel run by an enterprising English couple who came to Harris as teachers and fell in love with the place. It is an immensely civilised little hotel with a fine library, and is widely recommended for its cuisine. It numbers Cabinet Ministers among its guests and has been said by at least one connoisseur to serve 'the best breakfast in Britain'.

There must be some message for the future of Harris in the contrast between the menu at Scarista House Hotel in the 1980s and the unvarying diet of sand eels laboriously dug from the shore. But it is a complex message and somewhat difficult to read.

CHAPTER 14

Rockets, Twins and an Elopement

The centre of influence and power in Harris gradually moved away from Rodil when the link with the Macleods of Dunvegan was broken and Harris passed into the hands of the Dunmores.

In the late sixties of last century, the third of the Earls of Dunmore to own Harris built a turreted castle at Amhuinnsuidhe, in the North Harris deer forest, beside a fine salmon river where, in the appropriate conditions, the fish can be seen, at the end of their three-thousand mile trans-Atlantic journey, making a spectacular leap up a sheer rock-face, to gain access to the river and their ancestral spawning beds.

There is a story, possibly apocryphal, that when the young earl's bride – a daughter of the Earl of Leicester – saw the castle he had built for her, she commented drily that her father had bigger stables.

In any event, a wing was hastily added, as a result of which the Dunmores became financially embarrassed, and sold the castle and deer forest to Sir Edward Scott.

Parts of the forest have been designated as Sites of Special Scientific Interest and have been graded by the Nature Conservancy Council – like Roneval – as being 'of the highest international importance'. The North Harris deer forest is of biological as well as geological significance but its outstanding interest rests on the fact that 'it formed the seat of the most important local centre of ice dispersal in the Outer Hebrides and combines a fine suite of glacial landforms'.

The establishment of the deer forest imposed no new hardship on the community. Rather the reverse. The impact of change had struck North Harris earlier, when thirteen villages were cleared along Loch Resort and West Loch Tarbert, so that North Harris could become a sheep farm. The subsequent change from sheep farm to deer forest provided, at least, a modicum of employment for the dispossessed – those of them who still remained!

However, it wasn't only for the creation of sheep farms and deer forests crofters were evicted before the Crofters Act gave them security of tenure. Frequently they were evicted because of personal animosity on the part of ground officers and factors.

When the Napier Commission visited North Harris, John Macleod, a crofter in Ardhasaig, told the Commissioners that he had taken up fishing because he lost his land.

'How did you lose your land?' asked Sheriff Nicolson.

'There's a story behind that', replied Macleod. 'There was a lady in Uist and a gentleman in Skye, and my brother had a vessel. He came in the vessel with Donald Macdonald from Monkstadt (in Skye), and he went to Balranald (in North Uist) to remove from there the young lady, whose parents were not willing that she should marry the young gentleman in the ordinary way. They wanted her to marry the man who was factor on the estate, but this man took her away.

'The factor, Macdonald, had his revenge on me and my two brothers for this act, though we were quite innocent of it. One of my brothers was at that time in Borve, and another in Scalpay, and I had a sister in West Tarbert. The four of us had lands at the time but he deprived us of them all.'

The evictions took place at the first rent day after the elopement!

The story of the elopement is well remembered in Skye and Uist as well as in Harris. At their first attempt the eloping couple were driven into Rodil by adverse winds. There, relatives of the girl seized her and locked her in a bedroom of what is now Rodil Hotel.

Before her parents could come to collect her, young Macdonald returned from Monkstadt with his friends and besieged the house. While those within concentrated their attention on preventing the raiders from bursting in through the front door, where a mêlée was taking place, the girl was quietly removed through a window at the back. This time the lovers escaped to Australia where they lived to a ripe old age.

Even as a fisherman, Macleod told the Napier Commission, he felt oppressed. He complained that he was restricted in the mesh of net he could use and the locations in which he could fish, in case he caught any of the landlord's precious salmon by mistake.

Although the Scotts – and the Dunmores before them – had inherited, or purchased, the fruits of a crime – the forcible dispossession of the native population of North Harris by the Macleods to create the sheep farm – they were good proprietors and were highly regarded. As was their successor, T.O.M. Sopwith, the aircraft pioneer, who built the plane in which Hawker attempted the first trans-Atlantic flight, and whose yacht was crewed almost exclusively by Harrismen.

The Scotts are commemorated in the name of the Tarbert school which they endowed, and they used to hold extravagant regattas in Loch Tarbert in which the locals participated. The landlord's move from Rodil and Borve to Amhuinnsuidhe meant that Tarbert supplanted Rodil as the capital, and principal gateway, of the island.

The Visitors' Book of the Harris Hotel at Tarbert records that three of the leading literary figures of the day were there together in 1912: J.M. Barrie, then at the height of his fame as a playwright; Anthony Hope (Hawkins) who wrote *The Prisoner of Zenda*; and E.V. Lucas, novelist, biographer, contributor to *Punch* and the best-known essayist of his day.

They were in Harris as Barrie's guests, and he was there because he had rented Amhuinnsuidhe Castle to provide a holiday home for the orphaned Llewellyn Davies boys he had taken under his wing. The visit is described at some length in Andrew Birkin's *J.M. Barrie and the Lost Boys*.

It was in a sense a profitable holiday for Barrie and the British theatre. It was in Amhuinnsuidhe, in Barrie's own phrase, that he 'caught Mary Rose'.

The idea which eventually crystallised as *Mary Rose* was in Barrie's mind long before he ever saw Harris. The main theme of the play is to be found in the old Scots ballad of 'Bonny Kilmeny' with which he was familiar from childhood. The play itself was not written until seven years after he left Harris for good, and it owes another central element to the participation of the Anzacs in the first world war, which was not even a shadow on the horizon during that Harris holiday.

Barrie, however, used the Kilmeny story when he was in Harris to weave a fantasy for the Davies children round an island in Loch Voshmid which is, in that sense, the original of the 'island that likes to be visited'. And he picked up other elements in the play which clearly establish the Harris provenance.

Reference to a whaling station, for instance. The chimney

stack of Barrie's whaling station still stands beside the road at Bunavoneadar. It is now disused but in Barrie's day it was operated by a Norwegian whaling company and the smell, apart from anything else, made it one of the most unforgettable landmarks in Scotland.

And then there is a stage direction in Act II which identifies one of the best-known characters in the play – the erudite island gillie – as 'a young Highlander, a Cameron'. Cameron is not an indigenous Harris name but, on that famous holiday, one of Barrie's gillies was David Cameron, son of the family which still owns the Harris Hotel, earning some holiday pocket money, before going to St Andrews to train as a doctor.

David Foster, who wrote an interesting account of Barrie's Harris visit for the *Scots Magazine* in November 1984, records that David Cameron, the student gillie, had a second meeting with the author when Barrie, as Lord Rector of St Andrews University, delivered his celebrated address on courage, and introduced his alter ego or 'familiar spirit' M'Connachie to a puzzled world.

David Cameron, who was then completing his medical studies interrupted by war service, asked Barrie if he ever thought of going back to Harris. He shook his head. Two of the Davies boys were dead by that time. There were too many ghosts in Harris for the sensitive author. But one at least of the Davies boys went back: Nico spent a holiday in Harris in 1962.

North Harris is, as it were, bracketed between two islands. To the west, on the Atlantic coast, is Scarp. To the east in the Minch is Scalpay. Each has something important to say to us. Around 1900 there were 32 families in Scarp and the population was 120. At the time of the Napier Commission in 1884 one of the witnesses estimated the population at around 200. Today Scarp is uninhabited, although some of the former crofter tenants, now living on the mainland of Harris, still use the island for grazing their sheep.

The last of the old crofting inhabitants of Scarp – Angus Macinnes, his wife Margaret and a teenage son – left the island in December 1971. Two sons and two daughters had already left to pursue their education. That was the end of a long story of human occupation which, on the evidence of place names, goes back to the Vikings if not earlier.

Signalling for a boat to come across from Scarp in the days before the island had a phone or a landing stage. The photograph was taken on a pleasant spring day but the Atlantic swell was so heavy the signal went unanswered. After years of agitation a jetty was built at Husinish, the mainland terminus for Scarp — just in time for the last permanent inhabitants of the island to move out!

It is perhaps surprising that Scarp was inhabited so long. Although it is close to the mainland, its isolation is extreme at times in winter when huge seas from the open Atlantic surge into the narrow sound.

On Saturday, January 14th 1934, Mrs Christina Maclennan gave birth to a child in her home in Scarp, attended only by an 85-year old midwife because the doctor was unable to cross the sound. He couldn't even be consulted: Scarp had no phone. On Sunday Mrs Maclennan's condition was causing anxiety. By then it was possible to cross to Husinish where there was a phone but it was out of order. The postman's son had to travel seventeen miles to Tarbert by car to summon the doctor. The patient was eventually taken across to Husinish on an improvised stretcher laid across the seats of the ferry boat. She was then taken seventeen miles to Tarbert, over one of the worst roads in Scotland, lying on the floor of the local bus. Finally she was taken from Tarbert to Stornoway by private car. In Lewis Hospital she gave birth to a second child two days after the first. The twins were born in different islands, in different counties and in different weeks.

Mrs Maclennan fortunately was none the worse of her ordeal. The twins are still hale and hearty. One is married in Valtos, Uig, and the other in South Uist.

The incident focused attention on the plight of Scarp, and some improvements were made – a telephone, for instance – but always too little and too late. A jetty was finally built at the Husinish end of the ferry when it was clear that the island had reached the point of no return. It stands now as a symbol of official inertia: the unwillingness to move until it is too late, and the inability to stop once the wheels have been set in motion.

There was a strange sequel to the birth of the twins. A German inventor, Gerhardt Zucher, tried to sell to the British government the idea that mail and medicines could be delivered to remote islands, irrespective of wind or weather – by rocket! A demonstration was mounted at Scarp but the rocket blew up. Thirty thousand letters fluttered down on the sands, slightly singed along the edges. Although the experiment was a failure, Zucher later played a part in the development of the German rockets which caused such havoc in London during the war. Eventually, however, he fell foul of Hitler and was 'liquidated'. His ill-fated experiment gives one of the more isolated of Hebridean islands a tenuous link with man's journey to the moon.

Despite its isolation, Scarp has enriched the life of Britain with many teachers, ministers and doctors. One of them wrote me recently describing family worship in his uncle's house, with a black and white collie lying below the bench, howling lustily in chorus with the Gaelic psalms.

'Prayer was not patter-wise', he added. 'God was as real as the cow in the byre, and they spoke to Him as one man to another.

The end of the Rocket Mail experiment at Scarp — thirty thousand letters are scattered on the beach, slightly singed along the edges!

'There was no policeman, no crime, no foul-mouth, no booze, no divorce, seldom a love child, and poaching was not commercialised – only for the pot. The gamekeepers wisely didn't see or hear nothing.'

The most isolated inhabited village now in Harris is Rhenigidale, but it is on the mainland and is never completely cut off. When inaccessible by sea it can be approached on foot over a wild hill track. The Gatliff Trust maintains a modest youth hostel there in an old thatched house.

Scalpay, unlike Scarp, is still occupied by a lively, vigorous and relatively prosperous community. It has the advantages of good anchorages and access to the relatively sheltered fishing grounds of the Minch. It now also has the advantage of a vehicular ferry to the Harris mainland.

According to an 88-year old Scalpay fisherman named Macdiarmid, who gave evidence to the Napier Commission in 1884, the first attempt to develop the island failed. It came from the outside, and was mismanaged.

Captain Stilwell, the Earl of Dunmore's representative, tried to establish a fishing station by the old method of doubling the number of crofters in the island, thus halving the size of the holdings, and sending in a curer to buy the catches. The curer would have been of some benefit, if he had stayed. The other part of the programme proceeded on the popular but mistaken belief that the way to make crofters into fishermen was to starve them of land.

The effect of this Draconian approach to development was to antagonise the people of Scalpay and intensify their poverty.

'There seemed no way by which this population could make a living out of it at all', said Macdiarmid, 'but there was a native of the place who was able, through Providence, to set up a curing establishment and it may be said of him that he kept them going for the past 28 years since I came to this island.

'For the last two seasons the early fishing has failed. The fishermen suffered in consequence but this man provided for them so that, although there was scarcely any expectation of a return, it could be said that none of them went to bed hungry.'

There are still enterprising people in Scalpay. The Cunningham family, for instance, over a long period of years have owned small coasting vessels as well as fishing boats. More importantly, the family is involved in the local community cooperative. In Scalpay terms, business enterprise is not directed purely to self-aggrandisement.

The strength of the community is also demonstrated in other ways. On a wild night in December 1962, the people of Scalpay turned out *en masse* to go to the assistance of the Milford Haven trawler *Boston Heron* which was being smashed by heavy seas on an islet off the coast. Although the waves were breaking right over the vessel, the Scalpay fishermen attempted to get alongside. Six of them received citations for gallantry from the

Royal National Lifeboat Institution.

In assessing the significance of this rescue, it is necessary to recall that for the best part of a century there was a bitter conflict between steam trawlers from the big English and Scottish fishing ports, often fishing illegally, and the local fishermen whose livelihood they destroyed.

Two centuries earlier a shipwrecked Orcadian, giving his name as Sinclair, landed at Scalpay from a small boat with some of his shipmates. They were welcomed by the tacksman, Donald Campbell, and lived with him for some days while plans were made for their return to Orkney.

Young Sinclair took part in the activities of the household. He went fishing with Campbell's son and helped to rescue a cow from a bog. It is not clear at what stage Campbell discovered that the young Orcadian was Prince Charles Edward Stuart, trying to make his way to Orkney in the hope of getting a passage to France. Prince or Orcadian fisherman, it makes no difference in Scalpay: the door is always open!

While the Prince was still in Scalpay the minister of Harris, Rev. Aulay Macaulay, great grandfather of Lord Macaulay, the historian, arrived with a party to arrest him. Macaulay had been alerted to the movements of the Royal fugitive by his son, the Rev. John Macaulay in Uist.

Campbell made it clear that he was not prepared to breach the Highland code of hospitality. He told Macaulay that, if need be, he would fight to defend the Prince. Macaulay retired rebuffed but the Prince had to leave Scalpay in a hurry.

The Macaulays were already launched on the long march which took them from their ancestral home in Uig, Lewis, to become one of the leading families in the small group which has been described as an Intellectual Aristocracy, which practically dominated the political and cultural life of Britain in the nineteenth century. Their long history as philanthropists and reformers suggests that their desire to capture the Prince was motivated by political conviction rather than the price on the fugitive's head.

At the same time, the Macleods of Skye and Harris were also trying to capture the Prince. They were at the crucial point where a society based on human relationships was being transformed into a society based almost exclusively on money.

But whether or not they were out for the reward, they had another compelling motive: they had to keep in with the Hanoverian government because of their known part in the Finsbay abductions.

Although the Macaulays and the Macleods failed in their effort to capture the Prince, they frustrated his attempts to get to Orkney or hire a boat in Stornoway for France. He was forced back to Uist and escaped with difficulty through Skye, disguised as Flora Macdonald's Irish maid.

'Thus', writes Evan Barron in his book *The Prince's Pilot*, 'by the strange irony of circumstances the Macaulays were unconsciously responsible for the halo of romance round the head of the man they sought to hound to his death, and for a tale of heroism, of devotion, and of chivalry for which there is no parallel in history.'

The part played by Scalpay in the Prince's escape was commemorated for many years in a Gaelic inscription on the lintel of a modern house, built on the site of the little thatched cottage where the Prince sought refuge. The inscription was discreetly harled over when the house became a Presbyterian manse!

It may be that the phrase "n uair a bha e air alaban na fhogarach na Rioghachd dhleighich fhein' (when he was wandering as an exile in his own legitimate Kingdom) was too much for the law-abiding churchmen, but it does show how the continuity of island culture has been broken, not only by the convulsions of history but by petty acts of self-mutilation.

It takes more, however, than a dab of harling on the lintel of a manse to cut Scalpay off from its deep roots in the pre-Presbyterian, even the pre-Christian, past; or from the pressures of another culture, no longer kept at arm's length by the sea, but sitting in the living room, where the peat fire used to be, pouring out insistently the blandishments of another way of life.

So far Scalpay has had the strength to cope with television. When Jackie Morrison, a Scalpay man now living in Inverness, won a national competition in which the first prize was a walk-on part in the TV soap opera *Dallas*, he took it in his stride. 'Sue Ellen has many fans in Scalpay', he told the press. 'I'll maybe sing her a Gaelic love song. I'll do my best to persuade them to highlight Gaelic and Scalpay.'

What the long-term effect of television on Scalpay and the rest of Lewis and Harris will be remains to be seen. Changes are undoubtedly taking place, both good and bad, but some things endure, like the rocks still scored by the fingernails of moving glaciers in the last Ice Age.

When Norman MacCaig, the Edinburgh poet whose mother came from Scalpay, revisited the haunts of his childhood holidays after a long absence, he saw many evidences of change: the ferry 'wading' across the sound, the tarred road, the presence of motor cars, 'houses where no house should be' – and houses he had known now bulldozed away.

But when he summed up his experience in 'Return to Scalpay' in the *Collected Poems* published by the Hogarth Press, he focused rather on the people he had visited and the attitudes which distinguish them from our disintegrating urban communities which are 'dark years away' from the 'pure, hardheaded innocence' of the islands.

CHAPTER 15

How Harris Became Bigger Than Wales

Lewis and Harris may be regarded as one island masquerading as two but, from another point of view, they form a sort of scattered archipelago, covering a vast area of land and sea.

The Shiant Islands in the Minch, St Kilda and the Flannans in the Atlantic, and Rona and Sula Sgeir thirty miles north of the Butt of Lewis have historically been part of either Lewis or Harris and some of them still contribute marginally to the island economy.

This island domain was extended dramatically, if nominally, in 1972 when Britain annexed Rockall and solemnly passed an Act of Parliament decreeing that this inhospitable rock, inhabited only by seabirds, should be subject to the law of Scotland and form part of the district of Harris. Rockall is further from Harris than Land's End is from London! Harris, by Act of Parliament, has become very much larger than Wales!

The validity of the Act in international law is doubtful. The mainland of Ireland is closer to Rockall than is the mainland of Scotland; hence the description of Rockall as a pertinent of Harris. Even to call Rockall an island is an abuse of language. Certainly there were no bonfires lit in Harris to greet the passing of the Act. If the people of Harris reacted at all, it would have been with a wry smile: the Act so neatly encapsulates so much of Highland history.

The acquisition of Rockall may be of immense importance to Britain, if it is upheld internationally, and the area proves to be the rich oil province it is believed to be, but there will be no advantage for Harris. Servicing and terminal facilities will almost certainly be located on the mainland, and the only spin-off for the Hebrides will be the risk of pollution to some of the finest beaches in Europe.

The discovery of oil round Rockall could, however, convert a fantasy into a prophecy.

Shortly after the end of the second world war, when Highland development was first being spoken of seriously, James Mackintosh published a booklet suggesting the establishment of a city at Rockall.

He produced elaborate proposals for an hotel, community kitchens, dining rooms, laundry, school, hospital, church, theatre, cinema, sport and recreation rooms, bank, post office, bakery, distillery, shops, warehouses and stores, with an elaborate system of escalators, elevators, and travelling footpaths on a sort of giant aircraft carrier, pivoting round Rockall to keep its nose permanently into the wind, as it would need to, to survive.

It is difficult to understand what purpose could possibly be served by the creation, at fantastic cost, of a fragile city, with no economic base discernible at that time, in one of the most tempestuous regions in the world. Now, however, there is the possibility that an array of oil rigs, flaring in the night, may yet give the impression that the city of Rockall really exists unless, by that time, technology has reached the point at which oil is extracted by submarine robots, operated by engineers at a switchboard, comfortably ashore in Glasgow or London or even Dallas.

Sula Sgeir, a similar rocky pinnacle within the Lewis and Harris orbit, illustrates another facet of the relationship between the islands and the outside world.

For centuries the people of Ness have gone annually to Sula Sgeir for the young of the solan goose known locally as the 'guga'. The expedition takes place in autumn. 'When the barley is ripe the guga is ripe' was the old saying.

It was an exceedingly perilous expedition in the old days with open boats, which had to be hauled up the sheer cliff face, because there was no anchorage or landing place. The Nessmen took food and fuel with them for a stay of several weeks on the island, killing and curing the birds.

In 1912, just after a crew of ten had sailed for Sula Sgeir, there was one of the worst storms anyone then alive could recall. Fears were felt for the safety of the men, and HMS *Phoenix* was sent to make search. She circled the island, sounding her siren, and returned with the report that there was no sign of life on Sula Sgeir. A fortnight later the crew arrived home with a record harvest of guga!

Realising they could not land on Sula Sgeir in the conditions prevailing, the Nessmen had gone on to the slightly larger island of Rona, in the lee of which they rode out the storm. By the time HMS *Phoenix* arrived, or was thought to have arrived, the men were on Sula Sgeir harvesting the birds. It has never been explained how the *Phoenix* failed to see the Nessman and the Nessman the *Phoenix*. One theory is that the Navy went to Suleskerry off Cape Wrath instead of Sula Sgeir off the Butt of Lewis.

The guga is still a delicacy in Ness: a taste which Lewismen from other parts of the island regard, or pretend to regard, as somewhat eccentric if not perverted. George Morrison, the Tolsta humourist, has described the guga as 'better meat than any fish, and better fish than any meat'.

In time the custom of harvesting the guga will no doubt die out in Ness, as it has died out in other places, such as Edinburgh, which used to plunder the Bass Rock for the same reason, as readers of Stevenson's *Catriona* will recall. The guga is still, however, of some significance in the local economy of an area which has few exploitable natural resources.

Sula Sgeir is now a National Nature Reserve and the cull of young solan geese is controlled by the Nature Conservancy Council. The colony is under no threat but some freelance crusading conservationists are unwilling to leave the regulation of this reserve to the scientists of the Nature Conservancy and the good sense of the fishermen of Ness – a reminder that, on the fringe of any reforming movement, there are those whose missionary zeal is massively reinforced by original sin: man's innate desire, from which few break wholly free, to impose his will on other people, by force if necessary, without regard to their wishes or their interests – and all with an air of great self-righteousness.

At Rona, Sula Sgeir's larger neighbour – if 'large' can be applied, even in the comparative, to such a minuscule island – the Nessmen had an earlier and less successful bout with the conservationists. In July 1914, when poverty in Ness was persistent and at times extreme, Parliament passed an Act banning the killing of grey Atlantic seals during the breeding season. The Nessmen were neither consulted nor considered, although the seals on North Rona represented an important item in the economy of many families. The pretext for the legislation was the quite unfounded belief that the seals were in danger of extinction. The sealers, as it happened, were in greater danger than the seals. Most of them were naval reservists and, before the ban became effective, war had broken out.

Although sealing was banned, Rona continued to be of some economic importance to Lewis as a grazing for sheep but, even in that non-controversial area, the Nessmen fell foul of the bureaucrats.

During the first world war the grazing tenants were fined for failing to dip the sheep on North Rona, although it was quite impossible to get to Rona in wartime, even if there had been men at home to go; the sheep posed no risk of infection to any other stock; and no one could even be sure that the sheep were still there.

Many years later it emerged that, while the Nessmen were being fined, a German submarine was lurking around Rona, and occasionally sending a party ashore to replenish the larder by stealing the Nessmen's undipped sheep.

In the 1930s Sir Frank Fraser Darling, one of the pioneers of the science of ecology, lived on North Rona with his family for two successive summers. He describes it as a 'city of the seals'. In his fascinating book, *A Naturalist on Rona,* he describes the rough stone shelters used by the Nessmen. He makes no criticism of their banned activities but refers understandingly to the difficulties which they faced in their open boats. His view of conservation was wide enough (as it should be) to include human communities as well as birds, plants and animals, as his detailed study of the crofting townships in *West Highland Survey* clearly shows.

There is much more to North Rona than seals. The island sustained for many centuries one of the smallest and most isolated human communities on earth: five families, so completely cut off, even from Lewis, that, when a swarm of rats ate the corn, the whole population died of starvation before anyone knew of their plight. The steward of St Kilda discovered the tragedy when he was driven to Rona by contrary winds. On landing, he found a woman lying dead beside a rock with her child on her breast.

That was round 1685. Martin Martin, whose *Description of the Western Isles* was published in 1703, records that the island was

A rare photograph of the interior of a black house, taken in 1912 when William Grant, the founder of the *Stornoway Gazette,* was interviewing the crew of guga-hunters from Ness for whom the Navy had searched in vain.

subsequently resettled with families from Ness by the Rev. Daniel Morison, the minister of the parish, who had Rona as part of his glebe. It is a story of more than passing interest to me. According to family tradition, my mother was a descendant of the minister who resettled the island, while my wife is a great grand-daughter of the last child born on Rona, early in the nineteenth century.

According to the Rev. Daniel Morison, the islanders knew of his impending visit before it took place by a process similar to second sight. Sir Frank Fraser Darling, more than two centuries later, recorded that his own intuitions were sharpened remarkably while he was on Rona. 'Without any attempt at justification or explanation, and in the face of possible ridicule', he wrote, 'I say that during my months on Rona I have had knowledge and have spoken of coming events with an accuracy and clarity which have been disturbing.'

The history of Rona takes us back to the Dark Ages when, as Lord Clark pointed out in his TV series 'Civilisation', Western Christianity survived by clinging to isolated pinnacles of rock in the Gaelic west.

When on Rona, Sir Frank found relaxation from his scientific studies in excavating, and in part rebuilding, the ancient cell of St Ronan, from whom it is often asserted the island takes its name – although it is just as likely that the saint took his name from the island: 'Ron' being the Gaelic for seal!

Apart from the ravages of time, the cell was damaged by Sappers attached to the Ordnance Survey, oddly combining a little thoughtless vandalism with the preparation of maps which 'have proved invaluable to every visitor', according to Robert Atkinson whose book *Island Going* contains excellent photographs of the historic and sometimes puzzling stone structures on Rona, and a good deal of interesting detail. The ruins date from many different centuries and range from domestic uses, like low walls for the drying of fish, to a very old Celtic cross with three holes in it which, according to tradition, was put to uses which were a good deal more superstitious than religious. The cross is now in the 'temple' at Eoropie.

Beneath the altar in St Ronan's cell Sir Frank found a polished ball of green Iona marble 'the size and shape of a sheep's heart'. Apparently it was the custom of the Columban church, when a new religious centre was being established, to bury beneath the altar a piece of marble from the Mother Church. The stone is now preserved in the Nature Conservancy Office at Inverness.

Although Rona was isolated and the population small, the inhabitants were not uncultured. At the end of last century, when Alexander Carmichael was gathering the poems, legends, stories, charms, hymns and incantations which make his *Carmina Gadelica* such a fascinating book, he met an octogenarian in Ness who had lived for many years on Rona.

Angus Gunn had much oral lore and many stories which he told 'with great dramatic power'. His story of how St Ronan went to the island from Eoropie because 'the men quarrelled about everything and the women quarrelled about nothing' is worthy of a place in the *Arabian Nights*. According to Gunn's tale, the saint travelled to Rona on the back of a monster which flew with him over the sea 'in the twinkling of two eyes'. He found the island infested with biting adders, taloned griffins, poisonous snakes and roaring lions. When the beasts saw the holy man approach, they rushed off backwards into the sea, scratching the rocks with their claws as they fell.

Thus at one stroke the storyteller, with nothing but imagination to draw on, explained the almost complete absence of mammals on Rona and the striations left by the receding ice on the island's rocky surface ten thousand years before.

The Flannan Islands, which can be seen in good weather from the west of Lewis, like a flock of swimming seabirds or a fleet of ships in line astern, had much the same place as Rona in the history and economy of Lewis.

There are primitive ecclesiastical remains on the Flannans indicating a link with the old Celtic missionaries. In Martin Martin's day the people of Bernera went annually to the Flannans, making 'a great purchase of fowls, eggs, down, feathers and quills'. In more recent times the people of Bernera have used the Flannans for fattening sheep. Flannan Island mutton was esteemed a delicacy in Stornoway half a century or so ago.

The Flannans were still regarded as a place of special sanctity in Martin Martin's time. On landing, the fowlers used to uncover their heads, make a turn sunwise and thank God for their safe arrival. A number of strict taboos were also observed.

When Robert Atkinson visited the Flannans in 1937 in pursuit of Leach's Fork-tailed Petrel, he went out with Malcolm Macleod of Bernera who, at that time, had a let of the grazings. Atkinson describes the visit in *Island Going*.

Around the same time Malcolm Macleod took another visitor to the Flannans: Neil Gunn, the Scottish novelist, seeking local colour for one of the most dramatic scenes in his best-known novel *The Silver Darlings*.

The Silver Darlings is an excellent yarn and, although it deals with the fishing communities of the east coast of Caithness, which were in many ways different from those of the Western Isles, it gives the best account there is of social and economic developments which affected the whole north of Scotland around the same time and broadly in the same way.

The same applies to Gunn's earlier novel *Butcher's Broom*, dealing with the Clearances. There is no better account of the old Highland communities which the Clearances destroyed. And, with the possible exception of Iain Crichton Smith's *Consider the Lilies*, no better assessment of the damage done by the Clearances to the Highlands in cultural, emotional and spiritual, as well as material, terms.

Few people know of the link between the Flannan Islands and *The Silver Darlings*, but most people have heard of the Flannans in association with one of the great mysteries of the sea – the disappearance of three lighthouse keepers, the sole inhabitants of the island group, shortly after the lighthouse was built.

The Flannan Isles mystery has inspired a well-known poem and a very modern opera.

The poem by W.W. Gibson keeps reasonably close to the facts, although it introduces an element of the supernatural with its reference to strange birds 'too big by far for cormorant or shag', and sets the reader off on a false trail with its description of an unfinished meal and an upturned chair, suggesting an exit in panic from the keeper's dining room as a prelude to the tragedy.

The opera, by Peter Maxwell Davies, uses the mystery as launching pad for an excursion into a sort of Grand Guignol melodrama, with secret killings, illicit love and an outbreak of religious mania. In the end the keepers all go mad and are got rid of in some unspecified way by very implausible executioners: three officers from the Lighthouse Commission! It is good opera but it takes us a long way from Gibson's simple line about 'three men alive on Flannan Isle who thought on three men dead', and even further from the truth.

The light on the largest of the Flannan group came into operation on 7th December, 1899. On 26th December of the following year the crew of the lighthouse relief ship *Hesperus* were surprised that none of the usual signals were displayed at the lighthouse as they approached, and no preparations for landing were made at either of the landing stages. The *Hesperus* sounded its siren and, when this brought no response, fired rockets.

Finally the relief keeper was got ashore with some difficulty. He found the gate and door closed. The clock stopped. No fire lit. The living room and bedrooms empty. No sign of life anywhere. But the lamp was trimmed. The oil had been replenished. The lens and machinery had been cleaned since they were last in use. The kitchen was tidy, with all the pots and pans and dishes cleaned and polished. The last entry in the log was dated 15th December – eleven days before the tragedy was discovered.

Robert Muirhead, the Superintendent, who visited the island a few days after the discovery, came to the conclusion that the men had been trying to secure the gear at the west landing when they were overwhelmed by a huge wave and carried out to sea.

A lifebelt which had been fastened to the railing above the working platform was missing. Muirhead's first assumption was that it had been taken by one of the keepers to help a companion in difficulties. Examination, however, showed that it had not been removed by human hands. Although it stood 110 feet above sea level, it had been struck by a huge wave with such violence that it was torn from its moorings, leaving pieces of the canvas covering still adhering to the ropes.

Muirhead's theory has been questioned on the ground that three trained men, working on a perilous landing stage with huge seas running, would not have been so careless as to let themselves be caught by a wave which they could have seen approaching well before it reached them. There is an explanation, however.

George Macleod, a son of Malcolm who took Robert Atkinson and Neil Gunn to the Flannans, has pointed out that the west landing stage stands near the entrance to a long inlet which terminates in a cave. Often the mouth of the cave is completely submerged but, at certain states of wind and tide, when air is trapped within the cave, there is a return wave, very much more violent than the incoming wave, and directed straight at the landing stage like a bullet from a compressed air pistol.

Keepers who had only known the island for a single winter might well have watched a big wave pass, and decided they had a few moments before the next one came, to dash down and secure their equipment. They would not have been prepared for an even bigger wave coming on them from the landward side.

The Flannan Isles lighthouse is now an unmanned automatic station as a result of which one of the smallest and most exclusive golf courses in the world is no longer used! A very rough and ready course, made by the keepers themselves, it had five holes and a scratch score of 17!

None of the offshore islands is so well documented as St Kilda, lying almost fifty miles west of Harris and visible from many vantage points on a clear day.

The first, and one of the best, accounts of St Kilda was written by Martin Martin, a Skyeman, who submitted a report on the island to the Royal Society in 1698. He travelled to the island, by open boat from Harris, with the local minister, John Campbell. They struck a summer storm and were driven off course, missing St Kilda by about twelve miles. They might have missed it altogether if the crew had not taken a bearing from the innumerable sea fowl heading for their well-defined territories on the main island and the rocky pinnacles round about. 'Every tribe of fowls bends their course to their respective quarters, though out of sight of the Isle,' notes Martin. 'The inhabitants rely so much on this observation that they prefer it to the surest compass.'

A second account of life in St Kilda, just over half a century later, was written by the Rev. Kenneth Macaulay, grand uncle of Lord Macaulay. The redoubtable Dr Johnson, who met the Rev. Kenneth Macaulay and took a hearty dislike to him, declared unequivocally that he was incapable of writing such an interesting book. Someone must have written it for him! Perhaps, in an unusual exercise of Hebridean second sight, it was ghosted for him by the literary genius of his still unborn grand-nephew!

W.C. Mackenzie, the Lewis historian, wrote a not very successful novel based on the strange tale of Lady Grange, wife of a Scottish judge and pillar of the Church, who was abducted in 1742 with her husband's connivance, and incarcerated on St Kilda, while he concealed her disappearance by holding a mock funeral in Greyfriars cemetery in Edinburgh.

A later and more successful novel about St Kilda – lightly disguised – was written by Hammond Innes. *Atlantic Fury* does not, however, relate to the real St Kilda: the community of intrepid cragsmen who survived across the centuries by scaling for their food the most formidable rock faces in Britain, at one point dropping 1300 feet sheer to the sea.

The indigenous inhabitants were evacuated, at their own

This photograph, taken in the early '50s, indicates the rate of change in Lewis in the last thirty years. For anyone over forty in rural Lewis the memory of the daily trudge with buckets to a distant well is still vivid. The family wash was often done at a convenient stream or loch. Two huge iron pots heating the water can be seen in the background.

request, in 1931 and St Kilda was deserted except by the occasional scientist or birdwatcher, until 1957 when the British government established a tracking station there in connection with the rocket range on South Uist. It is the modern military use of the island that *Atlantic Fury* is concerned with.

While the old St Kildans lacked many of the basic amenities of life, the new St Kildans have it all laid on, including gymnasium and sauna.

The old St Kilda, however, was not destroyed by government neglect. Governments, both local and national, could certainly have done much more than they did to improve conditions, but that would not have averted the island's fate. The extinction of the old way of life had the inevitability, the pathos, and the irony of a Greek tragedy. Nothing could save the little community once its isolation had been breached, and its simple self-regulating operation, through the informal St Kilda Parliament, had come in contact with a wealthier and more sophisticated way of life.

Robin Prentice puts it well in *The National Trust for Scotland Guide:* 'For centuries a small, primitive, patriarchal society subsisted in almost total isolation in an inhospitable environment,' he wrote. 'It died of perplexity, lethargy and induced desires when contact with a meddlesome, mechanistic civilisation was thrust upon it'.

Prentice quotes with approbation Tom Steel's bitter comment in *The Life and Death of St Kilda* that the island had become 'the only human menagerie in the British Isles'. The annual influx of tourists, in the end, destroyed what they had come to see.

Charles Maclean in his book *Island on the Edge of the World* studies the process of cultural change in St Kilda in some depth: not so much to discover what went wrong with the primitive society of the St Kildans as in the hope of finding a cure for 'the social and environmental problems in the increasingly homogeneous wasteland of modern civilisation'. He foresees the collapse of modern industrial society and reaches the conclusion that 'the archaic social type', which St Kilda exemplified into the twentieth century, 'may provide the best and most adaptive response'.

'In the event of technological breakdown, widespread chaos, famine and disease', he writes, 'the small community formed out of necessity, rather than through idealism, may well be the basic unit for survival for those who wish to maintain freedom and stay alive.'

It is a gloomy conclusion, but others have seen St Kilda in much the same light.

When Martin Martin visited St Kilda, before it was corrupted by too much contact with the outside world, he commented: 'There is only wanting to make them the happiest people in this habitable globe viz. that they themselves do not know how happy they are, and how much above the avarice and slavery of the rest of mankind'.

Having visited Utopia, however, Martin Martin elected not to stay.

So would we all, but there may still be lessons to learn.

CHAPTER 16
Unique in North-West Europe

When E.J. Clegg, Regius Professor of Anatomy at Aberdeen University, studied blood group variations in Lewis, he discovered to his surprise that the island population 'is very different from all other N.W. European populations'.

The investigation was carried out in association with the British Museum and the University Autonoma in Madrid. It revealed sharp differences within the island, not only between Stornoway and rural Lewis, which might have been expected, but between the east of Lewis and the west.

In a paper in *Annals of Human Biology* (Vol. 12, No. 4, pp. 345-361) Professor Clegg has a table of genetic distances showing the populations of North-West Europe, from England to Iceland and Norway, in a cluster at one side of the page, and Lewis in splendid isolation at the other, in the same sort of relationship to the rest of Europe as Rockall bears to the Western Isles.

Lewis is closest to Iceland and Orkney, and closer to England and Denmark than to Eire, Northern Ireland, South-West Scotland or Wales.

'The genetic uniqueness of Lewis' – to use Prof. Clegg's own phrase – clearly raises a number of interesting issues.

There is an island tradition about an ancient race whose last refuge was on the rocky pinnacle called the Pygmies' Isle, or Eilean Luchraban, near the Butt of Lewis.

John Morison of Bragar, father of the Blind Harper of Dunvegan, refers to the pygmy tradition in an account of his native island written in the seventeenth century. He dismisses the story with contempt, maintaining that it arose because some small bones had been found there. 'I hold them to be the bones of small fowls which abound in that place', he wrote.

More than two hundred years later Dr Murdoch Mackenzie, the father of Agnes Mure Mackenzie, the historian, together with C.G. Mackenzie, the Procurator Fiscal at Stornoway, excavated a ruined building on Eilean Luchraban, recovering some pottery and the expected small bones. W.C. Mackenzie

tells in *The Book of the Lews* that, when he sent them to the
Natural History Museum at South Kensington, they were
identified as rock pigeon, razorbill, petrel and gull. There were
also some small bones from mammals: oxen, young lamb,
sheep and a dog.

That, however, does not dispose of the pygmies. Unlike John
Morison, Mackenzie does not believe that the story of the
pygmies arose because people found small bones. He believes
the small bones were assumed to be human because the
tradition of the pygmies was already well established.

He believes the tradition relates to a real race of small
stature, dramatised into pygmies by the storytellers. At the very
least, he concludes, there is 'an ethnological question which has
not yet passed out of the stage of investigation'.

Professor Clegg's recent research suggests that the
ethnological question might be even more important than
Mackenzie guessed. In any event the Professor's work on
'protein and polymorphism distributions' in the island of Lewis
gives relevance to the work now being carried out by the
Edinburgh University Archaeological Research Project under
the direction of Professor D.W. Harding, to which I referred in
an earlier chapter.

So far as serious archaeological study is concerned, Lewis
and Harris are still virtually 'terra incognita'. The Callanish
Stones have received a certain amount of attention, at various
levels of expertise but, as the Edinburgh Project team point
out, the basic field record for Lewis and Harris remains the
Inventory of the Royal Commission on Ancient Monuments
published in 1928, based on a survey which began before the
first world war.

The Edinburgh team have now undertaken, as a beginning,
the systematic study of an Iron Age broch, dating from around
700 B.C. at Loch Bharabhat, near the village of Kneep (or
Cnip), using modern techniques. The team report that the
original broch floor appears to have been below the level of the
adjacent Loch na Berie which raises 'considerable problems of
retrieval but clearly enormous potential for the survival of
organic materials in a primary broch context sealed in
antiquity'.

Apart from the importance of the Edinburgh University

work to our ultimate understanding of the remote past, in an area which has apparently some claim to uniqueness, the proposal to set up an open-air exhibition area at Callanish with visitor facilities could be of considerable significance for the island's growing, but still relatively small, tourist industry.

The Edinburgh Project is of great importance to the Islands, historically and economically, and it is essential that it should be adequately funded, which in these days probably requires outside contributions or sponsorship rather than reliance on the University's own funds.

While we must await the new light which the Edinburgh team will almost inevitably cast on the island's remote past, it is possible, even now, to identify some of the events and influences which, within historical times, have lodged in the folk memory and helped to shape island responses down to the present day.

The most obvious and all-pervasive influence has been the sea. Not just any sea, but the Western Ocean: thundering angrily on beach and cliff, simultaneously providing the sustenance which made life possible and the storms which made it precarious.

Fishing with open boats from open beaches, without even a barometer, let alone a weather forecast, was always hazardous. One of the worst disasters in the relatively sheltered waters of Broad Bay occurred in December 1894, because the haddock fleet sailed into the eye of a storm, not realising that the sudden calm would be short-lived as the hurricane returned from another direction.

They had to launch their boats in the darkness at 3 a.m. to catch the tide. There was no lighthouse then at Tiumpan Head. The villages of thatched houses round the bay gave no glimmer of light. When the storm was renewed the fishermen did not know from what direction it was blowing or where their vessels were being driven. The spindrift was so thick they could not see the shore until the boats had grounded, and the few who escaped could not see the land even when they struggled through the surf. Nineteen men were lost, including four fathers with their sons. One widow lost all three sons.

On the night before the disaster a Lewis divinity student, D.H. Morrison, then teaching in North Uist, dreamt that he was at a strange wedding held in the joiner's shop near his home. Seven of the guests, neighbours whom he recognised, attended the wedding in dripping oilskins.

Next day, on the journey home, he heard of the disaster. The seven men he recognised in his dream had all been drowned. At the time of his dream their coffins were being hurriedly prepared in the joiner's shop.

It is not difficult to read the print of the sea in the islanders' fatalism and disregard of personal danger.

The sea also strengthens the sense of community. An island is sharply defined; every departure, every arrival, has a dramatic quality which underlines the message, 'This is where I belong'. The effect has been muted but not obliterated by the advent of the plane and the roll-on roll-off ferries. An island still has a sense of separate identity no mainland parish, town or village ever feels. A separateness encapsulated in the Stornoway phrase for non-natives: they are 'from away'.

Even temporary visitors who have sojourned in the island for a year or two, as teachers perhaps or government officials, tend to identify with it in a way which would not have occurred without the encircling, defining sea.

Apart from the hazards of fishing, especially when the island economy was almost entirely dependent upon it, the sea had another attribute which has deeply influenced local attitudes: it is wide open to exploitation.

However poor his land, the farmer is secure within his marches. No neighbour has the right to step across the fence and take what he wants from the harvest. The fisherman, however, has no exclusive tenure of the sea.

The history of the island fishing industry is punctuated by conflicts between different and incompatible technologies in which the users of static gear like lobster pots and lines have come off worst, although now at last some attempt is being made to regulate the situation.

Much more importantly, the island fishermen, dependent largely, as I have said, on open boats launched from open beaches, were effectively expropriated by the steam trawlers from Fleetwood, Grimsby, Hull, Granton and Aberdeen, which not only fished out some of the more accessible grounds but frequently swept up the local fishermen's gear as well.

A familiar sight in Lewis not so very long ago — a knitting woman with a creel of peats. The pragmatic Lord Leverhulme was the only person, so far as I know, who ever tried to find out what was involved.

The struggle between the inshore fishermen of Lewis and Harris and the marauding trawlers from the big ports lasted for well over half a century and had a more devastating, if less dramatic, effect on the economy of the islands than the Clearances. Nominally there was a three-mile limit reserved for the inshore men. Even if it had been reserved it would have been inadequate, but the protection given by the Government's fishery cruisers was never complete and was often derisory.

In the 1890s, when a group of fishermen from Carloway

challenged a poaching trawler, the response was the command, 'Run the bloody Hielandmen down!' The small Carloway boat had to dodge among rocks where the trawler could not follow.

When, around the same time, a group of fishermen from Portnaguran boarded a poaching trawler in Broad Bay to make a citizen's arrest, the Government sent a gunboat to Stornoway. Not so much to protect the inshore fishermen as to make sure they did not take the law into their own hands again.

More than fifty years later Fleetwood trawlers were still fishing illegally in Broad Bay with the name and number of the vessel obliterated, the ship's bell hidden under a cloth, the builder's name-plate concealed and the crew masked.

An antiquated fleet of fishery cruisers tried ineffectively to enforce the law with little success, although on one occasion the fishery cruiser *Norna* finally identified a trawler after a running fight which took the vessels from Broad Bay round Tiumpan Head almost as far as Stornoway, and back again to the Butt of Lewis and into the open Atlantic.

The fine imposed (the maximum!) was less than the value of the catch, which the poacher was free to sell.

Around the same time another trawl skipper arrested by HMS *Doon* abducted the boarding party and headed for Fleetwood, disregarding the sluggish naval vessel's signals and even the blank shots fired across his bows. The case finished up in shoal water in the High Court where the offending skipper escaped most of the charges against him, on a technicality.

A very different situation exists now. With the advent of the EEC, policing the seas has become a matter of protecting national rather than local interests. Surveillance is more effective than it was when only the livelihood of the islanders depended on it, but conflicts between local and national interests and between different classes of fishermen remain.

Although the sea is unchanging, there is a dynamism and an element of relativity in effects and attitudes which must be taken into account.

At different times the sea has been a highway and a barrier, depending on the comparative ease of transport in other places and by other means. Historically everything is relative: isolation, wealth or poverty, education, culture, independence – even religion. The direction of movement and the basis of

In the far distance Bearasay where Neil Macleod made his last stand. In the middle distance Berie sands: an outstanding beach, even by Lewis and Harris standards. In the foreground Dun Barabhat where a team from Edinburgh University Archaeological Research Centre at Callanish is excavating an Iron Age site. The erection beside the dun is the team's photographic tower. Courtesy Prof. D W Harding.

judgement change from decade to decade: certainly from century to century. Island attitudes also change although some events are more deeply imprinted on the folk memory than others.

The process of change can also be traced in respect to the second great determinant of island attitudes – language. It is reflected clearly in the response to education.

When John Morison of Bragar wrote the seventeenth-century description of Lewis from which I have already quoted, he commented, 'the countrie is possessed and safelie governed by the Earle of Seaforth, to whose industrious care and benevolence, the people, formerlie inclined to rudeness and barbarity, are reduced to civilitie, much understanding and knowledge by the flourishing schooll planted and maintained by the said Earls all the tyme in the toun of Stornuway'.

The 'schooll' was no doubt a good one, but I doubt whether it had any effect except on the tacksmen and the townsfolk – the overlay of incomers or of natives, like Morison himself, moving from a Gaelic to an English culture.

It was very different with the schools established in the early years of the nineteenth century by the Gaelic Schools Society. N.C. Macfarlane records in *The Men of Lews* that when the Society opened a school at Bayble in 1811 there were three pupils on the first day, twenty on the second and sixty on the third.

Adults as well as children attended the schools. At Barvas a great grandmother asked the teacher whether she was too old to learn. The teacher actually bought twenty-four pairs of spectacles, out of his meagre salary, for his elderly pupils.

At Galson the teacher was sacked by the Society because he broke the rules by preaching as well as teaching. The people of the district built him a new school and paid his salary. When he died he left £150, half to his widow and half to the Gaelic Society which had dismissed him.

The Education Act of 1872, on the other hand, was greeted with considerable opposition in the rural areas. Compulsory education interfered with work on the croft, in which children had a part to play. Instruction was in English, often with a marked hostility to the native Gaelic. The school rate was a burden on crofters whose income was limited even when food and fuel were plentiful. And the schools were remote from the pupils. As a measure of economy most schools were established halfway between two villages, so that children five years old had to walk long distances, over exposed roads, in the bleak island winters, leaving home in the dark and returning in the dark, with nothing to eat between breakfast and supper.

The response of central government to the problems of education in the islands displayed a mixture of paternalism and insensitivity which is both revealing and characteristic. Compulsory attendance was enforced by the courts, widows being fined for keeping teenage sons at home to help with the croft, while special financial provision was made to help the poorer School Boards. The Treasury understands money: it does not understand people.

A general view of the Edinburgh University excavation at Dun Barabhat. In the foreground can be seen the paved entrance, and on the right the pivot stone for the door, temporarily used to support a ranging rod. In the background can be seen the entrance to one of the intra-mural galleries. Courtesy of Prof. D W Harding.

When the Lewis schools had their first medical inspection in 1912 – forty years after schooling became compulsory! – it revealed that the children's resistance to diseases such as consumption had been undermined in the classroom by cold, hunger and sodden garments. A decade later Lewis and Harris had the highest rate of tuberculosis in Europe, although before the introduction of compulsory education tuberculosis was almost unknown.

It is perhaps relevant to note in passing that the Medical Officer who realised the damaging side-effects of compulsory education on a model unsuited to the needs of a dispersed local community, and the special commissioner who helped to resolve the problems of the impoverished School Boards, were both islanders. The doctor – Donald Murray – became the first M.P. for the Western Isles when the constituency was created in 1918. The educationist – J. L. Robertson – became Senior Chief Inspector of Schools in Scotland. There is no substitute for local knowledge!

Despite the difficulties, in the period before school meals and buses the children of Lewis and Harris were avid for education. The production of professional men and women, largely to serve the needs of other places, became the island's most important industry.

Lewis and Harris now have the highest ratio in the country of pupils remaining at school after the legal leaving age and, to cater for them, two versatile and successful schools: the Nicolson Institute and Lews Castle College.

In addition to its range of academic subjects the Nicolson offers its 1350 pupils the choice of eighty different 'Friday afternoon activities', ranging from archery and astronomy by way of drama, hairdressing, karate, Scripture studies and slimming to woodturning and word-processing. Lews Castle College offers courses in Business Studies, including computer data processing, catering, engineering and indigenous industries, especially building, nautical studies, textiles and agriculture.

Since its foundation in 1873 the Nicolson has had seven rectors, six of them incomers, greatly enriching the life of the local community. The Castle College, more directly related to the island's traditional industries, has had four principals since 1951, all of them local.

On the other hand, while two-thirds of the Nicolson staff are local, the percentage of locals on the Castle staff is considerably smaller, indicating the extent to which the island's industries are being reinforced by skills imported from other places.

The existence of two such excellent schools implies a very considerable investment by the state in the welfare of the islands, and that leads directly to a great paradox.

When the process of social amelioration began in the middle years of last century, typhoid, typhus and diphtheria were rife but the schools were teeming with healthy children, and the infantile mortality was one of the lowest in Europe. Eighty years later, in the swinging sixties when Britain 'never had it so good', the killer diseases had been conquered and extreme poverty abolished, but schools were being closed for lack of pupils and the islands were burdened with a vast geriatric problem – a proportion of aged to working people far in excess of the Scottish, or even the Highland, norm.

The island economy was an empty shell, families were leaving at a rate which averaged one a week and there was a general air of despondency about the future.

The manner in which a century of benevolent, but misguided, government has produced this result on the periphery of one of the wealthiest nations in the world is of great significance for the Third World countries which are today seeking salvation in grandiose programmes of urban industrialisation: repeating the island disaster as a matter of public policy.

Of even more significance, fortunately, is the manner in which the dispirited island community of the sixties has been transformed into the vibrant island community of the eighties: still beset with problems, still underprivileged in many ways, but facing the future with vigour and a fair degree of confidence; showing an astonishing amount of initiative in the face of considerable odds.

CHAPTER 17

The Caterpillar's Wings

The ferment of activity in Lewis and to a lesser extent Harris in the 1980s has its roots, in an odd sort of way, in a row which rocked the islands in the 1930s, and the part played in that row by a lawyer from Inverness, a Free Church minister from Lewis, an M.P. whose speciality was Indian law, and a Bill which never became an Act of Parliament.

After the collapse of Lord Leverhulme's schemes, the destruction of the island's white fishing industry by competition from the big trawling ports, and the decline in the Scottish herring industry, the economy of Lewis and Harris rested almost wholly – and precariously – on Harris tweed.

The tweed industry would also have disappeared but for the amendment of the Orb trade mark in 1934, which permitted the mechanisation of the spinning and finishing processes, while retaining hand weaving and ensuring that all processes should be island-based.

The amendment was first proposed by Col. Neil Macarthur, an Inverness lawyer, who was consulted by some of the Lewis firms, when the industry seemed to be heading for complete disaster. The proposal produced a storm of controversy out of which nothing tangible might have emerged, had it not been for the negotiating skill of the Rev. Murdo Macrae, a Free Church minister, who represented the island weavers and, on one occasion, led a deputation of his ministerial colleagues to London on their behalf. T.B. Wilson Ramsay, the M.P. for the Western Isles, an Ayrshire man who practised as a barrister in Indian cases coming before the Privy Council, was largely responsible for persuading the Board of Trade to register the amendment. And some mainland interlopers who might have wrecked the settlement were frightened off by a Bill before Parliament – the Runciman Bill – which would have tightened up the protection given to certification trade marks but which, in fact, never reached the statute book.

In the wings, helping the process along, was the Dunmore family with whom it had all begun nearly a century before.

The amendment of the Orb trade mark was one of the few victories the islands won, in these grim years, in the struggle for survival.

In 1943 a group of business and professional men formed the Lewis Association to study the island's social and economic needs, and draw up progressive plans for development.

Over a period of years, reports were issued on town and country planning, agriculture, fishing, Harris tweed, hydro electricity, public health and transport. The reports were well received by the leading Scottish newspapers and magazines. The Fabian Quarterly, looking in from London, praised the careful research, the 'admirable clarity' of the reports and the freedom from local megalomania.

The work of the Association brought about the first Conference on the island's affairs in which the various government departments involved sat down with local councillors and others to look at the problem comprehensively.

Nothing came of it.

Lewis was ready for change. There were plenty of pent-up local initiative. Plenty of ideas. But the Government had no effective regional policy. The Association was talking to the deaf.

Neil Gunn, the Scottish novelist, who studied the work of the Lewis Association, commented: 'Whatever ultimately may come of it, of this I am certain – that in it we have a manifestation of the only kind of spirit which can truly build and enrich social life'. His words were, in a way, prophetic. He was proved right long after the Association had disappeared and he himself was dead.

The Association was the first abortive struggle by the island community to loosen the shackles of mainland control and take charge of its own destiny, as it is doing today to a greater extent than ever before.

Around the same time another example of local initiative did produce tangible and permanent results.

Lews Castle was used during the war as a naval hospital. Before the war it had been a white elephant. The Trustees in fact were advised to take the roof off to save rates. A ruin, they were told, would be cheaper than a habitable building.

A few leading members of the local Labour Party conceived

the idea of using the Castle as a Technical College when the Navy was done with it. They canvassed skilfully and successfully at both local authority and national level, and the College came into being in 1951 while the Labour government was still in power, although it was not formally opened until 1953, by which time Lord Home, who performed the ceremony, was Minister of State in a Conservative government.

The significant point, however, is that, on past form, it is extremely unlikely that a county council, located on the mainland, or central government, looking north from Edinburgh, would have accepted the idea of an innovative school in the Western Isles before Inverness or Dingwall were similarly provided. The decisive factors were the strength of the local campaign and the availability of a vacant building, going cheap, at a time when post-war restrictions inhibited the erection of new schools.

There was thus an element of luck, as well as of local initiative, in one of the most important island developments of the post-war period. It was, in one sense, a belated gift from Lord Leverhulme, a quarter of a century after his death.

During the naval occupation, a large hutted camp spread like a fungus around the Castle. When the Navy pulled out, the huts were abandoned. The great iron gates at the Porter's Lodge were slammed shut and padlocked.

In the night, outflanking the locked gates, a population of homeless islanders moved in by sea, to establish the first post-war squatters' camp in Britain. There had been births, marriages and deaths in the Stornoway camp before squatters' camps developed in the south of England and became national news.

When the squatters were eventually rehoused, an excellent golf course was established where the huts had been, within ten minutes' walk of the town centre. Again, luck and Lord Leverhulme played a part in the development.

Stornoway Golf Club had only been tenants, on a limited use basis, of the first-class seaside course which had existed before the war, where Stornoway Airport is today. But the Stornoway Trustees, set up under Lord Leverhulme's gift, succeeded in claiming compensation, provided they built a new golf course in the Castle Grounds.

A traditional industry which still contrives to move with the times. This was one of the winning designs in a competition mounted by the Harris Tweed Association in partnership with the makers of Drambuie, the Scottish whisky-based liqueur.

Although there was no effective government policy of regional development in the immediate post-war period, there were some notable government initiatives without which current developments could not have taken place.

Lewis and Harris were among the first islands to benefit from the activities of the Hydro Electric Board. Piped water and the elimination of the black house came a good deal later. In the early fifties one had the anomaly of villages with electric light but no running water: you could boil a kettle at the flick of a switch but, to get the water to fill it, you had to walk perhaps half a mile with a 'cearcal' (a frame to keep the buckets from bumping against the water-carrier's legs) and a couple of pails to a public and not always sanitary well.

The islands got electricity before running water simply because the social element in the development of Highland water power was riding on the back of an urgent national need for electricity.

The existence, and achievement, of the Hydro Board may have been counter-productive to some extent. John S. Gibson, in his history of the Scottish Office – *The Thistle and the Crown* – suggests that the Highlands might have got a Development Agency in 1947 instead of 1965 but for the existence of the Hydro Board with its social remit. Instead, the Government set up a Highlands and Islands Advisory Panel, which did excellent work within its limited remit, but had no executive power.

One of the Panel's most constructive initiatives was the Western Isles Fishery Training Scheme: the first effective attempt to reverse the long historic decline in the Hebridean fishing industry. But here too the idea and the driving force were local.

The Panel succeeded in persuading the Department of Agriculture and Fisheries for Scotland to take up and develop a proposal by a Lewis Committee that island crews, who accepted training in modern fishing methods, should be given the capital to acquire boats. The down payment on the first few Lewis boats was met from a fund established under the will of a Lewisman who died in Rhodesia.

Several elements in island history are drawn together by the story of Murdo Morrison from Ness. He left Lewis as a youth with little English and no money, made a modest fortune in Southern Africa, and left it to his native island, enabling a local committee, with no resources of their own, to entice a hesitant government department into an innovative experiment, which was later taken up by the Highlands and Islands Development Board and expanded into one of their most successful projects.

The setting up of the Highland Board was one of the major events in modern Hebridean history. From the start the Board ignored the Scottish Office advice to concentrate on the two ends of the Caledonian Canal, with their deepwater anchorages, and let the remoter hinterland sink or swim.

Robert Grieve, the first Chairman, put it firmly on the line that the Board's achievement would be judged by its success or failure in the peripheral crofting areas.

In the outcome, the Government's prestigious industrial developments in the favoured regions came to grief, but the release of local enterprise by the Board's offer of capital, training and advice has brought about a transformation which could well be cumulative and permanent, although it has not been so far on anything like the scale required to solve the islands' basic unemployment problem.

Of equal, perhaps even greater, importance in restoring confidence to the islands was the setting up of an all-purpose Islands Council in 1975 to replace the old-style colonial administration of Lewis from Dingwall and Harris from Inverness: a travesty of local government which enshrined in the Statute Book the unhappy and enervating accidents of history that had left the islanders for centuries without effective control of their own affairs.

The majority of the Wheatley Committee which advised the Government on local authority reform accepted the current fiction that size is everything and decided that the islands should remain appendages of a large mainland authority.

It was left to Russell Johnston, himself an islander, and Betty Harvie Anderson to make the percipient comment, 'The more dependent they are made on services controlled outside the island . . . the less likely (they are) to engender the self-reliance which alone makes island living possible'.

Fortunately, the Conservative Government accepted the minority view, and the reaction of the islanders to their new-found freedom quickly justified the decision, and vindicated Neil Gunn's comment on the importance of local initiative.

The new Islands Council proclaimed its faith in the indigenous Gaelic culture by adopting as the preferred title 'Comhairle nan Eilean' and introducing straight away a progressive, if somewhat patchy, bilingual policy.

With equal vigour the new Council, which had to equip itself from scratch with buildings and staff, having, unlike all the other authorities, no pre-existing structure to build on, set about tackling a vast backlog of infrastructural work in the most neglected part of Britain.

When the Comhairle took office, 70% of the 740 miles of road in its area was single-track and dangerous, a third of the housing stock was below tolerable standard, and the rate of unemployment was the highest in Britain.

The ingenuity with which the new authority approached its task is well illustrated by the manner in which it adapted – or bent – the Government's concept of Housing Action areas, designed for the inner cities, to the needs of a scattered rural community whose homes were subject to all the legal anomalies of crofting tenure.

In seven years the Comhairle established 133 Housing Action areas, while the two mainland districts of which the islands had previously been part had established one Action area each. In 1981 the Comhairle approved 233 applications for house improvement grants: the largest number approved by any authority in Scotland, except Glasgow which had 244.

By that time the Scottish Consumer Council was urging other local authorities to follow the lead of the Western Isles which, less than a decade before, had been a byeword for general backwardness and lack of enterprise.

The Comhairle made the same imaginative use of the Job Creation Programme and the Special Temporary Employment Programme. In a little over two years the Comhairle initiated nearly 350 schemes, sponsored by local communities and contributing permanently to the infrastructure of the townships.

The self-reliance on which Russell Johnston and Betty Harvie Anderson placed such store was not confined to the local authority: it was bubbling up in every corner of the island and in every activity – cultural, recreational, sporting and economic.

Kenneth Mackenzie Ltd., the largest firm in the Harris Tweed industry, has twice won the Queen's Award for Industry. In the first two years of the Livewire competition for young businessmen with ideas for development, Lewis provided the National winner. Students from Lews Castle College have on four occasions won the Kessock Bridge Trophy open to the whole of the Highlands.

In a single issue the *Stornoway Gazette* recently carried photographs of eleven university students who had just graduated, eight of them with Honours. Their subjects included Genetics, Business Studies, Politics, Modern Languages, Computing Science, Electronics, Publishing and Environmental Chemistry. The graduate in Modern Languages won a place at Harvard to study for a doctorate.

This was not an isolated occurrence. A list of the 1070 students who finished at the Nicolson Institute in the three years from 1982 to 1985 shows that 11.3% were at Scottish universities doing degree courses, 7.6% at central institutions, 29.5% in other forms of further education and 23.6% on Youth Training Schemes. Islanders believe in education!

Only one in five had found jobs, but three times as many of them were within the islands as on the mainland – a welcome change, although that balance will alter dramatically, both qualitatively and quantitatively, when those pursuing higher education complete their courses and come on the labour market. Other parts of Britain will then reap the island harvest. Lewis and Harris would be wealthy islands if there were transfer fees for university graduates, as there are for professional footballers. And why not?

The islands are still, to far too great an extent, net exporters of skill although, in this respect as in others, the establishment of the Comhairle has redressed the balance somewhat, increasing the number of professional jobs available in the islands.

One of the most encouraging features of the local scene has been the number of able young islanders, like John Murray and Finlay Macleod, who have remained in the islands or returned to them, sometimes at the sacrifice of career prospects, to take up what they saw as a challenge.

Their influence can be seen in the flurry of interest in Gaelic drama and in the establishment of Acair, a publishing company, based at Stornoway and supported by the Comhairle, the Highland Board and the Scottish Arts Council, primarily to produce Gaelic texts for children, but whose list ranges widely and richly in both Gaelic and English. It can also be seen in the imaginative use of Radio nan Eilean as a stimulator for the whole community.

Among the rural areas Ness was one of the first to respond to the new breeze blowing through the islands. It pioneered the local historical societies which have since mushroomed in almost every district.

Ness was also a leader in establishing Gaelic playgroups to support the language at its most vulnerable point. The first Care and Repair Project in the north of Scotland was set up in Ness, and in 1984 Ness Football Club pioneered the entry of teams from the Western Isles in the Highland Amateur Cup. This involved eight journeys across the Minch – twice as long and twice as turbulent as the crossing from Dover to Calais. They were rewarded by winning the cup, and more than three hundred island supporters travelled with them to the Final.

The Ness Football team has also established an excellent social club and in doing so has solved a long-standing problem – the bothans or unlicensed drinking places which came into existence because of the distance between Ness and Stornoway, where, under a misguided temperance policy (so called) the licensed premises in Lewis were for many years exclusively concentrated.

One of the most imaginative of the Ness initiatives was the publication of a local phone book in which subscribers were listed by their patronymics or nicknames. In an area where so many people share the same few surnames the phone book had an obviously utilitarian purpose but it is, I think, typical of the warm communal spirit of the islands that nicknames – not all of them flattering or polite – should be seen as an important ingredient in the social cement.

Ness is merely an example of a liveliness to be found in many different areas of the islands. In many forms of sport, social life, amateur drama, discos and dances there is a degree of activity which did not exist a quarter of a century ago.

A more trivial but still significant pointer to the change of mood has been the involvement of islanders in attempts to get into the *Guinness Book of Records,* by such exotic activities as smashing concrete slabs with a karate chop or high scoring in a marathon game of darts.

The amount of protest over the NATO presence at Stornoway is another indicator of a more independent spirit than prevailed for many years when the island was enervated by continual emigration although, to put things in perspective, the level of social protest over NATO has never remotely

Nearly 100 years ago W J Gibson, one of Scotland's great educationists, commented on the natural talent for drama displayed by Gaelic-speaking pupils in the Nicolson Institute of which he was Rector. Now at last this talent is being put to use. Lewis is developing an indigenous drama of its own. Here the Point Players are seen rehearsing a new play in Gaelic by Dr Finlay Macleod based on the life of the Megantic Outlaw: a folk hero both in Lewis and in Canada. Courtesy *Stornoway Gazette.*

approached the situation which existed in the islands at the time of the Aignish Riots, the Park Deer Raid, or the land troubles at Reef in Uig which smouldered on for decades, erupting occasionally into the Courts. The reason may be that the land agitation united the islands in protest whereas the presence of NATO, or the development of nuclear power, although emotive issues, have two sides to the argument.

It has not all been gain, of course; the islands have not been immune from drug abuse, and a rising standard of income among the young has increased the misuse of alcohol.

But one indicator which cannot be overlooked is the extraordinary level of fund-raising sustained in the islands for social causes – as well as for the churches. This is difficult to quantify or to find a firm basis for comparison but I would suspect that, in relation to the wealth of the community, the level of giving must be the highest in Britain.

Before the setting up of the Comhairle there was no museum or art gallery in the Long Island – apart from the little folk museum at Shawbost established by the schoolchildren. Now there is a good museum in the old Town Hall of Stornoway and a very adventurous art gallery, An Lanntair. They cooperated in 1986 in a programme celebrating the centenary of the first Crofters Act. It drew more than six thousand visitors: equivalent to an attendance of a million and a half at an exhibition in London. More importantly, the exhibition went on from Stornoway to tour the major towns and cities in Scotland. When the 'backward' islands begin to export cultural initiatives in this way, it is clear that a radical change has taken place in their status vis-a-vis the rest of Britain.

Another new element in the situation is the international interest in the islands. Twenty years ago the occasional journalist or sociologist wandered into the islands in search of the primitive or amusing. Since the islands have gained some limited measure of control over their own destiny, officials come from other maritime areas of the EEC, from the Third World and even from Japan, to study the problems of remote peripheral areas and the methods used to cope with them. The same change in the status of the islands induced a Dutch organisation – the Van Leer Foundation – to locate in the islands an important experiment in community education.

In some ways the EEC has been more responsive to the needs of the remote areas than British governments have very often been. An EEC initiative has involved the British government – a little reluctantly, by all appearances – in an Integrated Development Programme for the Western Isles from which Lewis and Harris have benefited greatly in infrastructure, land improvement, tourism and above all, in the development of fish farming. The integration, however, was not complete in that the programme omitted large areas of essential manufacturing and service industry, but these, of course, have had assistance from the Highland Board.

A young man or woman growing up in the islands today may still see them, quite legitimately, as a problem area with a high rate of unemployment, few indigenous industries, a considerable degree of social and recreational deprivation, an almost intolerable burden on initiative imposed by a position

This well-equipped electronics room at Lews Castle College raises the question whether recent developments in communications technology will enable the islands, at last, to compete on even terms with urban centres in the south. Courtesy *Stornoway Gazette*.

on the periphery of Europe, a remote and uncaring government, an aged population weighing heavily on the young and a local culture in disarray if not distintegration.

Anyone who has known the islands for the last fifty years, however, must see them as a phoenix rising from the ashes: a lively, bustling, enterprising community, vibrant with young life, confident – perhaps even brash – creative and culturally exciting.

In this respect the vision of the elderly is nearer the truth than the pessimism of the young. A memory of what was has given my generation knowledge of a dramatic change in the islands' fortunes while the young, unaware of the rougher road and the sharp corner behind them, see only the stiff climb ahead.

The desire to preserve the Gaelic language and culture is an important motivation for several of those who have come back to the islands or who have elected to stay. In the late forties and fifties the Lewis Association was presided over by two Gaelic speakers, who might have been regarded as Gaelic activists in the terms of their own day, but the Association never directed its attention to the preservation of the language. At that time nearly 90% of the population were Gaelic speakers, and the great majority of children had little or no English when they went to school. It was assumed that, if the economic problems of the islands were solved, the language would look after itself.

It was much later that the language was seen as an important development tool: an essential element in the restoration of confidence in the island community.

Among the first to recognise this were a Lewisman, Professor Derick Thomson, and a Harrisman, Finlay J. Macdonald, who together founded *Gairm,* which must rank as the most successful literary magazine founded in Scotland since the war.

Derick Thomson stayed firmly with his vision. He has given a great impetus to the extension of the Gaelic vocabulary to cope with modern life, to the production of Gaelic books, and to the understanding, among non-Gaelic speakers, of the richness of Gaelic literature.

Although a Gaelic poet in his own right, he has probably been more significant as a propagandist, not in any critical or pejorative sense, but as one who recognised the social, political and economic dimensions of the language issue.

For Iain Crichton Smith, on the other hand, Gaelic has been a problem and an inspiration rather than a cause. He is compelled to write mainly in English because it is there his market lies. But he feels the strong tug of Gaelic – the still unsevered umbilical cord – as he has revealed in interviews and in some of his short stories. English literature has been enriched by his binocular vision, his two separate, although not necessarily conflicting, views of the world.

Norman Malcolm Macdonald provides another variant of the Gaelic-English mix. He writes with greater fluency in his second language, English, because he was educated out of literacy in his native Gaelic by the bias in the Scottish educational system, but he is rooted deeply in a Gaelic base.

Sheila Macleod's childhood in an insular and Gaelic-speaking community seems irrelevant to her science fiction and literary criticism, but she has not forgotten the repressions based on

A historic class at Breasclete School in 1986. The first group of children in a Lewis School to be educated through the medium of Gaelic for more than a hundred years. Is this a dead end, or an important stage in a Gaelic renaissance which will create a bilingual community with access to the whole range of Anglo-American literature but still insulated from the mass media by a private culture of its own? The answer to the question — when it comes — may be of more than local interest. Courtesy W G Lucas.

religion and neighbourly interference, in a small rural village; and the traumatic change from egalitarian Lewis to the class-conscious south of England would appear to have been one of the causes of the anorexia nervosa of which she has written with an odd mixture of clinical detachment and morbid self-pity.

One of the arguments against making the Western Isles a local government area was the belief that the Presbyterians in the north and the Catholics in the south would inevitably quarrel and produce another Ulster.

At the first meeting of the new authority a Presbyterian minister was elected Convener with a Catholic priest as his deputy. The friendship between them set the tone for an almost wholly successful experiment in reconciliation.

But old attitudes die hard. There has been at least one attempt in the Comhairle to impose the Sabbatarianism of the Protestant majority on Catholic Barra, and, when the Harris Tweed Association awarded a commission to a young Shawbost photographer – Murdo Macleod – to make a study of life in the Western Isles, his visit to the Catholic islands clearly came to him as something of a revelation: a different Gaelic world from his own, newly discovered.

The exhibition of his photographs, in which the captions highlighted his new and broader view, was sharply criticised by the Free Church *Monthly Record* for what was seen as bias in favour of the Catholic islands. Finlay Macleod and Iain Crichton Smith were criticised in the same article for their attitudes to Presbyterianism.

The monolithic Calvinism of Lewis both creates – and needs – its critics. The dialogue between the two is one of the elements that give piquancy to island life, and the tension it induces stimulates the artistic and cultural activities Calvinism seeks to suppress. The Church also stands to gain from the friction. A church which does not have to defend itself is not triumphant: it is dead.

The conflict is contained within the framework of a strong community feeling. Attachment to the island is intense on both sides of the argument, and the Free Church *Record* has used Murdo's photographs as cover illustrations even though it criticises the artist who took them.

The Presbyterian churches which, more than any other organisation, have kept Gaelic alive, are now cutting back on their Gaelic services, at the very moment when the local authority, central government and the media, which in the past were hostile or indifferent, have stepped up their support for the language.

It is not possible to forecast the economic and social future of the islands, nor the ultimate fate of the Gaelic language. Gaelic literature is undoubtedly flourishing while at the same time there is a catastrophic decline in the use of Gaelic by school-children since the advent of television, a decline which Gaelic pre-school playgroups are strenuously trying to offset.

Gaelic may go the way of Manx and Cornish; it may revive as a rich literary language sheltered from the temptations of the mass market and the degradation that normally implies; it may flourish again as a popular language worn by the people as a badge of their independence; or it may become the private code of a small intellectual elite.

Whatever the future holds, the islands are not undergoing a process of fossilisation. The changes which are taking place are closer to the transformation of a leaf-bound caterpillar into a creature with wings.

Much will depend on the extent to which the people of the islands are permitted to control their own affairs and regulate the use of the assets on which survival depends.

These assets lie in the sea as much as on the land, and the future will be influenced by the policies of the EEC in regard to deep-sea fishing, and the activities of that anomalous institution, the Crown Estates Commission, in respect of fish farming.

For the next few decades, whatever happens, Lewis and Harris will provide a challenging and exhilarating environment in which to live, work and fight.

Further Reading

Books quoted from are marked with an asterisk and full acknowledgement is made to author and publisher.

Atkinson, Robert – *Island Going* (Collins)*

Barber, John – *The Western Isles* (John Donald)*

Barron, Evan – *Prince Charlie's Pilot* (Robt Carruthers)*

Boyd, John Morton – *Fraser Darling's Islands* (Edin. Univ. Press)

Buchan, John – *Montrose* (James Thin Ltd)*

Burl, Aubrey – *The Stone Circles of the British Isles* (Yale University Press)*

Cameron, A. D. – *Go Listen to the Crofters* (Acair)

Campbell, J. L. – *Hebridean Folksongs* (Oxford University Press)
      – *Highland Songs of the Forty-Five* (John Grant)

Campbell, M. S. – *The Flora of Uig* (T. Buncle & Co.)

Carmichael, Alexander – *Carmina Gadelica* (Oliver & Boyd)*

Clegg, Prof E. J. – paper on the genetics of Lewis (*Annals of Human Biology*)*

Countryside Commission for Scotland – *Scotland's Scenic Heritage**

Cunningham, Peter – *A Hebridean Naturalist* (Acair Ltd)*

Darling, F. Fraser – *A Naturalist on Rona* (Oxford University Press)*

Dunlop, Jean – *The British Fisheries Society* (John Donald)

Durkacz, V.E. – *The Decline of the Celtic Languages* (John Donald)

Feachem, Richard – *Guide to Prehistoric Scotland* (Batsford)*

Fenton, Alexander – *The Shape of the Past* (John Donald)*

Fenton, Alexander & Palsson, Hermann – *The Northern & Western Isles in the Viking World* (John Donald)

Foster, David – article on the Harris association with Barrie's Mary Rose (*Scots Magazine*)*

Grant, James Shaw – *Highland Villages* (Hale)
      – *Their Children Will See* (Hale)
      – *The Hub of My Universe* (Thin)
      – *Surprise Island* (Thin)
      – *The Gaelic Vikings* (Thin)
      – *Stornoway & the Lews* (Thin)

Grigor, I. F. – *Mightier than a Lord* (Acair)

Hunter, James – *The Making of the Crofting Community* (John Donald)*

Johnson, Alison – *A House By the Shore* (Gollancz)

Macaulay, Donald – *George Washington Wilson in the Hebrides* (Aberdeen University Press)*
      – *Modern Scottish Gaelic Poems* (Southside)

MacAulay, Rev. Murdo – *Aspects of the Religious History of Lewis**

MacCaig, Norman – *Collected Poems* (Chatto & Windus)

Macdonald, A. M. – *A Lewis Album* (Acair)

Macdonald, Donald – *Lewis* (Gordon Wright Publishing)*

Macdonald, Dr Donald – *Tales and Traditions of the Lews*
Macdonald, Murdo Ewan – *The Call to Obey* (Hodder & Stoughton Ltd)*
Macdonald, Norman Malcolm – *Calum Tod* (Club Leabhar)
Mackenzie, W. C. – *The Western Isles* (Gardner)
                          – *The Highlands and Islands of Scotland* (Moray Press)
                          – *The Book of the Lews* (Gardner)*
                          – *History of the Outer Hebrides* (Gardner)*
                          – *Col. Colin Mackenzie* (Chambers)
Maclean, Sorley – *Ris a Bhruthaich* Literary essays (mainly in English) on Gaelic themes (Acair Ltd)*
Macleod, Charles – *Devil in the Wind* (Gordon Wright)*
Martin, Martin – *A Description of the Western Isles of Scotland* (Thin)
Matheson, William – *The Blind Harper* (The Scottish Gaelic Texts Society)*
Miller, Karl – *Memoirs of a Modern Scotland* (Faber)
Murray, J. & Catherine Morrison – *Bilingual Education in the Western Isles* (Acair)
Murray, W. H. – *The Islands of Western Scotland* (Eyre Methuen)
Nicolson, Nigel – *Lord of the Isles* (Weidenfeld & Nicolson)*
Nature Conservancy Council – *Outer Hebrides: Localities of Geological & Geomorphological Importance*
Orr, Willie – *Deer Forests, Landlords & Crofters* (John Donald)
Prentice, Robin – *The National Trust for Scotland Guide* (Jonathan Cape)*
Proceedings of the Gaelic Society of Inverness – an invaluable source of material on a variety of island themes*
Ross, Neil – *Heroic Poetry from the Book of the Dean of Lismore* (Oliver & Boyd for the Scottish Gaelic Texts Society)*
Shaw, F. J. – *The Northern & Western Islands of Scotland* (John Donald)
Sinclair, Colin – *The Thatched Houses of the Old Highlands* (Oliver & Boyd)*
Smith, Iain Crichton – *Consider the Lilies* (Gollancz)
                          – *On the Island* (Gollancz)
                          – *The Last Summer* (Gollancz)
                          – *Selected Poems* (Carcanet)
                          – *Towards the Human* – Selected Essays
                             (Macdonald Publishers)
Stephen, Ian – *Malin, Hebrides, Minches* – in collaboration with Sam Maynard (Dangaroo Press)
Taylor, Michael – *The Lewis Chessmen* (British Museum Publications Ltd)*
Thomson, Francis – *Harris Tweed* (David & Charles)*
                          – *Harris and Lewis* (David & Charles)
                          – *The National Mod* (Acair)
                          – *Crofting Years* (Luath Press)
Thomson, Derick – *An Introduction to Gaelic Poetry* (Gollancz)*
                          – *Creachadh na Clarsaich* (Macdonald)
                          – *Why Gaelic Matters* (Saltire Pamphlets)

Watson, J. C. – *The Gaelic Poems of Mary Macleod* (Blackie & Son Ltd.)*
Withers, C. W. J. – *Gaelic in Scotland, 1698-1981* (John Donald)

This list is by no means exhaustive. In particular it includes only books in English or with an English translation. Readers who are interested in the wealth of Gaelic books now issuing from the islands are advised to consult the lists of the main Gaelic publishers such as Acair Ltd, Gairm and the Gaelic Texts Society.

Visitors who wish to learn something of Gaelic music can find innumerable tapes of the more popular songs and singers, but special reference must be made to the recordings by the School of Scottish Studies of Gaelic Psalms from Lewis (with explanatory leaflet) and, in conjunction with the Lewis-based publishing firm, Acair, of Gaelic hymns sung by Christina Shaw of Harris.

Only one of Iain Crichton Smith's many volumes of poetry has been listed, although all are relevant, directly or indirectly. The Carcanet volume contains a number of poems referring to Lewis and there is a tape available of his own reading of several of them with a commentary relating the poems to their environment.

Even more relevant is his book of essays – *Towards the Human* – with an introduction by his fellow islander, Prof. Derick Thomson. The book, incidentally, is published by another Lewisman, Malcolm Macdonald, whose contribution to literary publishing in Scotland at a difficult period has been recognised by an exhibition in the National Library.

In both English and Gaelic the Hebridean Islands (particularly Lewis and Harris) are currently making a contribution to British literature which is out of all proportion to their population. They are using a distinctive voice which utters from a cultural background long suppressed or disregarded but now beginning to reassert itself.

English and Gaelic Place Names

English names as used in the Ordnance Survey maps	Gaelic names as used by Comhairle nan Eilean
ACHMORE	ACHA MOR
ADABROCK	ADABROC
AIGNISH	AIGINIS
AIRIDHANTUIM	AIRIDH AN TUIM
AMHUINNSUIDHE	ABHAINN SUIDHE
ARDHASAIG	AIRD ASAIG
ARDROIL	EADAR DHA FHADAIL
ARDSLAVE	AIRD LEIMHE
ARDVEY	AIRD MHIGHE
ARDVOURLIE	AIRD A MHULAIDH
ARIVRUAICH	AIRIDH A BHRUAICH
ALINE	ATH LINNE
ARNISH	AIRINIS
BACK	BAC
BALALLAN	BAILE AILEIN
BALLANTRUSAL	BAILE AN TRUISEIL
BARVAS	BARABHAS
BAYBLE	PABAIL
BAYHEAD	CEANN A BHAIGH
BERIE	BEIRGH
BERNERA	BEARNARAIGH
BERNERAY	EILEAN BHEARNARAIGH
BORROWSTON	BORGHASTAN
BORRISDALE	BORGHASDAL
BORSHAM	BOIRSEAM
BORVE	BORGH
BOSTA	BOSTADH
BOWGLASS	BOGHA GLAS
BRAGAR	BRAGAR
BREACLETE	BREACLEIT
BREASCLETE	BREASCLEIT
BRENISH	BREANAIS
BROKER	BROCAIR
BRUE	BRU

BUNAVONEADAR	BUN ABHAINN EADARRA
BUTT OF LEWIS	RUBHA ROBHANAIS
CALLANISH	CALANAIS
CARISHADER	CAIRISIADAR
CARLOWAY	CARLABHAGH
CARMINISH	CAIRMINIS
CARNISH	CARNAIS
CARRIEGREICH	CARRAGRAICH
CAVERSTA	CABHARSTADH
CAW	CADHA
CLIFF	CLIOBH
CLUER	CLIUTHAR
COLL	COL
CROIR	CROTHAIR
CROMORE	CROMOR
CROSS	CROS
CROSSBOST	CROSBOST
CROWLISTA	CRADHLASTADH
CRULIVIG	CRULABHIG
DALBEG	DAIL BEAG
DALMORE	DAIL MOR
DIRACLEIT	DIRECLEIT
DRINISHADER	DRINISIADAR
EAGLETON	BAILE NA H-IOLAIRE
EARSHADER	IARSIADAR
EILEANANABUICH	EILEAN ANABAICH
EISHKEN	EISGEAN
EORODALE	EORODAL
EOROPIE	EOROPAIDH
ENACLETE	EINACLEIT
FEVIG	FIBHIG
FIDIGARRY	FIDIGEARRAIDH
FINSBAY	FIONNSBHAGH
FIVEPENNY	COIG PEIGHINNEAN
FLESHERIN	FLEISIRIN
FLODABAY	FLEOIDEABHAGH
GARENIN	GEARRANNAN
GARYNAHINE	GEARRAIDH NA H-AIBHNE
GARYVARD	GEARRAIDH BHAIRD
GESHADER	GEISIADAR

GISLA	GIOSLA
GLEN TOLSTA	GLEANN THOLASTAIDH
GOVIG	GOBHAIG
GRAVIR	GRABHAIR
GRESS	GRIAS
GRIMERSTA	GRIOMARSTADH
GRIMSHADER	GRIOMSIADAR
GROSEBAY	GREOSABHAGH
HABOST	TABOST
HACKLETE	TACLEIT
HAMNAWAY	TAMNABHAGH
HARRIS	NA HEARADH
HIGH BORVE	BAILE ARD
HORSACLETE	HORSACLEIT
HUSHINISH	HUISINIS
ISLIVIG	ISLIBHIG
KEOSE	CEOS
KENDIBIG	CEANN DIBIG
KERSHADER	CEARSIADAR
KINLOCH	CEANN LOCH
KINLOCHROAG	CEANN LOCH ROAG
KINTULAVIG	CEANN THULABHIG
KIRIVICK	CIRBHIG
KNEEP	CNIP
KNOCK	CNOC
KNOCKAIRD	CNOC ARD
KYLES SCALPAY	CAOLAS SCALPAIGH
KYLES STOCKINISH	CAOLAS STOCINIS
LACKLEE	LEAC A LI
LAXAY	LACASAIGH
LEMREWAY	LEUMRABHAGH
LEURBOST	LIURBOST
LEVERBURGH	AN T-OB
LICKISTO	LICEASTO
LIGHTHILL	CNOC AN T-SOLUIS
LINGERBAY	LINGREABHAGH
LINSHADER	LINSIADAR
LIONEL	LIONAL
LOCHGANVICH	LOCH A GHAINMHICH
LUNDALE	LUNDAL

LUSKENTYRE	LOSGAINTIR
MAARUIG	MARAIG
MANISH	MANAIS
MARVIG	MARBHIG
MANGERSTA	MANGURSTADH
MEALISTA	MEALASTA
MEAVAIG	MIABHAG NAM BEANN
MELBOST	MEALABOST
MIAVAIG	MIABHIG
NORTH DELL	DAIL BHO THUATH
NORTH GALSON	GABHSANN BIIO THUATH
NORTHTON	TAOBH TUATH
ORINSAY	ORASAIGH
PARK	PAIRC
PLOCKROPOOL	PLOCROPOL
PORT OF NESS	PORT NIS
PORTNAGURAN	PORT NAN GIURAN
PORTVOLLER	PORT BHOLAIR
QUIDINISH	CUIDHTINIS
RANISH	RANAIS
REEF	RIOF
RHENIGIDALE	REINIGEADAL
RODEL	ROGHADAL
SCADABAY	SCADABHAGH
SCALISCRO	SCEALASCRO
SCALPAY	SCALPAIGH
SCARISTA	SGARASTA
SEAFORTH HEAD	CEANN LOCH SHIOPHOIRT
SHADER	SIADAR
SHAWBOST	SIABOST
SHESHADER	SEISIADAR
SHIELDINISH	SILDINIS
SHULISHADER	SULAISIADAR
SKIGERSTA	SGIOGARSTAIGH
SOUTH DELL	DAIL BHO DHEAS
SOVAL	SOBHAL
STENISH	STEINIS
STOCKINISH	STOCINIS
STORNOWAY	STEORNABHAGH
STROND	SRANNDA

SWAINBOST	SUAINEBOST
SWORDALE	SUARDAIL
TARANSAY	TARASAIGH
TIMISGARRY	TIMSGEARRAIDH
TOLSTA	TOLASTADH
TOLSTA CHAOLAIS	TOLASTADH A CHAOLAIS
TONG	TUNGA
TARBERT	TAIRBEART
UIGEN	UIGEAN
UNGESHADER	UNGISIADAR
VALASAY	BHALASAIGH
VALTOS	BHALTOS
VATISKER	BHATASGEIR

Index

231